AMERICA'S BEST BEERS

America's Best Beers

Christopher Finch &
W. Scott Griffiths

Little, Brown and Company
Boston New York Toronto London

Art Direction by
Katherine Takahashi &
Richard Wilkes

Graphic Production by
Bret Chambers &
Ron Wong

First Edition

ISBN 0-316-28204-9
Library of Congress Catalog
Card Number 94-78577

10 9 8 7 6 5 4 3 2 1

RRD-OH

Published simultaneously in Canada
by Little, Brown & Company
(Canada) Limited

Printed in the United States of
America

Contents

Introduction

by Charles S. Finkel

AMERICA'S BEST BEERS IS A MUCH NEEDED GUIDE TO MICROBREWERIES AND BREWPUBS

ACROSS AMERICA. "MICROBREWERY" IS A NEW WORD IN THE VOCABULARY OF THE NINE THOUSAND YEARS OF RECORDED BEER HISTORY, YET THE CONCEPT OF CRAFT BREWING IN AN ARTFUL WAY HAS BEEN REVERED SINCE THE FIRST BEER WAS BREWED. THE WORD *BREWING*, FROM WHICH *BREWERY* ORIGINATED, IS OF GERMAN ORIGIN. COINCIDENTALLY, *BREAD* IS FROM THE SAME root word. Like other types of cooking, the earliest brewing was likely done at home to satisfy the requirements of one family. As tribes and individual cultures developed, communal and commercial breweries were constructed. ··· Today's

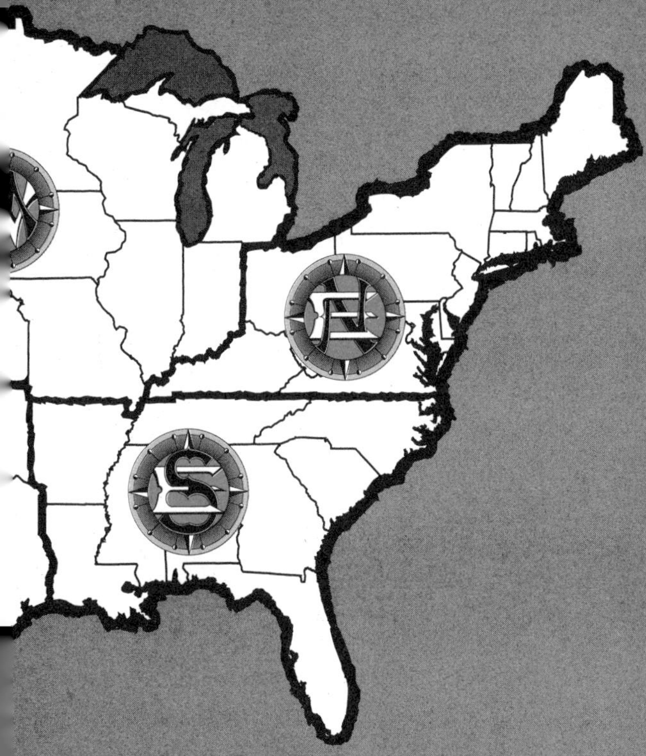

microbrewery enthusiasts might be surprised to learn that the first small-scale commercial breweries were created by the Middle Eastern clergy to brew faith offerings to the gods. The high priest and priestesses apparently drank the beer directly from the fermentation vessel through golden straws. The faithful were apparently rewarded with what was left over, giving some people a reason to speculate that beer significantly contributed to the early appeal of religion to humankind.

Microbrewing in Egypt is accurately recorded. One of the earliest examples of advertising is in the form of stones incised with the name of a beer brand. Since the hop, a natural preservative, was not to be introduced into beer for the first several thousand years of its history, most early beers had a very short "shelf life." Lest we think that the brewpub is a modern concept, most early breweries were brewpubs, with consumption and production taking place on the same premises.

Brewing can be traced from the earliest civilizations to the Western world by way of the Romans a little more than two thousand years ago. Like the gospel, beer culture was spread throughout Europe by the church. Monastic breweries popularized beer for its delicious taste and miraculous health-giving properties. Microbreweries were, next to the sanctuary, the most important part of the monastery. Monastic microbreweries such as the brewery at Orval Abbey in Belgium can trace their beer culture back more than 1,000 years, yet the quantity of beer produced at Orval is less than half as much as many of America's fast-growing microbreweries such as Anchor Steam, Redhook and Sierra Nevada.

The industrial revolution, with steam power replacing horsepower, gave rise to brewing as an industry. Other inventions significant to the development of brewing include artificial refrigeration, molded bottles, crown caps, high-speed transportation and metallic kegs. America had almost three thousand breweries, most of them micros, in the last century. Since repeal of Prohibition in America and the Second World War in Europe, commercial brewers have developed beer as an alcoholic fast food. The large sums spent convincing consumers that the advertised products were "beer" succeeded in forcing many microbreweries out of business in most of the Western world. By 1978, when Merchant du Vin Corporation began to introduce many of the classic brewing styles for the first time since pre-Prohibition, America had only one microbrewery. In England, thousands of local, high-quality breweries and their tied pubs decreased to hundreds at the hands of consolidators and mass-marketers. Ale, the predominant brewing type, yielded its market to lager. Belgium's wonderful specialties such as Lambic, Trappist, Red and White also lost more than half of their market to fizzy mass-marketed lagers, which copied their American counterparts, adding as much as 50% adjunct to the traditional malted barley. Germany, protected by its *Reinheitsgebot* (Bavarian Purity Law), remained the country with the most microbreweries.

While the term *microbrewery* dates from the late 1970's, it is *America's Best Beers* that finally defines the term, describing microbreweries as small, specialist, craft brewers who brew with mostly malt, hops, yeast and water using traditional recipes to craft the classic brewing styles.

It is obvious that the authors consider brewing at its best an art form. Christopher Finch and W. Scott Griffiths make it apparent that microbrewing is not a number but rather a philosophy. *America's Best Beers* is a labor of love. Both writers are real beer enthusiasts, immersed in the beer culture, Chris as the author of one of the most beautiful books ever done about beer and Scott as one of America's most talented beer marketers. Each contributes his individual talents—Chris as an art critic and Scott as a designer—to *America's Best Beers.* Their exhaustive research of more than 350 microbreweries and brewpubs, and their distinct, sometimes irreverent assessments, help them cut through the hyperbole surrounding the craft beer movement. With Finch and Griffiths as the judges, the jury is sure to gain an immediate insight into the fascinating world of American beer. So quickly is the industry changing, it is almost certain that as soon as *America's Best Beers* is released, a second edition will be appropriate. ■

Brewer, entrepreneur, graphic designer and publisher, Charles Finkel is one of the key figures in the American beer renaissance. Born in New York City and raised in Oklahoma, he began his career in the wine business, but since 1978 his Merchant du Vin company has been the premier importer of quality beers into the United States. Pike Place—Charles' Seattle microbrewery—observes the same high standards he set for himself as an importer. In addition, his importance as a spokesman for quality beer could hardly be exaggerated.

What is Great Beer?

What is great beer? There are probably as many answers to that question as there are beer drinkers, but a good way to answer is to compare great beer to great bread, that other staple made from grain, yeast, and water. Just as there are many kinds of bread, there are many kinds of beer. There are dark breads and white breads, dark beers and light beers. There are crusty breads and soft breads, each of which is appropriate under the right circumstances.

Similarly, there are "chewable" beers—like some ales—and refreshing beers such as pilsners, each appropriate to different occasions.

There is no one great sort of beer, any more than there is any one great sort of bread, yet it is not difficult to differentiate between the good and the bad. A freshly baked French baguette, an Italian country loaf, a handmade corn tortilla, a bagel from the Lower East Side of Manhattan, a Swedish rye bread, a German pumpernickel loaf—these are what bread should be and nobody is likely to mistake any of them for the kind of sliced bread you find in most supermarkets. Similarly, good beer—whether ale or stout or lager—has a satisfying wholesomeness that is never met in a six-pack of mass-market beer, no matter how well advertised.

There is a reason why the big commercial bakeries do not produce wonderful, crusty bread. It is expensive to make properly and it goes stale if it is not consumed immediately. Similarly there is a reason why the big commercial breweries show no interest in producing quality beer. It requires relatively expensive raw materials and it does not keep as well as those bland mass-market beers loaded with preservatives.

The chances of Anheuser-Busch coming out with a beer that is equivalent to a freshly baked baguette are remote. Even most of the smaller regional brewers cannot afford to produce such a beer, but luckily there is now enough demand for satisfying beer that during the past dozen years there has been a remarkable revival in the art of brewing in America, just as there has been a remarkable renaissance of quality baking. As far as brewing is concerned, we owe this almost entirely to the microbrewery/brewpub movement, which has been responsible for the revival of a variety of beer styles not seen in decades, and also of craftmade beers, which differ from the mass-produced article as an Indy car differs from a Geo Metro. This, then, is a book about craftmade beers but also about the microbreweries and brewpubs that craft them.

What is a *microbrewery*? There is no strict definition of the term, but typically it is a small craft brewery producing not more than 15,000 barrels of beer annually, though some successful micros have now exceeded this level of production without in any way lowering their standards. As for the term *brewpub*, that is a little easier to define. A brewpub is simply a pub supplied by its own small brewery. To complicate things, though, some businesses that started as brewpubs now produce and ship enough beer that they must also be thought of as micros. Contrariwise, some businesses that started as microbreweries now have on-site restaurants and bars that qualify them as brewpubs.

Whatever definitions are used, however, microbreweries and brewpubs are the best thing to have happened to American beer since the repeal of Prohibition. This book is a guide to the breweries and the brews that finally have given American beer fanciers something to cheer about.

HISTORY of BEER

AMERICA

When beer arrived in America with the early voyages of exploration, it was already thousands of years old. Archaeologists have speculated that nomads in prehistoric times made the discovery that wild barley, mixed with water and fermented by chance through contact with yeasts in the atmosphere, provided a beverage that was less likely to cause gastric problems than untreated water, and that had the added benefit of causing an agreeable state of euphoria when

HISTORIANS HAVE CALLED BEER THE NATIONAL DRINK OF ANCIENT EGYPT. THE PHARAOHS APPOINTED A "ROYAL CHIEF BEER INSPECTOR" TO PROTECT ITS QUALITY.

consumed. Many experts believe that beer predates wine, and it is even quite possible that beer predates bread, the other chief product made from grain, water and (later) yeast.

Brewing as a trade or profession is certainly as old as the great civilizations of the ancient Middle East. In both Mesopotamia and Egypt, many different kinds of beer were known. Most were made from malted barley or barley bread, mixed with water and fermented, perhaps even with the aid of cultured yeast, though nobody knows for sure when yeast was domesticated. It would be foolish to suppose, however, that these ancestors of Anchor Steam Beer and Sierra Nevada Pale Ale tasted anything like beer as we know it. Fermented barley malt has a distinctive, sweetish flavor that tends to be overpowering when unmodified by some flavoring agent. The ancients either cut the sweetness with the aid of bitter herbs, or exaggerated the sweetness with the help of honey or fruits such as dates.

Modern beer—its sweetness tempered with the bitterness of the hop—probably dates from the early Middle Ages and was known in most parts of Europe by the time of the great voyages of exploration. All classes and children and adults alike drank beer, it being valued as a source of nutrition and especially as a healthy alternative to water, which often came from contaminated sources (the fermentation process destroyed many malignant microorganisms). Beer was brewed in the humblest of homes and in the grandest of courts, at inns and in abbeys. It was likely to be found aboard just about any vessel undertaking a voyage of any significant duration and certainly beer was in the hold of many of the sailing ships that first tackled the Atlantic Ocean. It is well known that the Pilgrims, aboard the *Mayflower*, landed at Plymouth Rock instead of heading farther south, as planned, because they were running low on essential supplies, especially beer.

The pedigree of beer in the New World, then, is impeccable and the style that dominated here for the first two and a half centuries of European settlement was ale, along with its cousins such as porter. Beers of the ale family—brewed with top-fermenting yeast—were virtually the only types known in those days, but the kind that came to America with the Pilgrims and other early settlers was specifically the ale of England, and of a style that had become popular in the British Isles during the Tudor period, thanks largely to the arrival there of Flemish immigrants who favored heavily hopped beers that eventually evolved into the British draft ale style now known as Bitter (Pale Ale being the bottled version).

This Anglo-Flemish tradition was shared by the Dutch of New Amsterdam, so it can be safely assumed that the beers of colonial America had a good deal in common with beers that would have been found during the same period in London, Antwerp or Breda. Six-row barley was cultivated in the Americas from early colonial times, but it seems likely that for everyday brewing purposes, barley malt was often mixed with the native corn just as it is today. The best brews, however—those produced in some of the big houses, and later in city breweries—were all malt products, and much of the beer consumed in America in colonial times was actually brewed in England, then shipped across the Atlantic, probably with yeast pitched into the barrels to keep the beer "alive" during the long voyage.

LONG BEFORE THE TIME OF CONFUCIUS, THE CHINESE BREWED WITH MILLET, A CEREAL GRAIN. ACCORDING TO VERY OLD SACRED BOOKS, BEER PLAYED AN IMPORTANT ROLE IN EARLY CHINESE RELIGIOUS RITUALS.

In the earliest days of settlement, beer was usually drunk from black leather jugs called "blackjacks." Seventeenth-century New Yorkers preferred to sip their brew from pewter tankards, and it was only in the decades immediately preceding the Revolutionary War that Americans, even in the wealthier households, began to drink from glass vessels.

Ales were divided into four categories of strength: "small beer," the weakest (the sort drunk at home, even by the children), "ship's beer" next, followed by "table beer" and "strong beer." From the eighteenth century these were supplemented

COLONIAL AMERICANS USED THE TERM "SMALL BEER" TO DESCRIBE HOME BREW THAT WAS GENERALLY LOWER IN ALCOHOL CONTENT THAN COMMERCIALLY PREPARED "STRONG BEER." GEORGE WASHINGTON'S PERSONAL RECIPE CALLED FOR A GENEROUS MEASURE OF MOLASSES.

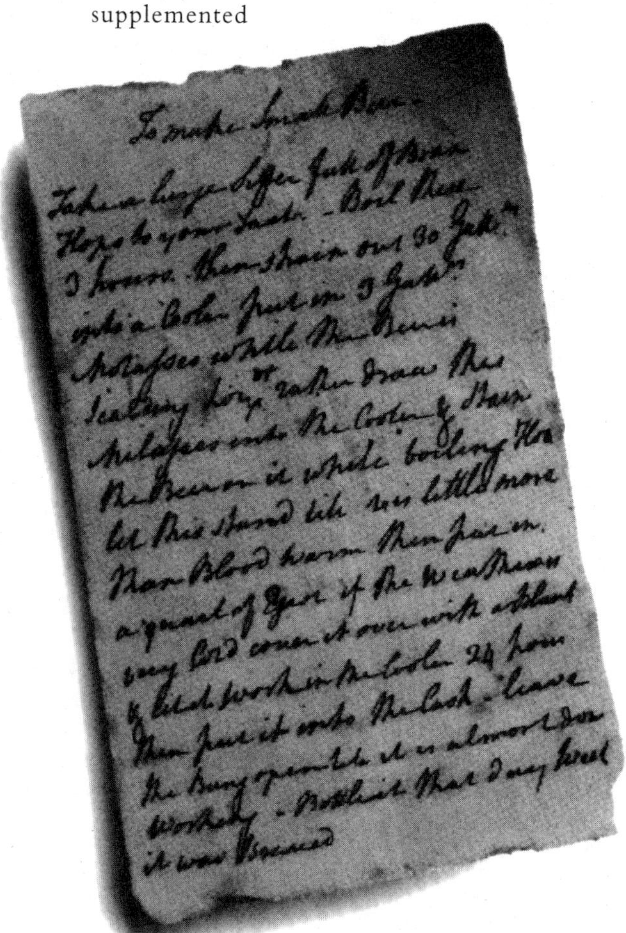
To make Small Beer-
Take a large Sifter full of Bran
Hops to your Taste. - Boil these
3 hours. then strain out 30 Gall[n]
into a Cooler put in 3 Gall[n]
Molasses while the Beer is
scalding hot or rather draw the
Molasses into the Cooler & strain
the Beer on it while boiling Hot
let this stand till it is little more
than Blood warm then put in
a quart of Yeast if the Weather is
very Cold cover it over with a Blanket
& let it work in the Cooler 24 hours
then put it into the Cask - leave
the Bung open till it is almost done
working. - Bottle it that day Week
it was Brewed

by porter, an almost black beer made from roasted, unmalted barley, which had first come to prominence in London and quickly caught on in America. It was a particular favorite of George Washington, who was especially fond of the porter brewed by Robert Hare of Philadelphia.

As early as 1770, Washington was one of those who—along with Samuel Adams, Jr., Patrick Henry, and others—lobbied for a boycott of British beer imports in order to bolster the health of the American brewing industry. After the Revolutionary War, imports of British beer did indeed cease for a while, and it was during this period that American brewing made significant strides. There was even talk of establishing a National Brewery, a notion that was supported by Thomas Jefferson, himself—like George Washington—an enthusiastic home brewer. In reality, however, what actually developed was something very much like the present-day brewpub and microbrewery movement. From Buffalo to Cincinnati and from Brooklyn to St. Louis, and in every other important American city, and in many small towns too, breweries sprang up to serve the local populace. Especially in the period before the railroads began to link population centers, the shipping of beer for any distance—except where water provided a natural highway—was virtually unheard of. The young nation, therefore, was served by hundreds of small breweries, most of them unknown outside their own metropolitan area, and sometimes barely known beyond their neighborhood.

Not that it was impossible to become wealthy from such a local brewery. A good case in point was the Eagle Brewery in Poughkeepsie, New York, founded in 1798 by Matthew Vassar, Sr. When the plant burned down in 1810, it was rebuilt by Matthew Vassar, Jr., who went on to take over competing breweries and create a small empire that enabled him, in 1860, to found the famous women's college that bears his name. Although the Vassar name had disappeared from the annals of brewing before the turn of the century, the college's ancestry is celebrated in the school song:

And so you see, for old V.C.
Our Love will never fail.
Full well we know
That all we owe
To Matthew Vassar's ale!

A similar tradition of local breweries evolved in Canada, where future dynasties had relatively modest beginnings. John Molson founded North America's oldest surviving brewery in Montreal in 1786, producing during its first year of operation just 4,000 gallons of beer—a quantity that today would qualify Molson's as a microbrewery. The Carling and O'Keefe breweries, which eventually combined to form the Carling O'Keefe multinational giant, were founded in 1840 and 1862, respectively, while the Labatt family has been in the business since it bought into the Balkwell brewery in London, Ontario, in 1847.

It was in the middle of the nineteenth century that American brewing began to undergo a revolution that would bring about its Golden Age. Lager beer—especially the pale, refreshing lagers of the pilsner type—had become all the rage in Europe, especially in Germany, Austria, Czechoslovakia and Scandinavia, areas from which immigrants were now reaching the United States and Canada in considerable numbers. They brought with them the technology to build lager breweries in America, and the special bottom-fermenting yeasts that made lagers so different in character from members of the ale family.

Lager quickly eclipsed ales and porters in popularity, but not to the extent that it destroyed the ale tradition. For almost 70 years, till Prohibition reared its ugly head, the British ale tradition and the Central European lager tradition thrived side by side as nowhere else in the world.

Initially the result of this was still more neighborhood breweries—some still specializing in ale, some now specializing in lager, and some producing both. In 1860, by which time the lager revolution had taken hold, there were already 1,269 brewery plants operating in America—some as far west as California, where a unique hybrid of ale and lager was developed (see page 50, Steam Beer). Things peaked around 1880, when 2,272 breweries were in operation in the United States.

By 1890 there were 94 breweries in Philadelphia alone, 77 in New York City, 38 in Brooklyn (still an independent city then), 41 in Chicago, 24 in Cincinnati, 33 in Detroit, 20 in Buffalo, 29 in St. Louis, and 26 already in San Francisco.

Milwaukee had just 14 breweries but largely because it was the city that, more than any other, was showing the way to the future—unfortunately, some would say. The citizens of Milwaukee were predominantly of German descent and so it was that lager was the style of beer favored there. Lager happens to be a more stable beer than ale. It keeps in good condition for longer periods and travels well, which is not true of all ales. It was almost inevitable, with the availability of rail transportation, that companies like Pabst, Schlitz, Blatz, and Miller should begin to think of themselves as regional brewers rather than neighborhood brewers. They began to ship their beer, bottled and on draft, to Duluth and Des Moines, to Iowa City and Indianapolis. By 1889, Pabst was producing more than 500,000 barrels a year, making it the industry leader, its nearest rival being the ambitious Anheuser-Busch company of St. Louis, which had embarked upon a similar expansion plan.

For the time being, there was plenty of room for expansion, so many of the local breweries survived for several decades more, though every year a few more closed. The 77 breweries found in New York City in 1890 had shrunk by 1910 to just 37.

While it lasted, though, this was a great period for the beer lover, and the variety of beers available in America was unrivaled anywhere else in the world. There were great ale centers, like Albany and Rochester, New York, and great lager centers, like Chicago and St. Louis, but everywhere you went, you

IN 1637, THE LEGISLATURE OF THE MASSACHUSETTS BAY COLONY MET TO FIX THE PRICE OF BEER. AFTER LENGTHY DELIBERATION, THE NEW PRICE WAS ANNOUNCED: "NOT MORE THAN ONE PENNY A QUART AT THE MOST."

FOR THE TIME BEING, THERE WAS PLENTY OF ROOM FOR EXPANSION, SO MANY OF THE LOCAL BREWERIES SURVIVED FOR SEVERAL DECADES MORE, THOUGH EVERY YEAR A FEW MORE CLOSED. could find an amazing variety of brews: ales, porters, stouts, pilsners, bocks, dunkels. The names alone conjure up a rich world of flavor treats. We would love to go back in time and taste Be-verwick Irish Cream Ale, Hornung's White Bock Beer, Centlivre's Nickel Plate Beer, Hohen-adel's Alt Pilsner, Rheingold Scotch Ale, Old Dutch Porter or Graf's Weissbeer. There was almost no style that could not be found.

But the big breweries got bigger, and the small breweries found it harder and harder to compete, so that even before Prohibition things were changing rapidly for the worse as heavily promoted beers like Budweiser and Schlitz gained bigger and bigger market shares.

This is not the place to recap the absurdities of Prohibition, but it is worth noting that the beer industry put up a strong fight in its attempt to be exempted from Prohibition on the grounds that beer is a drink of moderation. This strategy almost succeeded and if it had done so, America would have had a situation similar to that which existed in Belgium—also subject to a strong temperance movement—where partial Prohibition actually benefited the brewing industry by encouraging the production of a great variety of quality beers. As it was, Prohibition in America had exactly the opposite effect. For almost 14 years, from 1919 to 1933, the average American drinker had to be satisfied with substitutes such as near beer (bland tasting at best) spiked with moonshine grain alcohol.

This situation was not conducive to the encouragement of connoisseurship. By the end of Prohibition, most Americans under the age of 30 had never tasted real beer, and many older drinkers had half-forgotten what it was supposed to taste like. Some responsible brewers did try to go back to their pre-Prohibition standards—a few pre-Prohibition beers, like Ballantine India Pale Ale and Prior Double Dark, have actually survived to this day—but the lack of beer literacy that existed after the "Great Experiment" enabled the big breweries to become bigger and still bigger by flooding the market with beers that became more and more degraded as the years went by. The distribution of beer in cans, which began in 1935, was a boon to collectors of breweriana but otherwise simply presented brewers with a further opportunity to debase the product.

To be perfectly honest, there are people who prefer bland beer and would drink whatever was available at any price. The Constitution guarantees them the right to express their free will in this way, however perverse it may seem to anyone born with taste buds of reasonable sensitivity. Far more sinister is the scheme engineered by certain large brewery conglomerates to persuade the American public that bland is the way beer is *supposed* to taste. Millions of advertising dollars are spent on propaganda that endeavors to persuade Americans that they want something that tastes (to quote a British beer buff) like "Perrier water faintly tainted with hops." This has been going on for decades and has finally reached the point where further adulteration of the malt, or further dilution of the hops, is probably impossible without producing something that is barely distinguishable from seltzer.

In any case, it was against this background of the industrial abuse of the name "beer" that the American brewing renaissance—the return to small-scale, quality brewing—came into being. This was a renaissance

WILLIAM PENN WROTE THAT THE BEER IN HIS COLONY WAS MADE OF "MOLASSES... WELL BOYLED, WITH

SASSAFRAS OR PINE INFUSED INTO IT." THE TASTE OF SUCH A CONCOCTION MUST HAVE BEEN INTERESTING, ESPECIALLY FROM THE POPULAR DRINKING VESSEL OF THE PERIOD: A WAXED LEATHER TANKARD KNOWN AS A "BLACK JACK."

that owed a good deal to the survival of the American homebrew tradition that, for obvious reasons, had thrived during the Prohibition era, then had held on remarkably strongly, especially in regions such as the Pacific Northwest, in reaction to the blandness of supermarket beers. Another factor that contributed to this rebirth was increased international travel, brought about by cheap airfares, which introduced many Americans to great European beers for the first time. It is perhaps fair to say that the brewing renaissance was also one of the few worthwhile products of the yuppie period. Youngish business people who had made a killing in software or frozen yogurt decided to mix entrepreneurial spirit with pleasure by investing in brewpubs where they could show off to their friends by explaining the difference between half-and-half and *hefeweissbier* and at the same time make a few extra bucks by supplying the sawdust for the floor. This was to the benefit of all of us.

A key date in the prehistory of the renaissance is 1965 when Fritz Maytag purchased the Anchor Brewing Company, a floundering San Francisco brewery, established in 1896, which was the last company to produce the famous West Coast steam beer. Under Maytag's auspices, the company recovered and thrived. More importantly, it thrived by producing beers of the highest quality, which came to be sought out first locally, then regionally, then nationally. The success of Maytag's enterprise has been an inspiration to everyone who followed.

The first modern American microbrewery seems to have been the New Albion Brewing Company, in Sonoma, California, where Jack McAuliffe attempted to reproduce the styles of ale he had enjoyed in the British Isles while stationed in Scotland with the U.S. Navy. Beginning business in 1976, New Albion lasted till 1982 and was in effect absorbed by the better-financed Mendocino Brewing Company, which in 1983 opened one of California's first two brewpubs (the other is Buffalo Bill's Brewpub, in Hayward). These two ventures had been preceded, in 1982, by Bud Grant's Brewing and Malting Company, which had established a brewpub in the old Switzer Opera House in Yakima, Washington. Like Mendocino, Grant has gone on to brew a number of well-regarded beers that can be found hundreds of miles from the original brewpub. In this respect they are microbreweries with well-developed distribution systems. Perhaps the most successful of the early micros, however, are Sierra Nevada, founded in Chico, California, in 1981 and the Red Hook Ale Brewery, which opened for business in Seattle, Washington, the following year. Like all the other companies mentioned so far, both specialize in fine British-style ales with a strong American accent, though Sierra Nevada also brews a splendid bock.

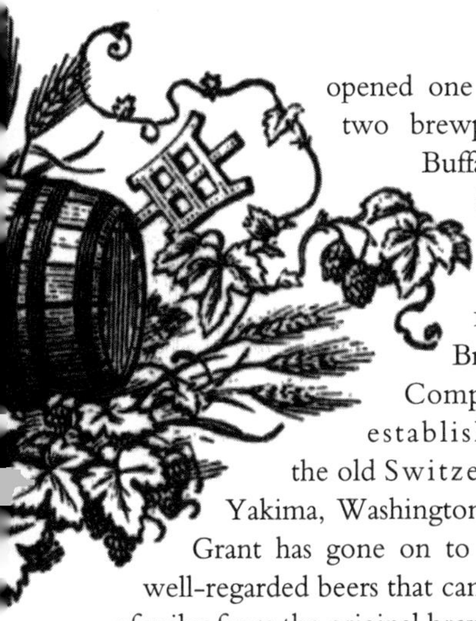

Other pioneers—Bill Newman in Albany, New York, Mike Hale in Colville, Washington, Charles and Diana Rixford in Berkeley, California—deserve to be mentioned, but the important thing is that by the early eighties the quality brewing renaissance was gathering momentum. A decade later, the Institute for Brewing Studies in Boulder, Colorado, was able to list 240 micros and brewpubs in the United States, plus 70 in Canada. The time had long passed when the discerning American beer drinker had to settle for bland substitutes.

the BREWING PROCESS

The Brewing Process

There is nothing complicated about the basic principles of brewing beer. A grain substance—classically malted barley—is blended with water and the mixture is encouraged to ferment, almost always through the agency of a yeast culture added at the appropriate time. Hops are added to flavor the brew, to temper its sweetness, to provide aroma, and to serve as a natural preservative.

As far as most great beers are concerned, these are the only ingredients used. A few wonderful specialty beers make use of other grains, such as wheat and oatmeal, and hops are very occasionally supplemented by other flavoring agents, such as fruit. For the most part, though, the world's best beers voluntarily obey the Bavarian law known as the *Reinheitsgebot,* which dictates that—except for a few noble exceptions—beer must be made from four basic ingredients: barley malt, water, yeast and hops.

Outside Germany, large commercial brewers are not subject to any such law so they will often cut their costs by blending their barley malt with cheaper grains such as corn or rice. These are known as adjuncts and even so-called super-premium beers—including many imports—often contained diluted barley malt with 20% to 30% inferior grains. Some cheaper American brands are composed of more than 40% corn in proportion to barley malt.

The use of inferior grains makes for inferior beers: It's as simple as that. The success of the brewpub and microbrewery movement in America is due in large part to the fact that almost all the small brewers who have made up the movement obey the strictures of the *Reinheitsgebot.* The discriminating drinker, even if he or she has not had the good fortune to grow up in Bavaria or Belgium, can quickly learn to differentiate between an all-malt beer and run-of-the-mill substitutes, however cleverly advertised.

The first stage, then, in understanding the art of the brewer is to learn a little about real beer's four basic ingredients.

Real Beer Ingredients

WATER: Anybody paying attention to the advertising put out by the big commercial brewers would assume that water is *the* key ingredient in beer, and in the case of some popular beers that might be true, because if brewers can't boast about their water—whether from the Rockies or elsewhere—they don't have much else to boast about. It's true that many of the world's great breweries did owe their original fame to the fact that they were located close to natural sources of water. The famous breweries of Burton in the English Midlands, for example—Bass is the best known—owed their success to the waters of the River Trent. Trent water, in its natural form, provided salts and minerals that added character to a certain kind of ale. In the days before master brewers had degrees in chemistry, this was important. For more than a century, however, it's been possible to take tap water and "Burtonise" it by chemical adjustment, thus making Trent-like water available to brewers from Syracuse to Sydney.

In ancient times, beer was flavored with such things as coriander, rosemary, and lupine. Eventually, the people of Northern Europe learned to use hops instead. Hops added flavor to beer, made it clearer, and helped preserve it. Anyone who has tasted beer flavored with coriander has reason to be grateful for this discovery.

BARLEY: Wild barley was known in prehistoric times and barley may well have been the first grain to be cultivated by man. Ancient Mesopotamians used barley as the base of a fermented drink at least 6,000 years ago, and beer-like beverages made from barley were well known to Egyptians of the dynastic era. The strains of barley favored for brewing in modern times are two-row barley—the aristocrat of the family—and six-row barley, which can be grown in a greater variety of climates. Before it is used for brewing, barley is malted: the hard grains are soaked in water in order to promote germination. This germinated barley makes up the malt. When it is dried, the malt is ready for use, but it can be further treated by roasting. The longer the malt is roasted, the darker the beer produced from it will be. The roasting process also alters the flavor and

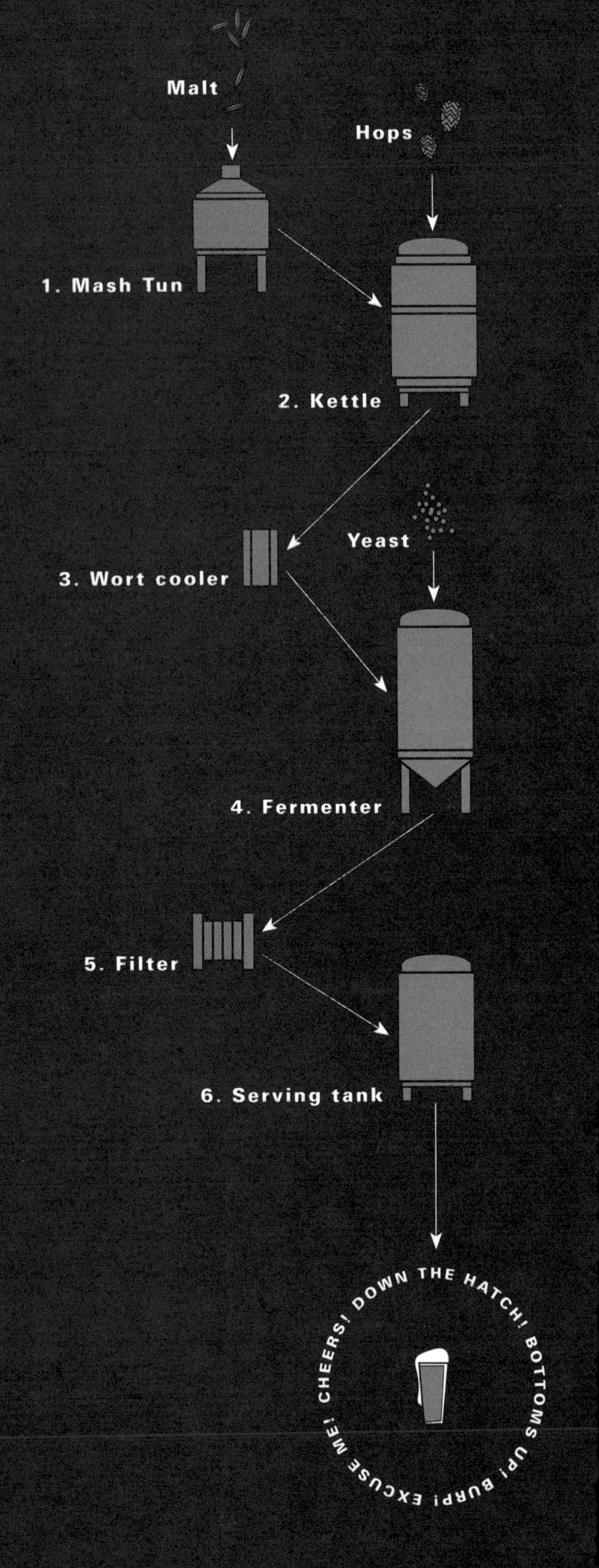
Malt
Hops
1. Mash Tun
2. Kettle
Yeast
3. Wort cooler
4. Fermenter
5. Filter
6. Serving tank
CHEERS! DOWN THE HATCH! BOTTOMS UP! BURP! EXCUSE ME!

aroma of the brew. Unmalted roasted barley is used in brewing porter and stout.

YEAST: In order for malt and water to become beer, fermentation must take place, and normally this is achieved by the introduction into the brewing process of carefully cultivated strains of yeast. Like wine, a few beers—such as the lambic beers of Belgium—are fermented through contact with naturally produced microorganisms, but these are very much the exception to the rule. Yeast is simply a fungus that can convert sugar into alcohol. Its chemistry was not well understood till the 1850s and prior to that time almost all beers were made with top-fermenting yeasts—yeasts that rise to the top of the wort (the barley and water blend) during the fermentation process. In type, these very much resemble baker's yeast and produce the beers of the ale family that have become extremely popular once more during the American small brewery renaissance. Lager—a relatively modern form of beer—is brewed at lower temperatures with bottom-fermenting yeast that sinks to the bottom of the wort during the brewing process.

HOPS: The hop is a climbing herbaceous plant that occurs in the wild in many parts of Europe, Asia and North America. The hop was domesticated by the Romans who liked to eat its shoots, and it is even possible that it was used as a flavoring agent in beer-like beverages at that early date. Certainly it was being widely used for this purpose by the late Middle Ages, replacing other flavoring agents such as various bitter herbs and juniper berries, which had been employed till then to ameliorate fermented barley's excessive sweetness. It is the hop, more than anything else, that makes modern beer different from its ancestors. The hop gives beer its characteristic bitterness and refreshing dryness, the active ingredient being a substance secreted by the glands of the female hop cone.

Different strains of hop have very distinct flavor and aroma characteristics, contributing greatly to the personality of various beer styles.

Prior to the Industrial Revolution, brewing was a crude, chancy, labor-intensive business dependent upon strong men who stirred bubbling liquids in huge, wooden vats with paddles big enough to row a galley. During the nineteenth century, however, the technology of brewing changed drastically—steam power and new metal-founding techniques revolutionized the industry—and a new kind of brewery came into existence. Today's brewpubs are the direct descendants of those Victorian behemoths; smaller, of course, and furnished in some cases with transistor-age control consoles, but essentially similar in concept and layout. That layout is basically vertical in order to take advantage of the force of gravity, the brewing process beginning under the roof and the end product emerging at cellar level, ready to be tapped for on-premises consumption or bottled for transportation.

Malt, brought from a malting plant, is fed into a mill where it is ground into grist. This grist is then transferred, by gravity, into the mash tun—the first of a series of metal kettles—which is furnished with steam and water inlets, and also with power-driven paddles or similar agitators. Hot water is introduced into the mash tun and is mixed with the grist to create a porridge-like semiliquid known as the mash. Important chemical changes, some influencing the alcohol content of the beer, occur during this process.

Next, the mash is fed into another metal vessel, known as a lauter tun. Here it is diluted and insoluble residues are filtered out until the gruel-like substance has been turned into a partially clarified liquid known as the wort. The wort is transferred into still another metal vessel—the brew kettle—where it is further diluted, then boiled. This is the actual brewing process, and while it continues, hops—either whole cones or pellets of concentrated hop oil—are added to the wort.

Next, hop solids are removed from the wort, which then passes through a whirlpool device to be cleansed of unwanted protein. Then the wort is decanted into a fermentation vessel. Yeast is pitched into the wort and the process of fermentation begins. If the end product is a lager beer, fermentation takes place at a relatively low temperature (beginning at about 47°F) and typically lasts from eight to ten days. In the case of ale, fermentation takes place at close to room temperature and is completed somewhat faster.

At the end of the fermentation period, the beer is removed to maturing vessels. Lager (the word means storage) benefits from long periods of maturation. Some lagers are kept for months before being shipped. Beers of the ale family mature more quickly, but the maturation period can be important for them too. In some instances, hops are added to the maturing brew—a process known as dry-hopping, which produces great complexity of aroma and finish. Other ales undergo a secondary fermentation at this time, a little yeast being pitched into the maturing vessels. The greatest ales continue to ferment in the cask or in the bottle until the moment they are poured for consumption.

STYLES of BEER IN AMERICA

Styles of Beer

It is one of the miracles of brewing that four basic ingredients—barley malt, yeast, hops and water—can be made to yield an incredibly varied array of end products, from malty winter ales, potent as brandy, to light, refreshing lagers, perfect to quench the thirst on a summer day. Add legitimate grain adjuncts such as wheat or oatmeal to the mash and the possibilities are multiplied.

Those basic ingredients, of course, are not as simple as they seem at first sight. For example, the malt may be made from two-row barley or six-row barley. It may be roasted to various degrees of darkness, or it may not be roasted at all. The yeast may be of the top-fermenting or the bottom-fermenting type and, being a living organism, can vary greatly in character from one brewery to another. Hops come in many different varieties. The aristocratic assertiveness of Saaz hops, from the former Czechoslovakia, is very different from the yeomanly robustness of Fuggles, a staple in English ales, or from the floral bouquet provided by Cascade hops, a favorite with American brewers. Yet each of these hop strains—and several others, such as Hallertau, from Germany, and Poperinge, from Flanders—is appropriate in the right context and lends its own character to the beer. Mountain streams are not as important to the quality of beer as the advertising industry would have us believe, but water too plays its part as the salts and minerals it contains can influence the way the beer will taste.

The temperature at which a beer is brewed is a crucial factor in establishing its personality, as is the alcohol content, which is determined chiefly by the proportion of barley malt to water in a given brew. This proportion establishes what is known as the beer's original gravity. The higher the original gravity (the more malt to water) the stronger the beer will be, everything else being equal—though other factors such as the length of time for which the brew is permitted to ferment can also make a beer marginally higher or lower in alcohol content.

A WOMAN DROVE ME TO DRINK AND I NEVER EVEN HAD THE COURTESY TO THANK HER.

—W.C. FIELDS

In addition to all of this, a beer that undergoes a secondary fermentation in the cask or bottle will have a character quite different from the same beer that has been pasteurized before being shipped. Subtle differences in style can be achieved by techniques such as *krausening* (adding a little fresh brew to a maturing beer to encourage further fermentation) or dry hopping

BY LAW, BEER IN COLONIAL AMERICA HAD TO BE SERVED IN STANDARD HALF-PINT, PINT, OR QUART PEWTER VESSELS. WHEN TIN COULD NO LONGER BE IMPORTED FROM ENGLAND, AMERICAN PEWTER PRODUCTION STOPPED.

(adding whole hops to an ale at the maturing stage to add bouquet and subtlety).

The master brewer, having been asked to make a specific beer—a pilsner, say, or a stout—orchestrates the basic ingredients to arrive at an interpretation of one of the classic styles. Knowing the examples used in judging—Pilsner Urquel, say, or Guinness—he draws on all his technical expertise to blend and balance the basic ingredients into something that will provide knowledgeable drinkers with a unique experience. It is not necessarily a matter of producing a beer that is greater than Pilsner Urquel or Guinness. It is more a question of adding one's own signature to something that has already gone through generations of superb interpretations.

Totally new styles of beer are not unthinkable, but they are certainly quite rare. Except for aberrations such as light beer—which is hardly deserving of being described as a style (unless non-fat milk is thought of as a style of milk)—no significant new styles of beer have emerged in the twentieth century. Like a Chinese poet, therefore, or a major league shortstop, the brewmaster is judged by the ability to perform with skill and personal flair within a traditional framework.

With a couple of remarkable exceptions—one of which, as will be seen, happens to be America's most significant contribution to the brewing tradition—all the classic styles of beer fall into two basic families. The older of these families, by far, is the ale family, which includes ales proper along with porters, stouts, alt beers and wheat beers. All of these brews are made at room temperature with top-fermenting yeast—yeast that rises to the top of the wort during primary fermentation—very similar to the yeast used by bakers to leaven their bread dough. The other family is the lager family, which also comes in many styles, from pale pilsners to espresso-colored bocks, which is made with bottom-fermenting yeast. Such beers are brewed at significantly lower temperatures than is the case with the ale family, and must be "lagered" (German for "stored") at cool temperatures for considerable periods of time. Although lagers had been known earlier in places like Bavaria—where there was a plentiful supply of ice and deep caves for lagering—they did not become commonplace until the 1830s and 1840s when industrial refrigeration and a scientific understanding of yeast made it possible to produce these styles of beer on a large scale.

The clarity and crispness of pale lagers such as pilsners and Dortmunders made them very popular with the world's drinkers, and the lagers' excellent storage characteristics—they are more stable than ales—made all lagers popular with brewers and beer retailers alike. For a while, the novelty and commercial advantages of lager threatened to wipe out the older ale family of beers, but ales—generally more robust and fruity—and their cousins remained dominant in a few countries such as the United Kingdom and Belgium and continued to find a healthy degree of support in other countries like France, Australia,

THOMAS JEFFERSON WROTE MUCH OF THE DECLARATION OF INDEPENDENCE IN PHILADELPHIA'S INDIAN QUEEN TAVERN. LATER, AFTER TWO TERMS AS PRESIDENT, HE EXPERIMENTED WITH BREWING TECHNIQUES DURING HIS RETIREMENT YEARS AT MONTICELLO.

Canada, the United States, and even Germany. Ale brewers fought back with lighter, clearer ales that offered some of the same advantages as the revolutionary pale lagers, yet retained their natural vinous character. Lately the ale family has enjoyed a considerable revival, notably in the United States and Canada.

AMERICA'S FIRST "HELP WANTED" AD APPEARED IN LONDON, ENGLAND IN 1609:

HELP WANTED: *NEW OPPORTUNITY—TWO BREWERS URGENTLY REQUIRED TO HELP SET UP A BREWERY IN THE BRITISH COLONY OF VIRGINIA. ONLY THOSE WITH EXPERIENCE NEED APPLY.*

It has been suggested that ales are the red wines of the beer world and lagers the white wines. To the beginner this is a confusing distinction, since there are pale-colored ales and reddish lagers, but there is an element of truth in the suggestion. Top-fermenting yeast lends most ales a very marked vinous quality, such as might be found in a fine claret or a California Cabernet Sauvignon. Lagers, on the other hand, can be made to provide the refreshing dryness that might be associated with, say, a white wine from the Loire Valley.

Like wines, beers seem to take on the character of the place where they are produced. This is perhaps most evident in the case of British ales. Everyone has heard jokes about the British sipping warm ale. In fact British ales are traditionally served at cellar temperature—that is to say cool but not cold—which makes great sense given the British climate. The British pubgoer is seldom escaping 90-degree weather or coping with overpowering central heating systems. More likely he or she is slipping into the saloon bar to dodge a passing shower, and the only heat comes from a few logs in an open fireplace. Under those circumstances, a frosty mug is highly unsuitable and unsatisfying. For that reason British ales are designed to be enjoyed at cellar temperature and naturally taste better that way. They can stand a certain amount of chilling, but serve them too cold and much of their flavor is lost—in fact their entire character is changed.

This is very relevant to the American microbrew movement. For a variety of reasons, English pale ale is the style of beer most often aspired to by America's independent brewmasters. There is no better style of beer to emulate, but most of the best American brewers of pale ale manage to produce an ale that has a distinctly American accent, and this is all to the good since it reflects a difference of environment and climate. Among the most authentically British of American ales are Ballard Bitter and the higher-gravity ESB produced by the Redhook Brewery of Seattle, Washington. Significantly, the Seattle climate is damp and cool—not far removed from that of the British Isles. In other parts of North America, where the climate is sometimes very different, the best pale ales are given a discreetly different balance so that they can quench thirsts on a blisteringly hot Fourth of July afternoon. For this to work, they must be gutsy enough to stand up to reasonable refrigeration while remaining subtle enough to take advantage of the special qualities of American hops.

This American accent was probably present in pre-Prohibition American ales, and survives in Ballantine's remarkable India Pale Ale, which has been around for more than a century. It is very encouraging that the accent has been picked up by the new brewmasters. It demonstrates the fact that pale ale has acclimatized itself to America, once more, and that is good news for everyone who wishes the microbrew movement well.

What follows is a listing of the styles of beer belonging to its two primary families, with notes on which styles have found a significant following among American microbrewers. (Probably every style has been tried out somewhere during the past decade or so, but some are much more popular than others.) At the end of the list is a discussion of a couple of anomalies that defy categorization, including America's one original beer style, the wonderful hybrid produced by San Francisco's Anchor Brewery and marketed as Steam Beer.

BITTER

The basic draft ale of the British Isles, bitter, is one of the classic styles of the beer world. Not necessarily high in alcohol content (though some versions are quite strong), bitter can be almost as pale as straw, or burnished like gold, or ruby red. It is a malty beer but the sweetness of the malt is offset by heavy hopping, hence the name bitter. Keg versions of British ales such as Bass are available in the United States but, good as these are by everyday standards, these keg versions are only pale imitations of the cask-conditioned bitter available in the United Kingdom. To get a sense of what these cask-conditioned bitters are like, visit an American brewpub and try its house pale ale on tap. It may have an American accent, but otherwise it will be as close to fine British bitter as you could hope to find.

PALE ALE

In Britain this term is generally used to describe the bottled version of a beer that in the cask would be called bitter. Some British brewers, however, use the term for both bottled and cask beers and that practice has become very common in the United States so that *pale ale* has, for all intents and purposes, evolved into a generic term for a well-hopped, British-style ale that may or may not be pale in color. Especially fine pale ales are sometimes called India Pale Ales (IPAs), a reminder of the days when such brews were shipped from Great Britain to India and aggressively hopped as a preserving agent for the warmer climate.

MILD

Mild is another style of British draft ale, once very popular but now hard to find except in certain areas. Mild is less vigorously hopped than bitter (hence its name) and is usually brewed from a relatively low original gravity. Most milds are dark, though pale versions exist. The style is beginning to attract some attention in America and good to excellent examples have been encountered at recent beer festivals.

BROWN ALE

Brown ales probably originated as the bottled versions of the classic dark style of mild ale. Over the years, though, some brown ales have become stronger and hoppier. The style has been successfully transplanted to the United States where brown ales come in both bottles and casks.

SCOTCH ALE

Scotland was once famous for strong, dark ales, and a few are still to be found there in both bottled and draft forms so that Scottish tipplers can still ask for "a wee heavy." On the whole, though, you are more likely to find a Scotch ale of the traditional sort in a Belgian cafe or an American brewpub. It is not yet a commonplace brew on this side of the Atlantic, but some excellent versions are available.

BARLEY WINE

Barley wines are very strong ales (sometimes called old ales or winter warmers) with a distinctly vinous character. They are drunk in small measures, like fortified wines such as port. Some splendid versions are brewed in America, usually as seasonal specials and often in celebration of the Thanksgiving/Christmas/New Year holiday season.

PORTER

An immensely popular brew in both Britain and America during the eighteenth and nineteenth centuries, this style has lately enjoyed a considerable revival, especially in the United States. Brewed from roasted, unmalted barley, porter has a coffeelike palate and is almost black in color. Traditional porters are extremely bitter. Many American versions are faithful to this tradition, but some are relatively sweet.

STOUT

This beer that evolved from porter is also brewed from roasted, unmalted barley. Stout is just as dark as porter, and has the same spectacular head, but it is more full-bodied and creamier. Some English versions are very sweet, but the classic Irish version—much imitated around the world—is distinctly bitter. Excellent examples are produced by American brewpubs and microbreweries.

BELGIAN ALES

Along with the United Kingdom, Belgium is the country most associated with the ale tradition. It is a place where the spirit of the small brewer still thrives, and there are almost as many styles of Belgian ale as there are Belgian brewers. Equivalents can be found there of every British style from pale ale to barley wine, in addition to which there are many eccentric ales that fall into no general category. Because Belgian ales are so idiosyncratic, they are seldom imitated, but American craft brewers are not easily intimidated, and local versions of various Belgian-style brews are occasionally encountered on this side of the Atlantic.

TRAPPIST ALES

Highly distinctive and very vinous, these are the most famous of Belgian ales. The authentic versions are brewed in Cistercian abbeys, but these ales are imitated by Belgian commercial brewers—and now occasionally by American craft brewers.

ALTBIER

Altbier—"old beer"—is the German equivalent of ale, a top-fermented brew still very popular in cities like Düsseldorf and Münster. Yeasty and well hopped, most versions are extremely vinous in character. In general they have more in common with Belgian ales than with British ales. Some splendid versions have been brewed in the United States.

KOLSCH

Kolsch is a brew very similar to altbier, but pale and more refreshing. Indigenous to the city of Cologne, it is seldom found elsewhere—except in a handful of American brewpubs.

WHEAT BEER

Like ales, wheat beers are brewed with top-fermenting yeast and have a distinctly vinous character. Wheat is mixed with malted barley in various proportions to produce an astringent, refreshing palate. The wheat beers of Berlin, for example, use about 25 percent wheat in the mash to produce a very light beer to which the aficionado adds a little raspberry syrup or essence of woodruff. The wheat beers of southern Germany are more full-bodied, being brewed from a higher original gravity and a mash that employs proportionately more wheat. Wheat beer is often drunk with a splash of lemon juice and has enjoyed a considerable revival in America during the past decade or so. Fruit-flavored versions of wheat beer have become popular on this side of the Atlantic.

BOTTOM-FERMENTED BEERS (LAGERS)

PILSNER

The style of beer known as pilsener, pilsner, or just plain pils, is the most popular in the world. Originating in the city of Pilsen, in the former Czechoslovakia, the pilsner is a pale gold, refreshing lager beer with an almost astringent sparkle to it. Many beers aspire to be pilsners, but to be a good example of the type—whether produced in Bohemia, Bavaria or Boston—the brew must be almost extravagantly hopped with top quality hops, preferably of the Saaz variety. Despite its universal popularity, this is a difficult beer for the microbrewer to do really well. Top-notch brewpub pilsners are much rarer than top-notch brewpub ales.

HELLES

A brew that is similar to pilsner but less aggressively hopped, this is the everyday pale lager of Bavaria. Most American microbrew pale lagers—even some that claim to be pilsners—are really local versions of the helles style.

MUNCHNER

The dark lager beer of Munich—"dunkel" to the local drinkers—tends to be malty and sweetish. It has always retained some popularity in the United States, though really distinguished munchners are quite rare on this side of the Atlantic.

VIENNA

While the pilsner style was sweeping the world, in the mid-nineteenth century, the citizens of Vienna developed a taste for a reddish, fruitier lager that soon became known as Vienna-style beer. This beer was the direct ancestor of the amber lagers that became very popular in

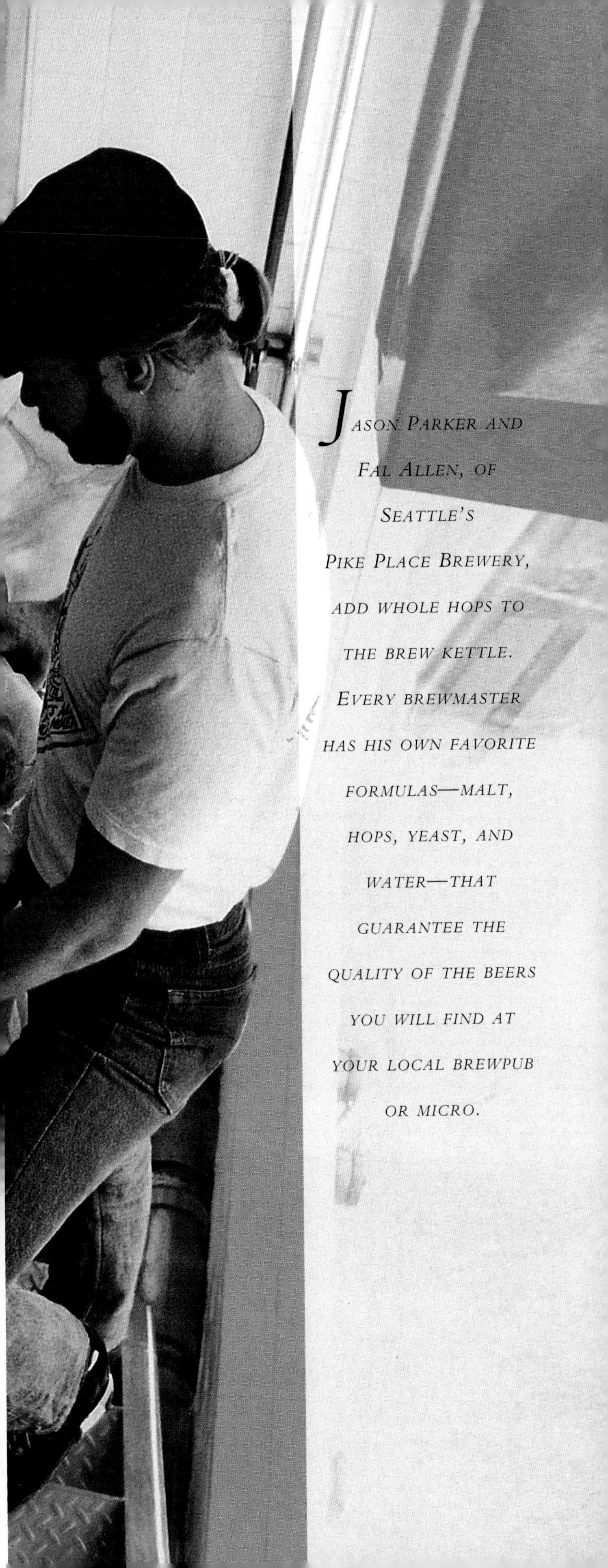

Jason Parker and Fal Allen, of Seattle's Pike Place Brewery, add whole hops to the brew kettle. Every brewmaster has his own favorite formulas—malt, hops, yeast, and water—that guarantee the quality of the beers you will find at your local brewpub or micro.

Photo courtesy of McCormick & Schmick and Full Sail Ale, the Pilsner Room

BREWPUBS COME IN MANY STYLES, FROM RUSTIC TO SOPHISTICATED TO DOWNRIGHT FUNKY. SOME RECALL BRITISH PUBS OR GERMAN BEER CELLARS, OTHERS ARE MORE LIKE FRONTIER SALOONS. THIS HANDSOME EXAMPLE HAS ITS BREWERY AVAILABLE FOR INSPECTION THROUGH PLATE-GLASS WINDOWS.

The holidays are for giving. That's why we share our profits with the African Wildlife Foundation.
WILLIAM & SCOTT'S
WINTERFUL™
BREWED IN
RHINO CHASERS®
A wonderful hearty ale to celebrate the winter season.
12 FL.OZ. (354 ml.)
SMALL BATCHES WITH THE FINEST INGREDIENTS

MANY CRAFT BREWERIES OFFER SPECIAL SEASONAL BEERS SUCH AS RHINO CHASERS® WINTERFUL™. CHEERS!

American cities and that lately have been resuscitated on this side of the Atlantic, especially by contract brewers claiming to revive traditional styles. Seldom as complex as, say, a pale ale, these amber lagers can nonetheless be both tasty and refreshing.

BOCK

The word *bock* is a shortened version of *zeigenbock*—"billy goat"—and these strong lagers have a definite kick. The style was first brewed in Saxony but is now especially associated with Bavaria. Bocks can be dark or light and are often brewed at special times of the year, and for special occasions, as is the case with Maibock. Great bocks are the most complex of the bottom-fermented beers, and some splendid versions have lately been produced in American brewpubs and microbreweries.

DOPPELBOCK

In Germany, a bock must contain at least 6 percent alcohol by volume. As the name suggests, a doppelbock must contain at least 12 percent alcohol by volume. This means that it has to be brewed from an extremely high original gravity, which in turn means that doppelbocks are so malty that even the heaviest hopping cannot entirely alleviate the cloying sweetness. To say that doppelbocks are an acquired taste is something of an understatement, and, perhaps for this reason, there have been few successful attempts at the style in the United States.

DORTMUNDER

Sharper than the helles of Munich, but less hoppy than a pilsner, Dortmunder lager was once considered a distinct branch of the pale lager tradition. Despite the fact that Dortmund is a major brewing city, however, the style has gone out of fashion and is seldom found anywhere except in a handful of American brewpubs.

ANOMALIES

GUEZE–LAMBIC

The beers of the gueze–lambic family—sometimes flavored with fruit—are unique in that they do not make use of a yeast culture but ferment through contact with natural microorganisms in the atmosphere. Brewed from a part-wheat mash, they come in several versions, all of which have a champagne-like sparkle. They are produced in the region of Belgium surrounding Brussels, and nowhere else.

STEAM BEER

Steam beer is the only style of beer indigenous to the United States, having its origins in California in the third quarter of the ninteenth century. Steam beer is made with bottom-fermenting lager yeast but is brewed at a temperature normally thought more suitable for an ale. The result is a beer that combines the clean drinking qualities of a lager with much of the complexity and fruitiness of an ale. In its sole remaining version, this is one of the world's great beers. Appropriately enough, steam beer is the one that launched the American brewing renaissance.

Tasting Notes

Tasting beer should be fun and if there's one drawback to writing a book that attempts to be as comprehensive as this one, it's that we, the authors, sometimes find ourselves having to become too professional, trying to cover the various styles of beer produced by a dozen brewpubs in a single day when it would perhaps be more fun to linger at one watering hole, sipping its seasonal specialty. Enjoying beer, after all, is a social activity that has much to do with circumstance and the company in which the tippler is found.

This is not to say that there are no objective standards involved in beer tasting. We suspect that few readers of this book would disagree with the statement that Anchor Steam Beer displays more hop character than Miller Lite and—while comparisons among craft beers are likely to be less exaggerated than this example—there are somewhat impartial standards that can be applied when rating brews that aspire to please the serious beer fancier. These have nothing to do with differences in preference among individual tasters. One educated beer drinker may favor hoppy ales while another may prefer malty bocks, but beer fanciers are not likely to disagree drastically about what constitutes good hop character or fine malt quality.

That said, the problem is that beers—especially superior-grade, unpasteurized, cask-conditioned brews—are perishable beverages that are greatly affected by temperature, transportation and handling. This means that it is impossible to be sure that one is giving certain brews a completely fair review unless one tastes them under absolutely optimum conditions, which sometimes means when the brews are not more than a few days old and have not been shipped more than a few blocks from the brew kettle.

It is said of certain wines that they do not travel well. In practice, however, most fine wines can be transported across continents and oceans without much damage, as long as they are handled properly and are permitted time to recover. A 1983 Chateau Margaux will taste much the same whether opened in Bordeaux or Boston. On the other hand, a delectable blueberry hefe-weizen brewed at the Crooked Creek Inn on Cape Cod may taste like diluted cough syrup by the time it has been shipped to some Back Bay oyster bar.

This is by way of a preface to saying that, while we have tried to taste the beers reviewed under the best possible circumstances, there is no way of guaranteeing that we have encountered every brew at the peak of its condition. When samples were obviously over-the-hill, we discarded them, but it is only fair to acknowledge that we have undoubtedly rated some beers that, while still very drinkable, were in fact past their prime to an unknowable extent.

When possible, we sampled beers on site at the brewery or brewpub. Ideally we would have tasted all the beers where they were produced, but even though each of us traveled thousands of miles in the course of our research, this was not possible, and so for the rest we relied on beer festivals, samples sent by brewers, and reliable retail outlets.

Brewers take great care to have their products at their best for events such as the Great American Beer Festival. Even so, the hustle and bustle of the event—and the inexperience of volunteer helpers—sometimes causes individual brews to suffer, while the reviewer is also faced with the fact that brewers have been known to make special batches of a given beer for a festival (hoping to impress the judges) so that the sample tasted there is in fact not strictly representative of what might be found back at the old ale house. Despite these drawbacks, we have found that beer festivals provide an excellent opportunity to taste many beers in good to very good condition.

By far the greatest number of beers tasted have been sampled under the circumstances covered by these first two categories. A smaller but still significant number of brews have come in the form of samples shipped directly to us by brewers. In general these seem to have arrived in very good condition (a statement that is supported by the fact that we have been able to cross-check some of these samples with others encountered at festivals and elsewhere). We have handled these samples as carefully as possible and have tasted them as promptly as practicable.

As for samples bought from retail outlets

(other than the breweries and brewpubs that produced the given item), these were purchased for comparison with samples of the same brew obtained elsewhere. They were always purchased from stores or hostelries we knew to treat beer with suitable respect.

In short, we have made every reasonable effort to taste beers at their best. As for our grading system, it utilizes a maximum of five units, with half-units permitted. By way of comparison, we would rate Michelob draft at 🍾½, Beck's (as sold in America) at 🍾🍾 and Heineken at 🍾🍾½. It will be seen, then, that 🍾🍾🍾 signifies a very respectable beer, 🍾🍾🍾½ indicates that a beer is pretty good, and 🍾🍾🍾🍾 is used for a brew that a real beer fancier will want to go out of his or her way to sample. Any score above that tells you that the brew in question is extraordinary.

The astonishing thing is that prior to 1980 it would have been impossible to find more than a handful of American beers that would have deserved a 🍾🍾🍾 rating, or better, by these same standards. Now the 🍾🍾🍾🍾 brews have become almost commonplace.

It should be noted that we do not attempt to list every beer produced by every brewery. To do so would be reckless since one of the joys of the American craft brewing renaissance is the fact that many brewmasters are constantly experimenting with seasonal beers and other specialty items. It would be impossible to keep up with every offering. We have, therefore, concentrated on each brewery's main beers, though we have reviewed seasonal and specialty brews when we have had the opportunity to sample them.

We wish we could have sampled at least one beer from every micro and brewpub in the country. That we have not done so is in large part a reflection of the rapid growth of the real beer movement in America. Literally scores of small craft breweries have opened since we began work on this book. To the extent that we are aware of their existence, and their beers, we list these newcomers even though we haven't had a chance to sample their wares.

Other longer-established beers go unrated because neither of us had the opportunity to visit the site and the brewer did not want the beers judged on the basis of shipped samples. Wanting the entry to be as complete as possible, we list what we know about these establishments so that the reader will have the chance to judge their products independently. As far as possible, we will update and expand our review coverage in future editions of this guide.

Finally, where possible we have listed the original gravity of specific beers. Original gravity ("og") is a measure of the density of fermentable matter in a given brew. The British system of expressing OG (as original gravity is often referred to) is the simplest to understand. In Britain an OG of 1.050 means that there are 50 parts of fermentable matter in 1,000 parts of water. Such a mixture is likely to produce a beer with an alcoholic content of about 5 percent by volume, though various other factors can influence the strength of the beer. Elsewhere in the world, it is more common to express the density of a beer in terms of degrees Plato, a system that is rather more difficult to explain. The same beer with a British OG of 1.050 will have a Plato density of about 12.5. A beer with an OG of 1.070 will have a Plato density of approximately 19.0.

Unfortunately there is no general agreement among American craft brewers as to how density should be expressed, so that some have provided us with figures utilizing the Plato system and others with figures utilizing the British system. For the sake of accuracy, we have printed those figures as they were supplied to us.

Breweries & Brewpubs

SOUTHWEST

Sou

Etna
Eureka
5
Redding
Red Bluff
Chico
Sacramento
San Francisco
San Jose
Santa Cruz
Monterey
5
San Luis Obispo
Santa Barbara
Los Angeles
San Diego
8
10
15
CALIFORNIA
80
NEVADA
Virginia City
Carson City
Las Vegas
84
Salt Lake City
Park City
UTAH
70
Moab
15
ARIZONA
40
17
Cave Creek
Phoenix
Tempe
Tucson
10
19
Bisbee

THWEST

Ft. Collins
Boulder
Brush
Steamboat Springs
Vail
Denver
76
70
COLORADO
Colorado Springs
25
Durango
Embudo
Taos
Santa Fe
Albuquerque
NEW MEXICO
25
Las Cruces
36
Tulsa
44
OKLAHOMA
Oklahoma City
40
27
30
Dallas
20
20
TEXAS
35
45
10
Austin
10
37

ARIZONA

Bandersnatch Brewpub
Black Mountain Brewing Company
Coyote Spring Brewing Co. & Café
Electric Dave Brewery
Gentle Ben's Brewing Company
Hops! Bistro & Brewery
San Francisco Bar, Grill & Brewpub

CALIFORNIA

Anchor Brewing Company
Anderson Valley Brewing Company
Belmont Brewing Company
Bison Brewing
The Boulder Creek Brewing Co.
Brewpub-On-The-Green
Brewhouse Grill
Brewski's Gaslamp Pub, Inc.
Buffalo Bill's Microbrewery & Brewpub
Butterfield Brewing Company
Callahan's Pub & Brewery
Crown City Brewery
Dempsey's Restaurant Brewery
Devil Mountain Brewery
Etna Brewing Company, Inc.
Fullerton Hofbrau
Golden Pacific Brewing Company
Gordon Biersch Brewing Company
Heckler Brewing Company
Heritage Brewing Company
Hogshead Brewpub
Humboldt Brewery
J & L Brewing Company at TJ's
Karl Strauss' Old Columbia Brewery
La Jolla Brewing Company
Lind Brewing Company
Los Gatos Brewing Company
Lost Coast Brewery & Cafe
Mad River Brewing Company
Manhattan Beach Brewing Co.
Marin Brewing Company
Mendocino Brewing Company
Monterey Brewing Company
Moonlight Brewing Company
Murphy's Creek Brewing Company
Napa Valley Brewing Company
Nevada City Brewing Company
North Coast Brewing Company
Pacific Beach Brewhouse
Pacific Coast Brewing Company
Pacific Tap & Grill
Pete's Brewing Company
Pizza Port / Solana Beach Brewery
Red, White & Brew
Redondo Beach Brewing Company
Rhino Chasers
River City Brewing
Riverside Brewing Company
Rubicon Brewing Company
San Andreas Brewing Company
San Diego Brewing Company
San Francisco Brewing Company
Sankt Gallen Brewery & Cafe Pacifica
Seabright Brewery
Shields Brewing Company
Sierra Nevada Taproom & Restaurant
SLO Brewing Company
Southern California Hofbrau
St. Stan's Brewery, Pub & Restaurant
Stoddard's Brewhouse and Eatery
Sudwerk Privatbrauerei Hübsch
Tied House Cafe & Brewery
Triple Rock Brewing Company
Truckee Brewing
Tuscan Brewing Company
Twenty Tank Brewery
Willett's Brewery
Winchester Brewing Company
Woodland Brewing Company

COLORADO

Baked & Brewed in Telluride
Breckenridge Brewery & Pub
Carver Brewing Company
Champion Brewing Company
Coopersmith's Pub & Brewing
Crested Butte Brewery & Pub
Durango Brewing Company
Flying Dog Brewpub
H.C. Berger Brewing Company
Hubcap Brewery & Kitchen
Irons Brewing Company
Judge Baldwin's
Mountain Sun Pub & Brewery
New Belgium
Oasis Brewery
Odell Brewing Company
Rock Bottom Brewery
Rockies Brewing Company
San Juan Brewing Company
Tabernash (Colorado Brewing Co.)
Telluride Beer
Walnut Brewery
Wynkoop Brewing Company

NEVADA

Holy Cow Casino, Cafe & Brewery

NEW MEXICO

Preston Brewery / Embudo Station
Russell Brewing Company
Santa Fe Brewing Company

TEXAS

Armadillo Brewing Company
Bitter End Bistro & Brewery
Celis Brewery
Waterloo Brewing Company

UTAH

Eddie McStiff's
Salt Lake Brewing Company/ Squatter's Pub Brewery
Schirf Brewing Company/Wasatch Brew Pub

B*—*Brewery
BP*—*Brewpub
R*—*Restaurant

B—Available in Bottles
K—Available in Kegs

BANDERSNATCH BREWPUB

B BP R *B*

This brewpub, near Sun Devil Stadium, features British style brews and German, Italian, and Irish food.

BEERS & RATINGS	**CF**
Bandersnatch Premium Ale *(1.048 og; 4.0 w)*	▮▮▮▮½
Bandersnatch Coyote Red *(1.055 og; 4.0 w)*	▮▮▮▮
Bandersnatch Holiday Ale *(1.045 og; 4.5 w)*	▮▮▮▮
Bandersnatch Milk Stout *(1.055 og; 4.0 w)*	▮▮▮▮
Cardinal Pale Ale *(1.045 og; 3.5 w)*	▮▮▮▮

Seasonals:
Jerry's Famous Edinbrew (1.055 og; 4.0 w)
Irish Red (1.055 og; 4.0 w)
Kilkenny Amber (1.045 og; 4.5 w)

Chris: "These brews are outstanding. The Premium Ale is a big-hearted beer with all the characteristics of a classic bitter."

---

125 East Fifth Avenue
Tempe, Arizona 85281
(602) 966·4438

Located 200 yards west of Sun Devil Stadium and 200 yards east of City Hall. Open daily 11-1 am. Jazz, folk, and Irish folk music.

BLACK MOUNTAIN BREWING COMPANY

B BP R *K B*

Black Mountain's beers are sold next door to the brewery in the Satisfied Frog restaurant, owned by the brewer's wife. In addition—and despite the brewery's limited output—the Cave Creek Chili Beer is widely distributed and even exported to England, where quality beer still has its supporters, and Japan, where dry beer was popularized.

BEERS & RATINGS	SG	CF
Ed's Original Cave Creek Chili Beer *(4.7 w)*	ıı½	ııı½
Ed's Original Cave Creek Beer	ıı	ııı

Scott: "To me, this chili beer tastes like diluted tabasco sauce."
Chris: "The hotness of chili is becoming a trendy way of disguising the blandness of mediocre beer. Black Mountain's basic lager is better than that, however, if a little on the sweetish side for my taste."

6245 East Cave Creek Road
Cave Creek, Arizona 85331
(602) 253·6293

15-20 miles north of Phoenix. Take 17th Avenue to Cave Creek Road. W-Sat Country Western singer; Fri-Sun live jazz.

COYOTE SPRING BREWING COMPANY AND CAFE

BP

Arizona does not yet have the reputation of Washington or Colorado where craft brewing is concerned, but it is home to a growing number of good quality micros and brewpubs. Coyote Spring Brewing Company and Cafe has taken over the business formerly known as Barley's Brew Pub and is off to a good start under brewmaster John Vogt-Nilsen.

BEERS & RATINGS	SG	CF
Coyote Gold *(1.047 og; 4.9 w)*	▮▮▮	▮▮▮▮
Nut Brown Ale *(1.048 og; 5.0 w)*	▮▮▮	▮▮▮½
Amber Ale *(1.048 og; 5.0 w)*	▮▮▮	▮▮▮▮
Seasonals:		
India Pale Ale		
Satin Stout		

4883 North 20th Street
Phoenix, Arizona 85016
(602) 468·0403

On the southeast corner of 20th & Camelback in Town & Country Shopping Center.

ELECTRIC DAVE BREWERY

B *KB*

The Electric Dave Brewery was founded in 1988 as one of the smallest micros in the country. The 7¼ barrel system is entirely homemade and makes use of plastic fermenters. The basic Electric Beer is krausened and unfiltered.

BEERS & RATINGS	CF
Ed's Original Cave Creek Electric Beer *(12.5 p)*	III

Chris: "Sweetish and full-bodied."

1A DD Street
South Bisbee, Arizona 85603
(602) 432·3606
Owner/brewer Dave Harvan says his brewery is out of town and is difficult to find; call for directions.

GENTLE BEN'S BREWING COMPANY

B BP *K*

This brewpub, adjacent to the University of Arizona, was established in 1991 and boasts Tucson's largest covered patio. Owner/brewmaster Dennis Arnold is self-taught, but no serious beer fancier who tries his brown ale will hold that against him.

BEERS & RATINGS	CF
Bear Down Nut Brown *(1.042 og; 4.3 w)*	🍾🍾🍾🍾
Copperhead Pale Ale *(1.052 og; 5.4 w)*	🍾🍾🍾½
Desert Big Horn Oatmeal Stout *(1.062 og; 6.3 w)*	🍾🍾🍾
Red Cat Amber	
Taylor Jayne's Raspberry Ale	

841 North Tryndall Avenue
Tucson, Arizona 85719
(602) 624·4177

One block west of University of Arizona.

HOPS! BISTRO AND BREWERY

B BP R *K*

Hops! is a brewpub that features American cuisine with Southwestern, Italian, and Oriental influences. The reason to seek out Hops!, however, is not dim sum burritos or risotto con carne. The food is fine but the beer can be outstanding. Brewmaster Peter McFarlane offers seasonal specialties to complement his three basic brews, a pilsner, an amber ale, and a hefe-weizen.

BEERS & RATINGS	SG	CF
Pilsner *(1.046 og)*		🍾🍾🍾
Amber Ale *(1.058 og)*		🍾🍾🍾½
Hefe-Weizen *(1.054 og)*	🍾🍾🍾🍾	🍾🍾🍾🍾
The Dictator's Little Sister *(17.0 p)*	🍾🍾🍾½	🍾🍾🍾🍾½

Seasonals:
Octoberfest (1.062 og)
Hops! Raspberry (10.5 p)

Scott: "A well-made, refreshing wheat beer."
Chris: "If I say that I'm very fond of the Dictator's Little Sister, I hope I won't be misunderstood. This is a very good, heady version of a South German bock."

7000 East Camelback Road
Scottsdale, Arizona 85251
(602) 945·HOPS

At intersection of Scottsdale & Camelback, in front of Scottsdale Fashion Square, downtown Scottsdale.
Open daily 11:30-1 am.

SAN FRANCISCO BAR, GRILL & BREWPUB

B BP R *K*

This establishment offers a full menu featuring fresh seafood and 25¢ oysters; mostly American cuisine. Live music and dancing on Friday and Saturday nights.

Cactus Lager *(1.052 og; 5.0w)*
Wildcat Ale *(1.054 og; 5.0 w)*
Amber Light *(1.037 og; 5.0 w)*
Mesquite Ale *(1.047 og)*

3922 North Oracle
Tucson, Arizona 85705
(602) 292·2233

At southeast corner of Roger and Oracle roads.
Open daily 11-1.

BAY AREA

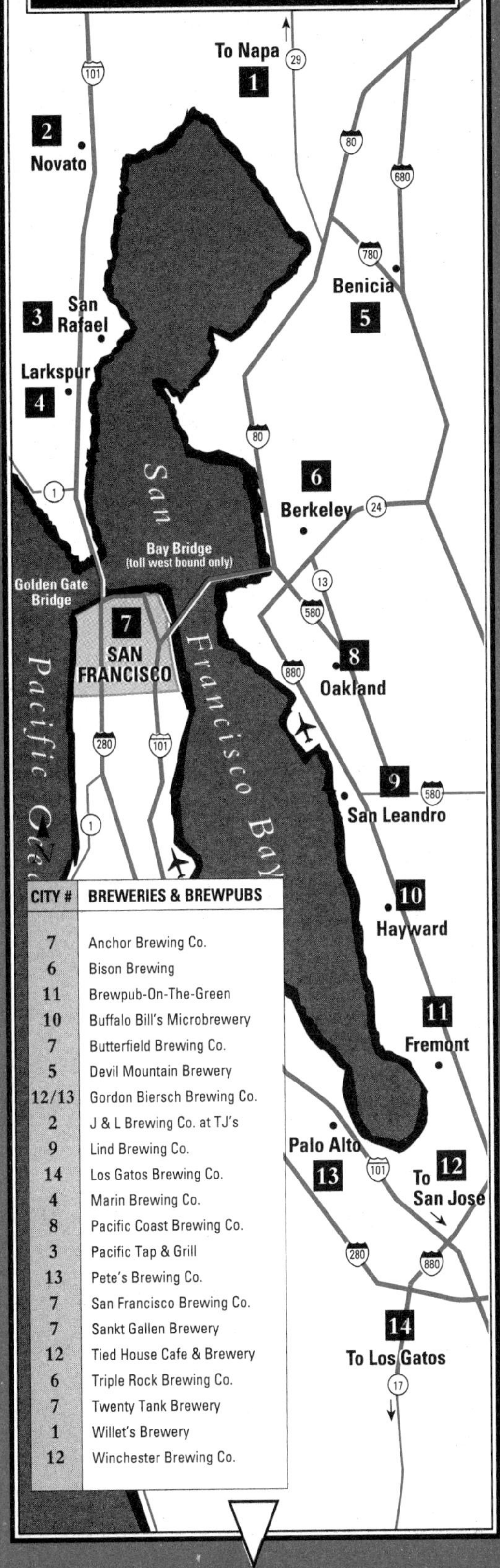

CITY #	BREWERIES & BREWPUBS
7	Anchor Brewing Co.
6	Bison Brewing
11	Brewpub-On-The-Green
10	Buffalo Bill's Microbrewery
7	Butterfield Brewing Co.
5	Devil Mountain Brewery
12/13	Gordon Biersch Brewing Co.
2	J & L Brewing Co. at TJ's
9	Lind Brewing Co.
14	Los Gatos Brewing Co.
4	Marin Brewing Co.
8	Pacific Coast Brewing Co.
3	Pacific Tap & Grill
13	Pete's Brewing Co.
7	San Francisco Brewing Co.
7	Sankt Gallen Brewery
12	Tied House Cafe & Brewery
6	Triple Rock Brewing Co.
7	Twenty Tank Brewery
1	Willet's Brewery
12	Winchester Brewing Co.

ANCHOR BREWING CO.

B KB *B*

Founded in 1896, the Anchor Brewing Company is not strictly speaking a microbrewery, yet it belongs in this book because—under the guidance of Fritz Maytag, who bought the then-floundering concern in 1965—it has been an inspiration to the entire craft brewing movement. Maytag restored Anchor's fortunes and made its basic product, the trademarked Steam Beer, world famous. Anchor also brews other excellent draft beers very much in the British tradition but with a strong American accent. The new brewery on Mariposa Street is a notable blend of the modern and the traditional. Its magnificent copper kettles alone would make it well worth a visit.

BEERS & RATINGS	SG	CF
Anchor Steam Beer	4½	5
Liberty Ale	4	4
Anchor Porter	3½	3½
Anchor Wheat Beer	3½	3½
Celebration Ale	4½	4
Old Foghorn *(barley wine)*	4½	4

Chris: "Anchor Steam Beer is not just a wonderful brew. It genuinely offers a unique taste experience, its palate being as distinctive as that of the best California wines.

1705 Mariposa Street
San Francisco, California 94107
(415) 863·8350

On the corner of Deharo and Mariposa.
Tours by appointment at least 2 weeks in advance.

ANDERSON VALLEY BREWING COMPANY

B BP *K B*

Located in Mendocino County, near the Garcia Highway, Boonville is a mecca for Deadheads and serious beer drinkers. Increasingly well distributed, Anderson Valley's top-fermented brews are best enjoyed at the brewery's own Buckhorn Saloon, which serves hearty American and Mexican food.

BEERS & RATINGS	SG	CF
Poleeko Gold Light Ale *(12.5 p; 4.5 v)*	3½	3
Boont Amber Ale *(13.5 p; 5.2 v)*	4	3
Deep Enders' Dark Porter *(12.9 p; 4.7 v)*	4	3
Barney Platt Oatmeal Stout *(15.5 p; 5.8 v)*	4	3½
High Rollers' Wheat Beer *(12.8 p; 4.8 v)*	3½	3

Chris: "The Anderson Valley brews are always reliable, but they have not yet found a distinctive personality that would make them stand out from the crowd."

14081 Highway 128
P.O. Box 505
Boonville, California 95415
(707) 895·BEER

In downtown Boonville. The trip to Boonville is a long trip on a beautiful winding road from the junction with Highway 101, approximately 2.5 hours from San Francisco. Open 11-10:30 weekdays, 11-midnight weekends.

BELMONT BREWING COMPANY

B BP *K B*

Established in 1990, Belmont Brewing is one of a handful of companies that is attempting to bring the excitement of craft brewing, so well established now in the north of the state, to Southern California. Happily Belmont is off to a good start and the friendly brewpub—near to downtown, the ocean, and a variety of Long Beach attractions—serves a small but promising selection of top-fermented brews.

BEERS & RATINGS	SG	CF
Top Sail Ale *(1.052 og; 4.5 w)*	ııı	ııı
Long Beach Crude *(1.060 og; 4.0 w)*	ııı½	ııı½

Scott: "Long Beach Crude is a porter that is almost as robust as a stout. Tasty, but not as fruity as I'd like."
Chris: "A strong accent of Cascade hops in these brews."

25 39th Place
Long Beach, California 90803
(310) 433·3891

Located on the beach at the foot of Belmont Pier.

BISON BREWING

B BP *K B*

The Bison Brewing Company is an establishment that displays the eclectic taste you would expect of a Berkeley brewpub. The kitchen menu is inexpensive and ranges from taters to tofu. All beers are seasonal and there is a tendency toward such relatively offbeat items as spiced ales. The bar also features the Rogue family of beers from Oregon, and Dry Blackthorn Cider, one of the great treats of the British pub world.

Smoke Scotch Ale *(1.066 og)*
Chocolate Stout *(1.067 og)*
Barley Wine *(1.094 og)*
Gingerbread Ale *(1.060 og)*

2598 Telegraph Avenue
Berkeley, California 94704
(510) 841·7734

Corner of Telegraph & Parker, half a mile from the U.C. Berkeley campus.

THE BOULDER CREEK BREWING COMPANY

B BP *K B*

Boulder Creek is a community in the Santa Cruz Mountains, not far from San Jose. The brewpub that bears its name has been open since 1990, and it is said that more than 30 styles of beer have been brewed on the premises since that time. This might seem overly ambitious, even by adventurous western standards, but the beers we have had the chance to taste justify brewmaster Michael Fisher's self-confidence.

BEERS & RATINGS	**SG**	**CF**
St. Severin's Kolsch *(11.75 p)*	IIII	IIII
O'Meal Stout *(14.75 p)*	IIII	IIII
Old MacLunk's Scottish Ale *(12.5 p)*	IIII	IIII
Seasonals:		
Brother Bob's Porter		
Buzzsaw Bock		
Logger's Lager		

Scott: "Chewy oatmeal flavor to the stout."
Chris: "The names of the beers tells you they're enjoying themselves at Boulder Creek. It's good to see American brewers trying their hands at brews like Kolsch, especially when it's done this well."

13040 Highway 9
Boulder Creek, California 95006
(408) 338·7882

Between Santa Cruz and Saratoga on Highway 9.

BREWPUB·ON·THE·GREEN

BP *K*

Brewpub-on-the-Green is one of the Bay Area ventures of Bill Owens, the man who practically invented the American brewpub. Bill's brewpubs are always reliable and always fun. This one is located on a golf course and attracts the sports bar crowd as well as serious beer fanciers. Typical pub fare—fish and chips, burgers, pasta—is served, and the house beers, brewed under the supervision of Geoff Harris, are handled with pride.

BEERS & RATINGS	**CF**
Mission Wheat *(1.048 og; 3.7 w)*	IIII

ESB *(1.080 og; 6.5 w)*	▮▮▮▮
California Amber *(1.050 og; 4.0 w)*	

Chris: "Yet another excellent wheat beer."

3350 Stevenson Boulevard
Fremont, California 94538
(510) 651·5510

2.5 blocks from the Fremont BART, 1.7 miles east of the 880. Open daily 11-midnight (opens 9 am on football Saturdays).

BREWHOUSE GRILL

***B BP** K*

This casual and cheerful establishment is located near Santa Barbara's picturesque downtown shopping area and a frisbee toss from the beach. The bar tends to be on the noisy side, but beer fanciers addicted to peace and quiet can find those commodities in a walled garden from which the Santa Barbara Mountains can be glimpsed.

BEERS & RATINGS	**CF**
East Beach Blonde	▮▮▮½
Old Town Brown	▮▮▮½

Chris: "Nice session beers, not too heavy after a day of sun and surf."

---

202 State Street
Santa Barbara, California 93101
(805) 963·3090

Two blocks from beach, near the Amtrak Station.

BREWSKI'S GASLAMP PUB, INC.

B BP *B K*

As the name suggests, this Southern California brewpub features an updated version of an Edwardian alehouse atmosphere. The bar surrounds the copper-clad brewhouse, where Mary Lou Moore—one of the owners—prepares a variety of British-style ales, porters, and stouts.

BEERS & RATINGS	SG	CF
Red Sails Ale *(12.5 p)*	3½	3
Aztec Amber Ale *(12.6 p)*	3½	3½
Pioneer Porter *(14.0 p)*	4	3
Seasonals:		
Original Honey Ale		

Scott: "Pioneer is one of those porters that has a chewiness which moves it towards the stout end of the spectrum. Very tasty."
Chris: "The dry-hopped Amber Ale has a pleasant, floral finish."

310 Fifth Avenue
San Diego, California 92101
(619) 231·7700

BUFFALO BILL'S MICROBREWERY & BREWPUB

B BP *K B*

Bill Owens is Mr. Brewpub. Nobody has done more to further the craft beer revolution in America than the publisher of *BEER, The Magazine* and *American Brewer*, who is also the proprietor of Buffalo Bill's Brewery, an establishment that might be taken as the epitome of the American brewpub.

For a dozen years before he opened his East Bay pub in 1983, Owens earned his keep as a photojournalist, freelancing for magazines like *Newsweek*, *Fortune* and *Esquire*. He also authored a book of photographs of suburbia that has become something of a classic. His publishing credentials, then, are impeccable, and as a publisher he is very much in the avant-garde of the beer renaissance.

At the same time, though, Bill Owens is the Jerry Garcia of the brewpub world—a healthy reminder of the gold rush days when craft brewing was a faintly funky activity and one batch of Pumpkin Ale might light up your Halloween more brightly than the next.

But it's hard to pigeonhole Bill Owens. His brewpub is still something of a happy throwback to the pioneer era, but recently he has challenged the new generation of entrepreneurs by going into the contract brewing business and distributing some of his favorites to supermarkets and other retail outlets. With Bill Owens, the only thing you can be sure of is that he will always be connected with good beer, one way or another.

BEERS & RATINGS	SG	CF
Buffalo Brew *(1.042 og; 4.2 w)*	3½	3
Buffalo Amber *(1.042 og; 4.5 w)*	4	3½
Buffalo Stout *(1.050 og; 5.0 w)*	4	4
Pumpkin Ale *(1.044 og; 5.5 w)*	4	4

Chris: "Bill Owens does things his own way—the feisty Black Eye Stout is bottom fermented—and his brews are not subtle, but they have an honest, home brew character that reminds us where the roots of the American brewing renaissance are to be found. I'm a fan."

1082 B Street
Hayward, California 94541
(415) 886·9823
On B Street at Foothill, across the street from Lucky's Supermarket.

BUTTERFIELD BREWING COMPANY

BP *K*

The Butterfield Bar and Grill is a modern, comfortable brewpub that attracts an upwardly mobile crowd and offers basic California-style food and beer brewed on the premises in a handsome and fully visible plant.

BEERS & RATINGS	**CF**
Bridal Veil Ale *(16.5 p; 5.0 v)*	▮▮▮
Strong Pale Ale	▮▮▮
Tower Dark *(17.0 p; 5.0 v)*	▮▮▮½

Chris: "Hoppy, aromatic beers. Tower Dark is almost like a dry version of a Scottish ale."

777 East Olive
San Francisco, California 97328
(209) 264·5521

1.5 miles east of Highway 99; take the Olive Avenue exit. Open M-Th 10:45 am-11; F 10:45-1; Sat 11-1; Sun 11-9.

CALLAHAN'S PUB & BREWERY

BP R *K*

Part of the perhaps surprising San Diego brewing renaissance, and located in the Mira Mesa Shopping Center, Callahan's is self-described as "A little hard to find, really hard to leave." Its 2,500-square-foot restaurant serves the usual pub fare, with some appropriate Gaelic touches. (We'll bet you can't wait to sample the Irish Nachos.) The beer is in the Anglo-Irish tradition.

Mesa Pale Ale *(1.048 og; 4.0 w)*
Bernardo Bitter *(1.060 og; 5.0 w)*
Callahan Red *(1.050 og; 4.5 w)*
Nameless Nut Brown *(1.058 og; 5.0)*
Black Mountain Porter *(1.058 og; 5.0 w)*
Lights Out Stout *(1.055 og; 5.0)*

8280 A Mira Mesa Boulevard
San Diego, California 92126
(619) 578·7892

In the Mira Mesa Shopping Center in North San Diego. Open M-Th 11- midnight; F-Sat 11-1; Sun 10-10.

CROWN CITY BREWERY

B BP R *K B*

Located in a 75-year-old former china factory, Crown City is a handsomely appointed brewpub that attracts a mixed crowd of yuppies, students, exiled Brits and Australians, and beer lovers of all stripes. The food is a cut above the average pub fare, and the service is especially friendly. About a dozen-and-a-half brews are offered on draft, and 150 bottled beers are available. The real attractions, however, are Crown City's own brews, made in a handsome modern facility that can be seen from the bar and restaurant through plate-glass windows.

BEERS & RATINGS	SG	CF
Mount Wilson Wheat Beer *(1.039 og; 3.4 w)*	▮▮▮½	▮▮▮½
Arroyo Amber Ale *(1.040 og; 4.0 w)*	▮▮▮▮	▮▮▮▮
Owen's Irish Stout *(1.044 og)*	▮▮▮▮½	▮▮▮▮
Black Cloud Oatmeal Stout *(1.044 og; 4.0 w)*		▮▮▮▮

Seasonals:
Doo-Dah Ale (1.040 og; 4.0 w)
Yorkshire Porter (1.045 og; 4.0 w)

Scott: "A bit off the main drag of Pasadena, well worth the visit. Not only are their beers excellent, Crown City offers an excellent selection of domestic micros."

300 South Raymond Avenue
Pasadena, California 91105
(818) 577·5548

In the Old Town district, at corner of Raymond & Del Mar, across from the Pasadena Amtrak Station. Open M-Th 11-midnight; F-Sat 11-1; Sun 10-9.

DEMPSEY'S RESTAURANT BREWERY

BP *K*

This brewpub, north of San Francisco, boasts a casual atmosphere and an "adventuresome" menu. The beers are in the Northern California Anglo-American tradition.

Golden Eagle Ale *(12.5 p; 4.0 w)*
Red Rooster Ale *(13.5 p; 4.8 w)*
Ugly Dog Stout *(16.0 p; 6.5 w)*

50 East Washington Street
Petaluma, California 94952
(707) 765·9694

In Golden Eagle Shopping Center in downtown area by the river. Open 7 days 11:30-10.

DEVIL MOUNTAIN BREWERY

B *KB*

Although it has relocated to more spacious premises in Benicia, a few miles north of Berkeley, this well-regarded brewery continues to supply the Devil Mountain Pub in Walnut Grove. The beers brewed in Benicia are very much in the British tradition—the Railroad Ale is reminiscent of the pale ales of London and the home countries—yet they still have a definite personality of their own.

BEERS & RATINGS	SG	CF
Diablo Gold	3½	3
Railroad Ale *(1.066 og; 6.0 w)*	3½	4
Devil's Brew Porter *(1.052 og; 5.5 w)*	3½	4
Devil Mountain Wheat	3	3½

Scott: "Great name for a brewery. The Railroad Ale is full-bodied and well-balanced. Diabolo Gold is quite good as lower-gravity micro beers go. The package design sucks."
Chris: "Malty but well-balanced British-style beers. At their best they can be very good."

2283 Camel Street
Benicia, California 94510
(707) 747·6961

ETNA BREWING COMPANY, INC.

B *KB*

The community of Etna grew up, in the 1850s, around the Rough and Ready flour mill, which was established to take advantage of the fertile farmland thereabouts. Later in the 19th century, a German immigrant named Charles Kappler established a brewery in Etna, and his tradition of craft brewing is carried on today by the present Etna Brewing Company—said to be the northernmost brewery in California—which produces both top-fermented and bottom-fermented beers, all of them unfiltered and unpasteurized.

BEERS & RATINGS	CF
Etna Ale *(1.048 og; 3.6 w)*	ııı½
Etna Dark Lager *(1.046 og; 3.4 w)*	ııı½
Etna Export Lager *(1.050 og; 4.0 w)*	ıııı
Etna Weizen *(1.038 og; 2.9 w)*	ıııı

131 Callahan Street
Etna, California 96027
(916) 467·5277

Off I-5 in northern California.

FULLERTON HOFBRAU

B BP *KB*

Located not far from Disneyland, the Fullerton Hofbrau has a Bavarian brewmaster, Andreas Starkmann, who, understandably, specializes in beers in the German lager tradition, though top-fermented brews are also available. The food offered includes German and American favorites. The sausages served are made in the German delicatessen next door.

BEERS AND RATINGS	CF
King's Lager *(1.05 p; 4.0 w)*	ııı½
Prince's Pilsner *(10.5 p)*	ııı½
Duke's Bock *(18.0 p; 7.0 w)*	
Pale Bock *(16.0 p; 7.0 w)*	

323 N. State College Boulevard
Fullerton, California 92631
(714) 870·7400

One block west of Hwy. 57 and one mile north of Hwy. 91. Open M-Sat 11-1. Closed Sunday.

GOLDEN PACIFIC BREWING COMPANY

B BP KB

Once better known as Thousand Oaks Brewing, Golden Pacific's beers—mostly belonging to the lager family—enjoy an enthusiastic following in the Bay Area.

BEERS & RATINGS	SG	CF
Golden Bear Lager *(1.048 og; 3.8 w)*	▮▮▮½	▮▮▮½
Golden Bear Dark Lager *(1.048 og; 3.8 w)*	▮▮▮½	▮▮▮
Seasonals:		
Cable Car Classic Lager (1.045 og)		
Winter Ale (1.056 og; 5.0 w)		

5515 Doyle Street
Emeryville, California 94608
(510) 655·3322

GORDON BIERSCH BREWING COMPANY

BP R *K B*

The Gordon Biersch brewpubs are classy operations serving not only well-crafted beer but also an eclectic selection of food—California-style, Southwestern, German, Italian, and Thai—in surroundings designed to satisfy the clientele of Silicon Valley and the Stanford University Campus.

Gordon Biersch
BREWERY RESTAURANT

BEERS & RATINGS	SG	CF
Pils *(1.052 og)*	▮▮▮	▮▮▮
Export	▮▮▮½	▮▮▮½
Dunkles *(1.052 og)*	▮▮▮	▮▮▮
Marzen *(1.062 og)*	▮▮▮½	▮▮▮
Doppelbock *(1.085 og)*	▮▮▮½	▮▮▮
Hefe Weizen		▮▮▮½

Scott: "Three cheers for style! Gordon Biersch brewpubs are nicely designed, from the interiors down to the menus. The beers display good flavor and balance."

640 Emerson Street
Palo Alto, California 94301
(415) 323·7723

33 East San Fernando Street
San Jose, California 95113
(408) 294·6785

41 Hugus Alley
Pasadena, California 91103
(818) 449·0052

HECKLER BREWING COMPANY

B *KB*

Founded in 1993, Heckler is a contract brewing company whose beers are produced by the well-regarded August Schell Brewery of New Ulm, Minnesota. Owner Keith Hilken served apprenticeships at the Paulaner Brewery in Munich and at the Bamberger Brauhaus, also in Bavaria. It is his aim to carve a niche for Bavarian-style lagers in what he describes as the "ale-saturated" northern California market.

BEERS & RATINGS	CF
Hell Lager *(12.5 p; 4.9 v)*	▮▮▮½
Fest Marzen *(13.5 p; 5.5 v)*	▮▮▮▮
Doppel Bock *(18.0 p; 7.4 v)*	

P.O. Box 947
Tahoe City, California 96145
(916) 583·2728

HERITAGE BREWING COMPANY

B BP *KB*

Dana Point has more of a surfing heritage than a brewing heritage, but John Stoner and Mark Merikle, who founded Heritage in 1987, have a good understanding of beer traditions, and their seven-barrel brewery produces distinguished British-style ales.

BEERS & RATINGS	**SG**	**CF**
Sail Ale *(1.056 og)*	▮▮▮	
High Seas Oatmeal Stout *(1.060 og)*	▮▮▮	▮▮▮▮
Seasonals:		
Black Fox Stout (1.060)	▮▮▮	
White Fox Porter (1.056)	▮▮▮	

Chris: "Sail Ale is hoppy with a fragrant finish. The oatmeal stout is firm and appropriately rich."

24921 Dana Point Harbor Drive
Dana Point, California 92629
(714) 240·2060

At the corner of Dana Point Harbor Drive & Golden Lantern in Pavilion Center, across from the beach. Open Sun-Th 11:30-midnight; F-Sat 11:30-2.

HOGSHEAD BREWPUB

B *K*

This basement brewpub is located in "Old Town," —the restored historic district of Sacramento.

Hogshead Lager
Hogshead Pale Ale

---

114 J Street
Sacramento, California 95814
(916) 443·BREW

In Old Sacramento, in the basement, half a block from the Pony Express statue.

HUMBOLDT BREWERY

B BP *K B*

This popular brewpub was founded in 1987 by Mario Celotto, formerly of the Oakland Raiders, and at the time of this writing the brewery itself is undergoing a major expansion that, along with the installation of a bottling line, will make Humboldt's beers available throughout the Northwest, from northern California to Washington.

BEERS & RATINGS	SG	CF
Gold Rush Pale Ale *(1.042 og)*	▮▮▮▮	▮▮▮▮
Oatmeal Stout *(1.058 og)*	▮▮▮▮½	▮▮▮▮
Red Nectar *(1.048 og)*	▮▮▮▮	▮▮▮½
Storm Cellar Porter *(1.053 og)*	▮▮▮½	

Chris: "Basically British in general style, but the hopping is floral in a way that gives these beers a very American jauntiness."

---

856 10th Street
Arcata, California 95521
(707) 826·BREW

One block from the Historic Plaza in downtown Arcata. Open M-Th 11:30-11; F-Sat 11:30-2; Sun 11:30-10.

J & L BREWING COMPANY AT TJ'S

B BP *K B*

Owned by head brewer Jim Hyde, and sales manager Lee Strauss, this Marin County brewpub specializes in malty ales. Its restaurant features both a pub menu and a full dinner menu, and there is a beer garden.

San Rafael Amber *(1.052 og; 5.0 w)*
San Rafael Golden *(1.048 og)*
San Rafael Diamond *(1.050 og)*

7110 Redwood Boulevard
Novato, California 94947
(415) 459·4846
101 North Rowland Blvd. west to Redwood. Pub open weekends 11-2 am; brewery by appointment only.

KARL STRAUSS' OLD COLUMBIA BREWERY AND GRILL

BP R *K*

Old Columbia is located in a busy section of downtown San Diego, where the hearty food and fresh beer attract a lively crowd, both at lunchtime and after the workday is over. Karl Strauss is a German-born brewmaster who served as a consultant to a number of micros and brewpubs before his involvement in Old Columbia, the oldest brewpub in this part of California. Although a couple of Old Columbia's beers are described as ales, this is basically a lager brewery, and a good one. The Amber lager is available on tap in a growing number of outlets in San Diego County.

BEERS & RATINGS	SG	CF
Karl Strauss Amber Lager *(12.5 p)*	▮▮▮	▮▮▮
Horton's Hooch *(17.0 p)*	▮▮▮½	▮▮▮▮
Point Loma	▮▮▮½	
Lighthouse Light *(8.1 p)*	▮▮▮½	
Karl's Cream Ale *(13.5 p)*	▮▮▮½	
Gaslight Gold Ale *(13.8 p)*	▮▮▮▮	

Chris: "Horton's Hooch is an excellent example of a paler, almost brass-colored bock, well-attenuated and reminiscent of Einbecker Maibock."

1157 Columbia Street
San Diego, California 92101
(619) 234·BREW

In the heart of downtown San Diego. Near the southeast corner of Columbia & B streets, between B & C streets. Open M-Th 11:30-midnight; F-Sat 11:30-1; Sun 11:30-10.

LA JOLLA BREWING COMPANY

B BP *K*

Established in 1990, the La Jolla Brewing Company is a beach town brewpub located a few minutes drive north of downtown San Diego. The 10-barrel brewhouse is visible behind a mahogany bar. The restaurant offers a varied menu and reasonable prices. (There is also an outdoor patio.) Beers are served from the cask and are named for local landmarks and favorite "surf breaks."

Blitzen Ale *(1.078 og)*
Pumphouse Porter *(1.066 og)*
Red Rooster Ale *(1.053 og)*
Big Rock Bock

7536 Fay Avenue
La Jolla, California 92037
(619) 456·BREW

Located just north of Pearl Street. Open Sun-Th 11-11; F-Sat 11-2.

LIND BREWING COMPANY

B *KB*

The Lind Brewing Company is a tiny microbrewery that distributes its wares, on tap only, in the San Francisco Bay Area where the ales named for Sir Francis Drake (who visited this part of the world in 1579) are deservedly well regarded by local beer enthusiasts.

BEERS & RATINGS	SG	CF
Drake's Ale *(1.054 og; 5.5 v)*	▮▮▮▮	▮▮▮▮
Sir Francis Stout *(1.066 og; 4.9 v)*	▮▮▮▮	▮▮▮▮
Drake's Gold *(1.054 og; 5.5 v)*	▮▮▮▮	
Seasonals:		
Drake's Pale Ale (1.056 og; 5.5 v)		
Drake's IPA (1.066 og; 6.0 v)		

Chris: "Despite its relatively high gravity and alcohol content, Sir Francis Stout is a delightfully easy-drinking brew, very soft on the palate but with plenty of hop bite in the background."

1933 Davis Street #177
San Leandro, California 94577
(510) 562·0866

In the Westgate Mall. West of the 880 freeway.

LOS GATOS BREWING COMPANY

BP

This brewpub serves California cuisine, makes a feature of Sunday brunch, and offers German-style beers.

Los Gatos Lager *(11.0 p; 4.2 v)*
Octoberfest *(13.5 p; 4.8 v)*
Dunkel *(13.0 p; 4.7 v)*

130 G North Santa Cruz
Los Gatos, California 95060
(408) 395·9929

Open Sun-Th 11:30-11; F-Sat 11:30-1.

LOST COAST BREWERY & CAFE

B BP *K B*

One of the few micros or brewpubs run by women, Lost Coast is largely the brainchild of Barbara Groom, who switched to brewing when she became bored with the drugstore business. The on-premises pub offers the usual burgers and salads, but also specializes in imaginative Cajun-Creole dishes and home-baked bread. The beers to date are predominantly in the British idiom with typical West Coast inflections.

BEERS & RATINGS	SG	CF
Lost Coast Pale Ale *(1.050 og)*	▮▮▮½	▮▮▮½
Downtown Brown Ale *(1.050 og)*	▮▮▮	▮▮▮½
Lost Coast Amber *(1.050 og)*		
Lost Coast Porter *(1.052 og)*		

Chris: "Lost Coast presents its beers with real flair. A brewery that shows considerable promise."

617 Fourth Street
Eureka, California 95501
(707) 455·5726

On the edge of Eureka's Old Town shopping district, southbound on Hwy. 101, between G & H streets. Open M-Th 11-11; F-Sat 11-midnight; Sun 9:30-9:30.

MAD RIVER BREWING COMPANY

B *KB*

Located in Humbolt County, where dairy country meets the redwoods, and close by the beautiful city of Eureka, this brewery takes both its name and its water supply from the river that runs through town.

BEERS & RATINGS	SG	CF
Steelhead Bitter	ııı	ııı½
Steelhead Extra Pale Ale	ıı½	ııı½
Steelhead Extra Stout	ıı½	ııı

195 Taylor Way
Blue Lake, California 95525
(707) 668·4151

East of Arcata on State Highway 299. Open M-Sat 9-5.

MANHATTAN BEACH BREWING COMPANY

B BP *K*

A lively brewpub overlooking the ocean, popular with the singles crowd both for its beer and its casual atmosphere. The location is near Manhattan

CALIFORNIA

Beach Pier and the oceanfront boardwalk and bike path. This is a year-round mecca for skateboarders, roller-bladers, volleyball players and sunworshippers. A large oak bar dominates the room, where gourmet pizzas are available, along with burgers, sandwiches and salads.

BEERS & RATINGS	SG	CF
Manhattan Beach Blonde *(1.040 og)*	ııı½	ııı½
South Bay Bitter *(1.044 og)*	ııı½	ıııı
Rat Beach Red *(1.054 og)*	ııı½	
Dominator Wheat *(1.042 og)*		ııı½

124 Manhattan Beach Boulevard
Manhattan Beach, California 90266
(310) 798·2744

Take 405 Freeway to Inglewood south, ¼ mile to Manhattan Beach Blvd. west, to the beach and pier. Cross streets are Manhattan Beach Blvd. and The Strand. Open Sun-Th 11-midnight; F-Sat 11-1.

MARIN BREWING COMPANY
CALISTOGA INN

B BP R *K B*

Located in the Larkspur Landing Shopping Center, adjacent to the Larkspur Ferry Terminal (and handy to San Quentin Prison), Marin's brewpub serves some of the best beers in the San Francisco Bay Area and also offers food that is a cut above the pub average, with a variety of Italian specialties, as well as burgers, sandwiches, and ribs. Popular with both the upscale commuters of Mill Valley and San Anselmo and with grizzled veterans of the Altamont Generation. (Grateful Dead videos are a special attraction the first Tuesday of every month).

BEERS & RATINGS	SG	CF
Mount Tam Pale Ale *(1.058 og; 5.0 v)*	▮▮▮▮	▮▮▮▮
Point Reyes Porter *(1.065 og)*	▮▮▮▮	▮▮▮▮
San Quentin Stout *(1.072-76 og)*	▮▮▮▮½	▮▮▮▮½
Main Weiss *(1.055 og; 4.5 v)*	▮▮▮½	▮▮▮▮
Seasonals:		
Blueberry Ale (1.055 og; 5.0 v)	▮▮▮	▮▮▮½
Raspberry Trail Ale (1.060 og)	▮▮▮½	▮▮▮▮

Scott: "The stout has a delicious toffee flavor. The pale ale displays a nice hoppiness. The porter has rich coffee overtones."

11809 Larkspur Landing Circle
Larkspur, California 94939
(415) 461·HOPS

Located in Larkspur Landing Shopping Center, across the street from Larkspur Ferry Terminal in Marin County. Open M-Th 11:30-midnight; F-Sat 11:30-1; Sun 11:30-midnight.

MENDOCINO BREWING COMPANY

B BP *K B*

It is only appropriate that a town called Hopland should be the site of California's first modern brewpub, opened there in 1983 with equipment purchased from New Albion, America's first modern microbrewery. Founded by Michael Leybourn, Mendocino is widely known for its well-distributed Red Tail Ale, but it also produces a number of other highly-regarded beers that are California interpretations of classic British styles. The brewpub is located in a century-old brick building that was once a post office. The food served is an imaginative version of western American cuisine, featuring such specialties as hot beer sausages.

BEERS & RATINGS	SG	CF
Red Tail Ale *(1.054 og; 5.25 w)*	IIII½	IIII½
Blue Heron Pale Ale *(1.054 og; 5.0 w)*	III½	IIII
Black Hawk Stout *(1.054 og; 4.5 w)*	IIII	IIII
Peregrine Pale Ale *(1.0 og; 4.0 w)*	IIII	IIII

Scott: "My rating of Red Tail Ale is based on tasting a fresh batch on tap. It has great balance, but I've sometimes been disappointed with this beer in the bottle."
Chris: "For me Red Tail Ale is one of the benchmarks of West Coast brewing. I love its creaminess and complexity."

13551 South Highway 101 South
Hopland, California 95449
(707) 744·1361

In Downtown Hopland on Hwy. 101.
Open M-Th 11-10; F-Sat 11-1; Sun 11-10.

MONTEREY BREWING COMPANY

B BP *K B*

Founded in 1988, this brewpub is located near the aquarium and wharf. Appropriately, its menu places an emphasis on fresh seafood, though pizzas, smoked sausages and other favorites are also available.

BEERS & RATINGS	SG	CF
Killer Whale Amber Ale *(1.046 og)*	▮▮½	▮▮½
Sea Lion Stout *(1.066 og)*	▮▮▮½	

638 Wave Street
Monterey, California 93940
(408) 375·3634

Near the aquarium and wharf; across from the Cannery Row Garage. Open M-Sat 11-2; Sun 11-11.

MOONLIGHT BREWING COMPANY

B *K*

This micro is located just north of Santa Rosa, in an area that has become a hotbed of brewing activity. Brian Hunt began this one-man operation in the fall of 1993, having assembled his equipment from "the bones of at least fifteen breweries."

Moonlight Pale Lager *(12.0 og; 3.9 w)*
Twist of Fate Bitter Ale *(13.6 og; 4.5 w)*
Death and Taxes Black Beer *(12.0 og; 3.9 w)*
Santa's Tipple Strong Ale *(15.5 og; 5.0 w)*

P.O. Box 316
Fulton, California 95439
(707) 528·2537

Just north of Santa Rosa (not open to the public)

MURPHY'S CREEK BREWING CO.

B *K B*

The only brewery since Prohibition in Calaveras County, Murphy's Creek distributes its products in both bottles and kegs and offers beer to go.

Murphy's Red Ale *(12.5 p; 4.3 w)*
Murphy's Golden Wheat *(14.3 p; 3.0 w)*
Murphy's Black Gold Stout *(14.0 p; 4.0 w)*

P.O. Box 1077
4557 French Gulch Road
Angel's Camp, California 95222
(209) 736-BREW

Off Hwy. 4 in Angel Camp. Turn left onto Murphy's Grade Road and then 2.5 miles up. Tasting hours: Saturday & Sunday 11-5.

NAPA VALLEY BREWING COMPANY CALISTOGA INN

B BP R *K B*

Located in a turn-of-the-century building, in what was till recently thought of as wine country, the Calistoga Inn is a rarity among American brewpubs in that it offers comfortable accommodations to overnight visitors and has a kitchen that provides patrons with imaginative fare altogether too sophisticated to describe as pub food. It's tempting to say that the Calistoga Inn is not a pub at all until one remembers that many of the best British pubs are housed in country inns much like this, and are occasionally furnished with fine restaurants that belie Britain's reputation for mediocre food. The brewery itself is located in an old water tower on the premises.

BEERS & RATINGS	SG	CF
Calistoga Golden Lager *(1.048 og)*	2½	2½
Calistoga Wheat Ale *(1.044 og)*	3	2½
Calistoga Red Ale *(1.056 og)*		

1250 Lincoln Avenue
Calistoga, California 94515
(707) 942·4101

At the corner of Lincoln & Cedar.
Open 11:30-midnight daily.

NEVADA CITY BREWING COMPANY

B *KB*

Founded in 1986, this brewery offers Saturday afternoon tours and beer to go. Its principle product is Nevada City Brew, a draft lager that is neither filtered nor pasteurized.

Nevada City Brew
California Gold Lager *(4.0 w)*
California Dark Lager *(4.0 w)*

---

75 Bost Street
Nevada City, California 95959
(916) 265·2446

Off Searle behind SPD. Saturday tours 1-5; Friday 3-5. Just come on in.

NORTH COAST BREWING COMPANY

B BP *B*

Located on the California coast, near several state parks, North Coast Brewing makes its headquarters in an attractive 1916 building. The kitchen provides patrons with basic burgers, salads, and pasta. It's the beer, though, along with the scenery, that makes Fort Bragg a worthwhile destination.

NORTH COAST BREWING Co

BEERS & RATINGS	SG	CF
Centennial Ale	III½	IIII
Red Seal Ale *(1.057 og)*	IIII	IIII
Old 38 Stout *(1.058 og)*	IIII½	IIII
Scrimshaw Pilsner *(1.045 og)*	III	III½

Scott: "An excellent stout with burnt coffee and toffee flavors."
Chris: "Big, chewy, well-rounded beers with a dry, satisfying finish."

---

444 North Main
Fort Bragg, California 95437
(707) 964·2739

At corner of Pine Street & Main Street,
across from the Skunk Train.
Open T-Sat 2-11; closed Sunday & Monday.

PACIFIC BEACH BREWHOUSE

B *B*

A new San Diego-area establishment located near La Jolla, Sea World and several college campuses.

Crystal Pier Pale Ale
Pacific Beach Blondes
Over the Line Stout
Sunset Red

4475 Mission Boulevard H-1
Pacific Beach, California 92109
(619) 274·ALES

PACIFIC COAST BREWING COMPANY

B BP *KB*

Not many hostelries offer the ambiance of pre-Prohibition imbibing as impressively as the Pacific Coast Brewing Company. Located in downtown Oakland, PC's carefully restored 1876 building provides just the right atmosphere for sampling traditional brews, and, happily, the beers made on the premises fit the bill very nicely.

BEERS & RATINGS	SG	CF
Gray Whale Ale *(1.052 og; 5.0 v)*	▮▮▮▮	▮▮▮½
Blue Whale Ale *(1.070 og; 7.0 v)*	▮▮▮▮½	▮▮▮▮
Killer Whale Stout *(1.055 og; 5.0 v)*	▮▮▮½	▮▮▮▮
Imperial Stout *(1.080 og; 8.0 v)*		
Seasonals:		
Amethyst Blackberry Ale (1.048 og; 4.0)	▮▮▮▮	▮▮▮▮
Humpback Alt (1.050 og; 5.0)		

Scott: "I like the hint of smokiness in the Gray Whale Ale and the hops character of the Blue Whale Ale. The Blackberry Ale has a nice nose and good follow-through on the fruit. Very refreshing."
Chris: "Dry hopping lends Pacific Coast's excellent ales a complex and subtle finish."

906 Washington Street
Oakland, California 94607
(415) 836·2739

PACIFIC TAP AND GRILL

BR *K*

Established in 1993, Pacific Tap and Grill features a beer garden where Sunday brunch is served.

Mission Gold Ale *(1.046 og; 4.5 v)*
Bootjack Amber Ale *(1.048 og; 5.0 v)*
Noah's Dark Ale *(1.048 og; 5.0 v)*
Riley's Wheat *(1.044 og; 4.0 v)*

---

812 Fourth Street
San Rafael, California 94901
(415) 457·9711

Central SR exit off 101 north. Open daily 11:30 am-12 midnight. Occasional live music.

PETE'S BREWING COMPANY

B

Pete Slosberg was an enthusiastic home brewer and Silicon Valley marketing executive when in 1986 he joined forces with Mark Bronder—another beer enthusiast—to found the Palo Alto Brewing Company. Palo Alto's six-packs were embellished with the image of Pete's pit bull, Millie, and the Latin legend "Cave Canum Nidentum" (Beware of the white dog). About that time, Budweiser's advertising wise guys came up with the concept of Spuds McKenzie, and Palo Alto was slapped with cease and desist letters. Pete was able to prove that his use of Millie predated Bud's use of Spuds, and Anheuser-Busch backed down. Unfortunately, consumers assumed that Palo Alto was imitating Bud, so Slosberg was forced to rethink his marketing concept from scratch.

It was at this point that Slosberg brought in new management with solid experience in the business of distribution, and since then Pete's Brewing Company, as the company is now called, has become a considerable presence on the real beer scene. Their basic products are brewed by Minnesota Brewing Company and are widely available. Slosberg is well known among beer enthusiasts as an ardent preacher of craft brewing gospel, traveling the country as an advocate for the cause.

BEERS & RATINGS	**SG**	**CF**
Pete's Wicked Ale	▮▮▮▮	▮▮½
Pete's Gold Coast Lager	▮▮▮½	▮▮▮

Scott: "Pete's Wicked Ale is a great name and it has great packaging."
Chris: "Pete's brews lack complexity, but they do display an agreeable gutsiness."

514 High Street
Palo Alto, California 94301
(415) 328-7383

PIZZA PORT/SOLANA BEACH BREWERY

B Ṙ *K Party Pigs*

Located a block from the beach, Pizza Port features customers in shorts and tank tops, "anti-wimpy" gourmet pizzas and top-fermented beers that, judging by their OGs, must pack a potent punch.

Shark's Bite Red Ale *(1.053 og; 5.3 w)*
Port's Porter *(1.058 og; 5.8 w)*
Swami's India Pale Ale *(1.068 og; 6.8 w)*

135 North Highway 101
Solana Beach, California 92075
(619) 481·7332

One mile north of Del Mar Racetrack.
Open 11:30-11, midnight on Fridays & Saturdays.

RED, WHITE & BREW

BP *Jugs To Go*

This is a recently opened brewpub in the Lake Shasta area. The kitchen offers appetizers along with lunch and dinner specials.

Lassen Lager
Trinity Trail Pale Ale *(1.068 og; 5.5 w)*

2181 Hill Top Drive
Redding, California 95814
(916) 447·BREW

Open daily 11-11.

REDONDO BEACH BREWING COMPANY

BP

A younger cousin of the nearby Manhattan Beach Brewery, this is another lively brewpub with a laid-back, surfside atmosphere. David Zizlis—a partner in both establishments—is also the owner of Bohemian Brewery Importers, so, not surprisingly, a handsome Czech-built ten-barrel brewplant is the centerpiece of this establishment, which is built on two levels, with two bars and two outdoor patios. The menu features California-style pub food with an emphasis on pizzas, pastas, burgers, salads and sandwiches.

BEERS & RATINGS	**CF**
Redondo Beach Blonde *(1.046 og)*	▮▮▮▮
Dominator Wheat *(1.052 og)*	▮▮▮½
Pier Pale Ale *(1.058 og)*	▮▮▮½
Rat Beach Red *(1.054 og)*	

135 North Highway 101
Solana Beach, California
(619) 481·7332

RHINO CHASERS

B *KB*

Since Scott Griffiths is CEO of William & Scott, he disqualifies himself from giving an objective rating of the Rhino Chasers range of beers. Since I am not an employee of William & Scott, I have no such scruples. First, a smidgin of history.

Although some of William & Scott's proceeds are contributed to the African Wildlife Foundation, the beer was not, in fact, named for anything to do with the large African mammals, let alone the men who hunt them. Rather it was named for another kind of hunter, the surfers who seek out the largest and most radical waves in Hawaii. The legend goes back to when Greg Knoll, in 1960, was the first to ride Waimea, on the North Shore of Oahu. The surfboards were nicknamed guns. On a big day they would use their Elephant Guns, on a huge day, their Rhino Guns. Greg and his buddies became legendary, and a surfboard called the "Rhino Chasers" was designed in 1969 by Dick Brewer to commemorate the extreme surfers.

Rhino Chasers beer had its origins in the

late eighties, when Scott Griffiths ran a marketing design firm that sponsored a team in the Los Angeles Advertising Softball League. After games, he would serve beer, and he decided to have his own team beer. The players enjoyed it so much, he put it into a restaurant that he's involved with, where they sold twenty cases in the first month. Pretty soon restaurants all over the area were carrying Rhino Chasers, and the distributors began calling.

As of this writing, Rhino Chasers is distributed in 45 states. They are underway to open their first brewpub toward the end of 1995.

Rhino Chasers is not only an excellent beer, but it also supports a great cause.

RHINO CHASERS®
GREAT AMERICAN LAGERS & ALES

BEERS & RATINGS	CF
Rhino Chasers Amber Ale *(4.0 w; 1.014 og)*	🍾🍾🍾🍾
Rhino Chasers American Ale *(3.6 w; 1.010 og)*	🍾🍾🍾🍾½
Rhino Chasers Lager *(3.8 w; 1.013 og)*	🍾🍾🍾½
Rhino Chasers Dark Lager *(3.9 w; 1.012 og)*	🍾🍾🍾🍾
Rhino Chasers Hefe-weizen *(new)*	
Seasonals:	
Rhino Chasers Winterful (14.1 p)	🍾🍾🍾🍾

Scott: "I respect Chris' refined taste, but everybody's entitled to an off day.

Oh, by the way, I just tasted our new hefe-weizen and it's a 🍾🍾🍾🍾🍾."

8460 Higuera Street
Culver City, California 90232
(800) 788·HORN

No brewery tours (contract brewer).

RIVER CITY BREWING

BR

Opening its doors to the public in December 1993, River City brews German and Austrian-style beers to accompany the food on its unusually ambitious Western-accented menu.

River City Lager *(1.050 og; 4.0 w)*
Vienna Lager *(1.054 og; 4.2 w)*
Maibock *(1.068 og; 5.5 w)*

---

545 Downtown Plaza
Sacramento, California 95814
(916) 447·BREW

At Third & K streets.
Open Sun-Th 11:30-midnight; Fri-Sat till 1:30.
Occasional live music.

RIVERSIDE BREWING COMPANY

BP *KB*

Launched in the summer of 1993, this ambitious brewpub is located a couple of blocks from the famous Mission Inn, in the old Fruit Exchange Building, which, around the turn of the century, was the clearinghouse for the area's citrus growers. The pub-style menu features a few unusual twists, such as a buffalo burger and "frickles" (deep-fried breaded kosher dill pickles).

BEERS & RATINGS	CF
Golden Spike Pilsner *(11.3 p; 5.1 v)*	▮▮▮½
Pullman Pale Ale *(13.0 p; 5.8 v)*	▮▮▮½
Victoria Ave Amber Ale *(15.0 p; 5.8 v)*	▮▮▮▮
7th Street Stout *(14.5 p; 6.0 v)*	▮▮▮▮
Cream Ale	▮▮▮▮

Seasonals:
Cherry Kölsch (10.8 p; 5.0 v)
Oktoberfest (13.5 p; 6.4 v)
Christmas Bock (17.0 p; 7.7 v)

Chris: "Each beer has a clearly defined character, yet there is a definite house style. I especially liked the Cream Ale, which has something of the feel of a good British sipping beer, dry and satisfying."

3397 Seventh Street
Riverside, California 92501
(909) 682·5465

Located on the corner of 7th and Lime—
one block north of the 91 Freeway,
two blocks south of the Mission Inn.

RUBICON BREWING COMPANY

B *KB*

Rubicon is a brewpub that opened its doors in 1987. It seats approximately 100 people and offers typical pub food to go along with its very dependable beers, which are mostly top-fermented, though a pilsner is sometimes available.

BEERS & RATINGS	SG	CF
Rubicon Wheat *(1.045 og)*		▮▮▮▮
Rubicon IPA *(1.058 og)*	▮▮▮	▮▮▮½
Rubicon Stout *(1.061 og)*		▮▮▮½
Rubicon Amber Ale *(1.053 og)*		▮▮▮½
Seasonals:		
Rubicon Irish Red Ale (1.064 og)		
Rubicon Pilsner (1.048 og)		

Chris: "Unashamedly West Coast-style beers. The IPA will satisfy any fan of American hops."

2004 Capital Avenue
Sacramento, California 95814
(916) 448·7032

On the corner of 20th & Capital, next to America's Italian Restaurant.

SAN ANDREAS BREWING COMPANY

B BP *K B*

A popular brewpub, located disquietingly near the celebrated fault, San Andreas also bottles some of its excellent beers for wider distribution. The brewpub is located in the old Baywood Creamery building, and has something of the atmosphere of a beverage museum, its walls decorated with many historical photographs and items of breweriana.

San Andreas Brewing Co.

BEERS & RATINGS	SG	CF
Earthquake Pale Ale *(1.036 og)*	iiii	iiii
Seismic Ale	iiii	iiii
Earthquake Porter *(1.042 og)*	iii½	iiii

Chris: "Earthquake Pale Ale is a good example of the fact that a beer with a relatively low original gravity (1.036) can still display plenty of flavor and character. Such brews are often found in England but remain something of a rarity on this side of the Atlantic."

737 San Benito Street
Hollister, California 95023
(408) 637·7074

Hwy. 101 south of San Jose to Hwy. 25, south of Gilroy, continue to 737 San Benito. Open T-Th 11-10; F-Sat 11-11; Sun 11-10; Closed Monday.

SAN DIEGO BREWING COMPANY

BP *K*

San Diego is rapidly becoming the brewpub capital of Southern California, This 1993 entry is centrally located and features pub fare, pastas, and salads along with a range of top-fermented brews.

BEERS & RATINGS	SG
Blueberry Wheat Ale *(1.040 og; 3.8 v)*	iiii
Grantville Golden Ale *(1.045 og; 4.0 v)*	iiii
San Diego Ale *(1.050 og; 4.5 v)*	iiii

10450 Friar's Road,
San Diego, California 92120
(619) 284·2739

Near Jack Murphy Stadium. Open M-Th 11-midnight; F-Sat 11-1; Sun 10-midnight.

SAN FRANCISCO BREWING COMPANY

BP *KB*

Located in the shadow of the TransAmerica Pyramid Building, this brewpub is located in a building that has some real history attached to it. Originally it housed the Andromeda Saloon and later the somewhat notorious Albatross Tavern, where Baby Face Nelson was arrested and Jack Dempsey was a bouncer. The place still looks as if Baby Face might walk in through the door, having been sprung from the local slammer, and the beer has the character to go along with the period decor.

BEERS & RATINGS	SG	CF
Albatross Lager	▮▮▮	▮▮▮
Emperor Norton Lager	▮▮▮	▮▮▮½
Oatmeal Stout	▮▮▮	▮▮▮▮
Alcatraz Stout		
Seasonals:		
Grace Darling Bock		
Andromeda Wheat Beer		
Year of the Dragon Ale		

Scott: "The lagers are notably malty. The oatmeal stout has a full flavor and a dry finish."
Chris: "San Francisco's brews are good and have improved since I first tasted them. The silky oatmeal stout demonstrates what this brewery is capable of."

155 Columbus Avenue
San Francisco, California 94133
(415) 434·3344

Two blocks from the TransAmerica Pyramid Building at the corner of Columbus & Pacific.
Open M-Th 11:30-12:30; F 11-1:30; Sat 12-1:30; Sun 12-midnight.

SANKT GALLEN BREWERY AND CAFE PACIFICA

B BP *K B*

Given the location, the Cafe Pacifica part of the name needs no explanation. It is the retail outlet of the Sankt Gallen Brewery, and interestingly enough it serves Chinese food. As for Sankt Gallen, this is the name of the Swiss monastery where the oldest written records of brewing in Europe are to be found. Those records date from the 8th century. If the combination of European-style craft beer and Chinese food seems eclectic, the beers themselves tend towards eclecticism too. Sankt Gallen Dark Ale is described as "our top-fermented interpretation of the great dark beers of Europe, especially Munich and Kulmbach." And why not? Respect for tradition has lent substance to the American beer renaissance, but it is experimentation and acceptance of eccentricity that has given that renaissance its own flavor.

Amber Ale *(4.7 w)*
Pale Ale *(4.7 w)*
Dark Ale *(4.7 w)*

---

333 Bush Street
San Francisco, California 94104
(415) 296·8203

Between New Montgomery and Kearny.

SEABRIGHT BREWERY

B BP *KB*

This cheerful brewpub, located near the beach—the patio provides an ocean view—attracts a young crowd and offers seasonal specialties along with an eclectic selection of food that ranges from Cajun to Mexican to locally caught fish.

BEERS & RATINGS	**SG**	**CF**
Seabright Amber Ale *(13.2 p)*	🍾🍾🍾½	🍾🍾🍾
Banty Rooster India Pale Ale *(13.5 p)*	🍾🍾🍾½	🍾🍾🍾
Pelican Pale Ale *(13.0 p)*	🍾🍾🍾½	
Black Cat Imperial Stout *(13.25 p)*	🍾🍾🍾🍾	
Seasonals:		
Pleasure Point Porter (13.5 p)		
Seabright Gold (12.0 p)		
Seabright Extra Special Bitter (14.0 p)		

519 Seabright Avenue Suite 107
Santa Cruz, California 95062
(408) 426·2739

At the corner of Seabright & Murray Streets; 2 blocks from the beach, between the Harbor & Beach boardwalk. Open Sun-Th 11:30 am-midnight; F-Sat 11:30-12:30.

SHIELDS BREWING COMPANY

BP *KB*

Ventura's historical district is a paradise for antique mavens and book browsers. Miraculously, it has not yet been tarted up. Shields is located on the northern edge of this colorful neighborhood in an unprepossessing industrial building of absolutely no historical interest whatsoever. Nor has the idea of suspending a few beach balls from the ceiling done much for the brewpub's interior, though the very functional-looking brewery equipment fully visible behind the bar is somewhat reassuring. In short, this is not a place to which you would bring someone who keeps *Architectural Digest* in the bathroom. If, however, your friends appreciate fresh beer, better-than-average pub food, and friendly service, Shields is definitely the place to head for after an afternoon of haggling over the price of Deco salt shakers and vintage *Mad* magazines.

BEERS & RATINGS	**CF**
Channel Islands Ale *(1.045 og)*	III½
Gold Coast Beer *(1.040 og)*	
Shields Stout *(1.055 og)*	
Seasonals:	
Bobby's Bock (1.065 og)	IIII
Oktoberfresh (1.055 og)	

Chris: "Bobby's Bock is an aromatic and deceptively gentle version of the Maibock style with a crisp, satisfying finish."

---

24 East Santa Clara Street
Ventura, California 93001
(805) 643·1807

Corner of Ventura Avenue and Santa Clara in historic downtown Ventura. F-Sat 11:30-10; Sun-T-W-Th 11-9; closed Monday.

SIERRA NEVADA TAPROOM & RESTAURANT

B BP R *K B*

Founded in 1981 by longtime home brewers Ken Grossman and Paul Camusi, the Sierra Nevada Brewing Company has been one of the great success stories of the microbrewery renaissance. Its products are primarily in the British tradition—ranging from a classic, pale ale to a formidable barleywine—though an excellent bock is also brewed. These enjoy a wide distribution and well-deserved high reputation throughout the West, but the best place to enjoy them is in the brewery's own attached taproom and restaurant, opened in 1990. The food served matches the beer; wholesome and tasty.

Sierra Nevada beers can hold their own with the best in the world and set a standard by which other microbrews must be judged.

SIERRA NEVADA BREWING CO.

BEERS & RATINGS	SG	CF
Sierra Nevada Draft Ale *(1.045 og; 3.9 w)*	▮▮▮▮½	▮▮▮▮½
Sierra Nevada Pale Ale *(1.052 og; 4.4 w)*	▮▮▮▮½	▮▮▮▮½
Sierra Nevada Porter *(1.052 og; 4.7 w)*	▮▮▮▮	▮▮▮▮½
Sierra Nevada Stout *(1.064 og; 4.8 w)*	▮▮▮▮½	▮▮▮▮½
Seasonals:		
Sierra Nevada Celebration Ale (1.064 og; 5.1 w)		▮▮▮▮½
Sierra Nevada Bigfoot Barleywine (1.096 og; 8.48 w)	▮▮▮▮½	▮▮▮▮½
Sierra Nevada Pale Bock (1.064 og; 5.2 w)	▮▮▮▮	▮▮▮▮

Scott: "The pale ale is always a treat. The stout is marvelously exotic. Bigfoot is astounding."
Chris: "Superb American interpretations of classic European styles."

1075 East 20th Street
Chico, California 95928
(916) 893·3520

In Northern California town of Chico, some 100 miles north of Sacramento or 165 miles northeast of the San Francisco Bay Area.
Open T-Sat 11-11; Sun 10-2. Closed Mondays.

SLO BREWING COMPANY

B BP *K*

Opened in 1988, this brewpub became the first brewing establishment to operate in San Luis Obispo since Prohibition. It is located upstairs in the turn-of-the-century Hanna Hardware building. The kitchen menu features typical American style pub fare.

Brickhouse Pale *(1.048 og)*
Cole Porter *(1.064 og)*
Garden Alley Amber *(1.054 og)*

1119 Garden Street
San Luis Obispo, California 93401
(805) 543·1843

Going north on the 101, take the Marsh Street exit, turn left on Garden Street. Coming south on the 101, exit at Santa Rosa Street, turn right on Sta. Rosa. Go right at Higuera and left on Garden Street.
Open M-W 11:30-10:30; Th-Sat to 12:30; Sun noon-5.

SOUTHERN CALIFORNIA HOFBRAU

B *KB*

Formerly known as Alpine Village Hofbrau, this micro is located a short drive away from Los Angeles International Airport, as part of a complex of Bavarian-flavored stores and food outlets. The beers are perhaps best enjoyed at the inn next door to the brewery, which, while technically not a brewpub, does provide good German food and a Hofbrauhaus atmosphere.

BEERS & RATINGS	SG	CF
Hofbrau Superior Pilsner *(1.042 og; 4.0 w)*	2½	
Hefe-weizen *(1.050 og; 4.0 w)*	4½	4
Hofbrau Bock *(1.064 og; 8.0 w)*	4½	3½

Scott: "I have been pleasantly surprised by these beers. The bock is well-balanced and fruity."

833 West Torrance Boulevard
Torrance, California 90502
(310) 329-8881

ST. STAN'S BREWERY, PUB & RESTAURANT

B BP *KB*

The pride of beautiful downtown Modesto, St. Stan's has quickly become something of a landmark. Located in a building with a Bavarian-style bell tower, the brewpub is large and lively, featuring a bar that is overlooked by a huge animatronic mural created by Disney artists and starring the establishment's patron saint, a bibulous friar of some dubious mendicant order. A goodly variety of foods, from burgers to designer pizzas, is served. The beers brewed here are many and various, ranging from a pumpkin ale to a notably heady barleywine. St. Stan's is most famous, however, for its top-fermented, German style alt beers, which, luckily, are quite well distributed. They are worth seeking out.

BEERS & RATINGS	SG	CF
St. Stan's Amber Alt *(1.048 og)*	▮▮▮½	▮▮▮▮
St. Stan's Dark Alt *(1.052 og)*	▮▮▮▮½	▮▮▮▮½

Scott: "These are fruity, distinctive brews, and they make a nice break from the more popular styles, but the packaging makes them look like root beers."

821 L Street
Modesto, California 95354
(209) 524·4PUB
(209) 524·BEER

Across the street from the 15-story Red Lion Hotel/Convention Center in the heart of downtown Modesto.
Open M-Th 11-11; F-Sat 11-midnight; Sun 11-9.

STODDARD'S BREWHOUSE AND EATERY

BP *K*

This new addition to the San Francisco Bay Area brewpub scene is owned and operated by Bob Stoddard, formerly associated with Pete's Brewing Company and the Tied House in Mountain View. Located in the historic section of downtown Sunnyvale, a few miles south of the Palo Alto campus of Stanford University and handy for the high-tech businesses of Silicon Valley, Stoddard's offers an ambitious menu and a distinctive range of brews. (The porter, for example, is deep red in color rather than black.)

Kolsch *(13.7 p)*
Pale Ale *(14.2 p)*
Porter *(14.4 p)*
ESB *(14.2 p)*
American Wheat *(14.0 p)*

111 S. Murphy Avenue
Sunnyvale, California 94086
(408) 733·7824

SUDWERK PRIVATBRAUEREI HÜBSCH

B BP *K B*

This is a large brewpub that features an even larger beer garden, where American-style pub grub is available but the real attraction, as far as the cuisine is concerned, is authentic German food, including both popular favorites and dishes that will be unfamiliar to most Americans. Especially noteworthy are the sausage dishes, featuring a variety of *wurst* such as might be found in Bavaria. The beer, needless to say, is very much in the German style.

BEERS & RATINGS	SG	CF
Hübsch Brau Pilsner *(1.048 og)*	▮▮▮½	▮▮▮
Hübsch Brau Märzen *(1.052 og)*	▮▮▮▮	▮▮▮½

Scott: "The Pilsner is strongly accented with Hallertau hops. The Märzen is excellent."
Chris: "One of the better West Coast lager breweries."

2001 Second Street
Davis, California 95616
(916) 756·2739

Corner of Pole Line Road & Second Street, behind the Post Office. Open T-W 11:30-11:30; Th 11:30-12:30; F-Sat 11:30-1; Sun noon-11:30.

TIED HOUSE CAFE & BREWERY

B BP *K B*

Located on San Pedro Square, this is a spacious, beer-hall type of establishment with the kitchens and the brewing equipment open to view. The food ranges from burgers to mildly adventurous pastas, with the fresh seafood being especially popular with some regulars.

BEERS & RATINGS	CF
Tied House Amber Ale	
Tied House Dark	
Tied House Dry	
Tied House Pale Ale	
Seasonals:	
Alpine Pearl Pale	▮▮▮
Andrechs Stout	▮▮½

65 North San Pedro,
San Jose, California 95110
(415) 965·BREW

Between Castro Street & Shoreline Boulevard. Open M-Tues 11:30-11; W 11:30-midnight; Th-Sat 11:30-1; Sun 4-11

TRIPLE ROCK BREWING COMPANY

B BP *K*

Located in a 70-year-old brick building, Triple Rock is a brewpub that offers honest pub food and its own honest brand of traditional beer. Not a bad combination.

BEERS & RATINGS	SG	CF
Pinnacle Pale Ale	▮▮▮½	▮▮▮
Red Rock Ale	▮▮▮½	▮▮▮
Triple Rock Stout	▮▮▮▮	▮▮▮▮

Seasonals:
Tree Frog Alt (1.072 og; 5.7 w)
Hop of the Rock (1.060 og; 5.3 w)
Passed Stout (1.064 og; 5.0 w)

Scott: "A big, chewy stout—nicely hopped."

1920 Shattuck Avenue
Berkeley, California 94704
(415) 843·2739

Take I-80 to University Avenue, left on Shattuck and one and a half blocks farther. Open M-W 11-12:30 am; Th-Sat 11-1:30; Sun 11-12:30.

TRUCKEE BREWING

B R *K B*

High in the Sierra Nevada, Truckee was originally a lumber camp, then became a railroad town serving the Southern Pacific near the point where the right-of-way clings picturesquely to the mountainside, protected by snow sheds from winter blizzards. Appropriately, the brewery is located in a boxcar and caboose. The food served is Italian. The beer is in the German style.

Truckee Amber *(4.0 v)*
Truckee Dark *(4.0 v)*
Boca Bock *(6.5 v)*
Boxcar Bock *(7.0 v)*

11401 Donner Pass Road
Truckee, California 95734
(916) 587·7411

One quarter mile west of Safeway.
Open daily 11-11.

TUSCAN BREWING COMPANY

BR *KB*

This tiny micro, at the northern end of the Sacramento Valley, opened in the summer of 1993.

Pale Amber
Stout

Red Bluff, California
(916) 527·7048

Located near the world-famous 1900 Tuscan Springs, 10 miles south on 99 east.

TWENTY TANK BREWERY

BP

A glass-fronted brewpub that mixes the old and the new—an old wooden bar set off against post-modern, high-tech decor. In case this sounds a little off-putting, it should be emphasized that the Twenty Tank Brewery is a decidedly friendly place. The food is basic but good, with a hint of a health-food bias. The standard of brewing is ambitious and the results are very well worth sampling.

BEERS & RATINGS	SG	CF
Red Top Ale	IIII	III½
Hefe Weizen	IIII	IIII½
Kinnikinick Stout	IIII½	IIII

Scott: "Lots of character here."
Chris: "A very promising relative newcomer. The Hefe Weizen is one of the best American wheat beers I've tasted."

316 11th Street,
San Francisco, California 94103
(415) 255·9455

South of Market Street. Open M-Sat 11:30-1:30; Sun 5:30 am-1:30 am.

WILLETT'S BREWERY

B BP *K*

Charles Willett Ankeny, the proprietor, is descended from the family that once owned the Hamm's breweries in Minnesota and California. (Remember the Hamm's bear? "From the land of sky-blue water.") Willett's is located in the picturesque Napa Valley in a tiled deco building with a riverside terrace. It features an extensive and inexpensive kitchen menu and—since this is Napa—the brewpub offers a selection of local wines along with its own beers.

Ace High Cream Ale *(13.3 p; 4.2 w)*
Victory Ale *(13.5 p; 4.4 w)*
Tail Waggin' Ale *(13.5 p; 4.5 w)*
Willy's Lager *(12.1 p; 3.9 w)*

---

902 Main Street
Napa, California 94559
(707) 258·2337

Downtown at the dead end of Second at Main on the Napa River. Open M-Sat 11:30-midnight; Closed Sunday.

WINCHESTER BREWING COMPANY

B BP

This colorful brewpub is named for the Winchester gun-making family, which gave its name to the boulevard on which the pub stands. Sandwiches and full dinners are served. Some of

Winchester's beers are currently brewed by Angeles Brewing in Chatsworth.

BEERS & RATINGS

	SG	CF
Spence's Pale Ale	▮▮▮½	▮▮½
Spence's Red Ale	▮▮▮½	▮▮½

Chris: "Drinkable beers, but without much individuality."

820 South Winchester Boulevard
San Jose, California 95128
(408) 243·7561

A few blocks south of I-280 and the Winchester Mystery House. Open Sun-Th 11-11; F-Sat 11-midnight.

WOODLAND BREWING COMPANY

B BP *K B*

This establishment was formerly known as the Dead Cat Alley Brewery. It has been described as "not quite a biker brewpub," though it also functions as something of a local sports bar, and even as a comedy club. The kitchen menu is varied.

Oprah House Pale Ale
Victorian Red Ale
Harvester Oatmeal Stout

667 Dead Cat Alley
Woodland, California 95695
(916) 661·2337

Off Main Street on Dead Cat Alley. Open M-W 11-11; Tues 11-12; F 11-1; Sat 11-1; Sun 10-10.

DENVER & VICINITY

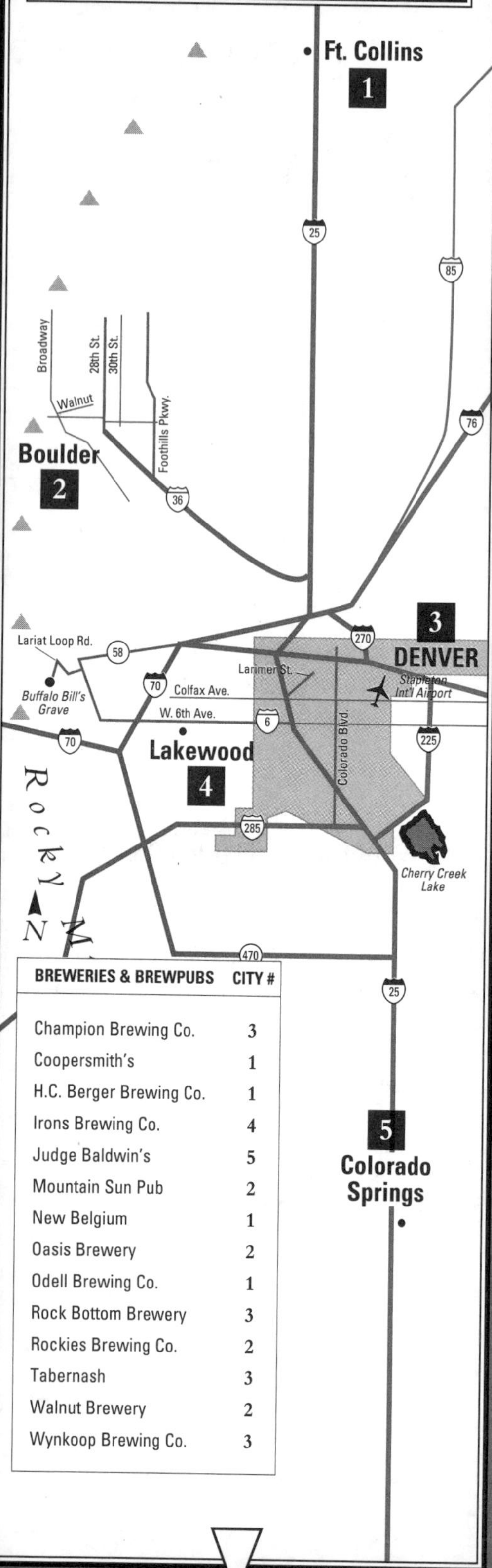

BREWERIES & BREWPUBS	CITY #
Champion Brewing Co.	3
Coopersmith's	1
H.C. Berger Brewing Co.	1
Irons Brewing Co.	4
Judge Baldwin's	5
Mountain Sun Pub	2
New Belgium	1
Oasis Brewery	2
Odell Brewing Co.	1
Rock Bottom Brewery	3
Rockies Brewing Co.	2
Tabernash	3
Walnut Brewery	2
Wynkoop Brewing Co.	3

BAKED AND BREWED IN TELLURIDE

BP *K 1/2 Gallon Bottles To Go*

Since the 1970s, this company has baked a variety of pastries and breads, including what is claimed to be the Best Bagel in the West. Since 1991 its tiny brewery—*a one-barrel kettle!*—has enabled Telluride customers to enjoy fresh-brewed beers, too.

BEERS & RATINGS	CF
Pandora Porter *(14.0 p)*	ııı
Snow Wheat *(9.5 p)*	
Runner's High *(13.5 p)*	
Stormy Stout	ııı½

127 South Fir Street
Telluride, Colorado 81435
(303)728·4705

Half block south of Main Street, red warehouse.
Open daily 5:30-10 pm; beer 11-9.

BRECKENRIDGE BREWERY AND PUB

B BP *K B*

Breckenridge brews British- and German-style brews at 9,600 feet in the Rocky Mountains. The altitude does not seem to do any harm to the beer. Breckenridge was once a gold mining town but the brewpub is now frequented by skiers and other tourists, as well as by locals. Breckenridge already bottles Avalanche Ale and Mountain Wheat, along with its Oatmeal Stout and IPA, for statewide distribution. At the time of this writing, the company is in the process of building a micro-brewery in Denver that will greatly increase its capacity and, we hope, make Breckenridge's name known further afield.

BRECKENRIDGE
MOUNTAIN WHEAT
HANDMADE ALE • 100% NATURAL

BEERS & RATINGS	SG	CF
Avalanche Ale *(1.054 og; 4.5 w)*	▮▮▮½	▮▮▮
Mountain Wheat *(1.050 og; 4.3 w)*	▮▮▮½	▮▮▮
Oatmeal Stout *(1.052 og; 4.4 w)*	▮▮▮▮	▮▮▮½
India Pale Ale *(1.056 og; 4.7 w)*	▮▮▮½	▮▮▮
Blue River Bock *(17.0 p)*	▮▮▮½	▮▮▮½
Seasonals:		
Märzen/Oktoberfest (13.0 p)	▮▮▮½	▮▮▮½
Christmas on the Mountain (7.0 w)		

Scott: "Breckenridge's lesser-known German-style beers have good character. Both the bock and the Märzen are full bodied and satisfying. The Märzen has a nice, spicy finish."

---

600 South Main Street
Breckenridge, Colorado 80424
(303) 453·1550

At the foot of the Breckenridge Ski Resort.
Open M-Sat 11-2; Sun 11-midnight

CARVER BREWING COMPANY

B *KB*

The Carver Brewing Company is a 1989 addition to a pre-existing restaurant and bakery in the historic section of downtown Durango. About 500 barrels a year of various brews are produced chiefly for consumption on the premises.

CARVERS BAKERY CAFE BREWERY

BEERS & RATINGS	SG	CF
Purgatory Honey Pilsner *(1.046 og; 5.0 w)*		
Animas City Amber Ale *(1.050 og; 5.0 w)*		
Iron Horse Stout *(1.054 og; 4.8 w)*		
Seasonals:		
Raspberry Wheat Ale (1.048 og; 4.8 w)	▮▮▮	▮▮▮▮
Carver's Oktoberfest (1.058 og; 5.4 w)		
Bavarian Weizer (1.042 og; 4.2 w)		

Scott: "The only beer we've tasted from Carver is the Raspberry Wheat Ale—40% wheat malt, 60% barley malt—which is a good, clean-tasting brew, though a little light on the raspberries for my taste."
Chris: "This is an instance of begging to differ. I like this particular brew a lot precisely because it is more subtle with its raspberry flavor than some other American fruit beers, and this permits more of the wheat beer character to come through."

1022 Main Avenue
Durango, Colorado 81301
(303) 259·2545

Five blocks north of the Narrow Gauge train station. Open M-Sat 6:30 am-10 pm; Sun 6:30-2.

CHAMPION BREWING COMPANY

B *KB*

This Denver brewpub opened for business in 1991. It's a place to watch Monday Night Football (especially if the Broncos are playing) or shoot pool. American-style food—from hotdogs to catfish to apple pie—is available.

BEERS & RATINGS	SG	CF
Home Run Ale *(13.5 p)*	II	II
Norm Clarke's Lager *(12.5 p)*	II	II
Stout Street Stout *(13.5 p)*	II½	II½

1442 Larimer Square
Denver, Colorado 80202
(303) 534·5444

Located in historic Larimer Square. Valet parking $2 with restaurant validation.

COOPERSMITH'S PUB AND BREWING

BP *K*

This is almost a copybook example of what a brewpub should be. Occupying the old J. H. Hohnstein Building in historic downtown Fort Collins, CooperSmith's offers an atmosphere that is traditional by association, yet modern in its lack of formality. It has a cozy interior, perfect for snowy winter evenings, and a spacious terrace, ideal for long summer brunches. It offers pub basics—highland cottage pie, western buffalo sausage—and touches of sophistication such as a spectacular selection of single-malt scotches. The management is efficient, the service friendly. Best of all, the beer is first rate.

If brewpubs—even some quite good ones—have a generic fault, it is a tendency for all of a brewmaster's beers to taste somewhat the same.

The great brewpubs offer a range of beers that are varied and distinctive. This is very much the case with CooperSmith's, which provides a choice of brews that range from a Bavarian-accented DunkelWeizen to a Bitter that is as British as any you'll find this side of the Atlantic.

BEERS & RATINGS	**SG**	**CF**
Albert Damm Bitter *(1.044 og; 3.8 w)*	4	4
Punjabi IPA *(1.051 og; 4.0 w)*	3½	3½
Not Brown Ale *(1.048 og; 4.0 w)*	4	4
Horsetooth Stout *(1.050 og; 5.0 w)*	4	4
Montana Avenue Wheat *(1.044 og; 3.8 w)*	4	3½
CooperSmith's DunkelWeizen *(1.050 og; 4.0 w)*	4	4
Peach Wheat		4
Sigda's Green Chili Beer *(1.048 og; 4.0 w)*	4	4
Pedestrian Ale *(1.042 og; 3.9 w)*		

Scott: "The way it should be."

Chris: "The great advantage of a brewpub is that the beer can be served in optimum condition. On our visit to CooperSmith's, freshness was as much an ingredient of the beers as hops or barley."

#5 Old Town Square
Fort Collins, Colorado 80524
(303) 498·0483

One block east of College on Mountain Avenue.
Open M-Sat 11-1:30 am; Sun 11-midnight.

CRESTED BUTTE BREWERY AND PUB

***B** K Bottles Only for Red Lady Ale*

Yet another newish Colorado brewpub—opened in 1991—that is producing good to very good beers. The styles are sophisticated and all are brewed with a great deal of confidence. The Raspberry-Oatmeal Stout is decidedly innovative—you won't run into that on your pub tour of the British Isles—and it's an experiment that has been carried out with considerable aplomb.

BEERS & RATINGS	SG	CF
Red Lady Ale *(1.050 og; 4.1 w)*	▮▮▮½	▮▮▮▮
Bucks Wheat *(1.048 og; 3.9 w)*	▮▮▮	▮▮▮½
3-Pin Grin Porter *(1.049 og; 3.99 w)*		▮▮▮½
Seasonals:		
Raspberry-Oatmeal Stout (1.052 og; 4.0 w)	▮▮▮▮	▮▮▮▮
Spiced Pumpkin Ale (1.048 og; 3.6 w)		

Scott: "The Raspberry-Oatmeal Stout is a fun idea. A great dessert beer."
Chris: "Red Lady Ale is a strong entry with a touch of astringent bitterness and a fragrant finish."

P.O. Box 906
Crested Butte, Colorado 81224
(303) 349·5026

Across the street from the Post Office.
Open 11:30-2 am daily.

DURANGO BREWING COMPANY

B *K and Jugs*

Durango is a small brewery that is dedicated to producing fresh beer for the town of Durango and the surrounding ski areas. Durango Dark is the year-round basic product, but Durango also brews seasonal specialties.

BEERS & RATINGS	CF
Durango Dark Lager *(1.050 og)*	▮▮▮½
Seasonals:	
Colorfest (1.048 og)	▮▮▮½
Durango Pale Lager Anasazi Wheat	

3000 Main Street
Durango, Colorado 81301
(303) 247·3396

Twenty blocks up Main Street from downtown Durango.

FLYING DOG BREWPUB

B BP *K B*

Perhaps the best thing about this lively brewpub, two blocks from the gondola, is that its owners and brewmaster have learned the art of producing quality beer without taking themselves too seriously. The names of the beers—from Doggie Style to Hair of the Dog—broadcast the message that this is a place to have fun. A taste of one of the better brews may tempt the beer fancier to linger.

FLYING DOG BREW PUB

"The Beer of Aspen"

BEERS & RATINGS	SG	CF
Doggie Style *(1.048 og; 5.0 v)*	iiii	iii½
Ol' Yeller Golden Ale *(1.048 og; 5.0 v)*	iiii	
Seasonals:		
Airedale Pale Ale (13.0 p)	iiii	iii½
Bulldog Stout (1.080 og; 7.0 v)	iiii½	iiii½
Gnarly Barley Wine (1.096 og; 9.0 v)	iiii	iii½
Greyhound Honey Ale (1.044 og; 5.0 v)	iiii	iiii

Scott: "Good beers. Great packaging concept." ***Chris:*** "The brewer's name is Dennis Miller. Couldn't be the same guy, could it? In any case, these are definitely Saturday Night Live beers."

424 East Cooper
Aspen, Colorado 81611
(303) 925·7464

On Cooper Avenue Mall, one block from Skier Shuttle Buses and two blocks from the gondola. Open 11:30-2 am daily. Flying Dog Bluegrass Band on Sunday nights.

H.C. BERGER BREWING COMPANY

B *KB*

Fort Collins holds an enviable position in the American brewing renaissance. At least five breweries and brewpubs are located within the city limits and four of them are taking part in the craft brewing adventure. Owners Sandy and Karen Jones named this enterprise for their grandfather, H.C. Berger.

BEERS & RATINGS	SG	CF
Inego Pale Ale	iiii	iii½
Whistlepin Wheat	iiii	iii½
Seasonals:		
Katcher's Rye Ale	iiii	
Vienna Gold IPA	iiii	

1900 East Lincoln Avenue
Fort Collins, Colorado 80524
(303) 493·9044

East on Lincoln Avenue across from HaufBrau Restaurant. Open M-Th 8-5; F 8-6; Sat 1-5.

HUBCAP BREWERY AND KITCHEN

B BP

This brewpub is located smack in the middle of Vail—part of the Crossroads Shopping Center—an easy walk from the ski lifts. The setting is high-tech—stainless steel walls and a glass-enclosed brewhouse—and the atmosphere relaxed. The kitchen serves what is appropriately described as "good, honest food," and head brewer Wayne Waanenen produces a variety of unfiltered and unpasteurized beers that are served on-site and from the keg in restaurants. A certain amount of Hubcap's product is hand-bottled in 22-ounce "bombers" for local liquor stores.

BEERS & RATINGS	SG	CF
White River Wheat *(11.0 p)*		▮▮▮
Camp Hale Golden Ale *(11.7 p)*	▮▮½	▮▮▮½
Ace Amber Ale *(11.7 p)*		▮▮▮½
Beaver Tail Brown Ale *(12.0 p)*		▮▮▮½
Rainbow Trout Stout *(12.8 p)*	▮▮▮½	
Seasonals:		
Solstice Ale (14.3 p)	▮▮▮½	▮▮▮▮
Bock N' Roll		▮▮▮

143 East Meadow Drive
P.O. Box 3333
Vail, Colorado 81658
(303) 476·5757

On the Crossroads Shopping Center.
Open 11-2 am daily.

IRONS BREWING COMPANY

B *KB*

Another addition to the growing list of Colorado craft breweries, Irons was founded in 1992 with brewmaster Larry Irons in charge of the kettles. At the time of this writing, his product includes a brisk American ale and two German-style lagers. Future plans call for a *dunkel* as well as seasonal and specialty brews.

BEERS & RATINGS	CF
Green Mountain Ale *(4.0 w)*	▮▮▮½
Alpine Pilsener *(4.0 w)*	
Irons Amber Lager *(12.0 P)*	▮▮▮½
Rocky Mountain Red Ale *(4.0 w)*	
High Plains Porter *(4.5 w)*	
Europa Lager *(3.2 w)*	

12354 West Alameda Parkway, Unit E
Lakewood, Colorado 80228
(303) 985·BEER

Sixth Avenue & Union. I-6 south on Union, west on Alameda.

JUDGE BALDWIN'S

B *K*

Colorado Springs' first brewpub, Judge Baldwin's features beer that is brewed in full view, right behind the bar.

BEERS & RATINGS	SG	CF
Amber Ale *(1.046 og; 4.5 w)*		▮▮½
Porter *(1.068 og; 6.5 w)*	▮▮▮	▮▮▮▮
Pale Ale *(1.046 og; 4.5 w)*	▮▮▮	▮▮▮
Nut Brown Ale *(1.057 og; 5.5 w)*		

Chris: "This is the kind of small operation where the beers are likely to differ in quality from batch to batch—the porter can be very good, with a dryish, hoppy finish—but they're always fresh and that in itself is a big plus."

4 South Cascade Avenue
Colorado Springs, Colorado 80903
(303) 473·5600

Located in the Palmer Center, next to the Antlers Doubletree Hotel. Open Sun-Th 11-midnight; F-Sat 11-1.

MOUNTAIN SUN PUB AND BREWERY

BP *Jars*

This newcomer to the Boulder brewpub scene offers spectacular scenery, pub food (with daily pasta specials), and top-fermented craft brews.

Thunderhead Stout *(1.066 og; 6.0 w)*
Quinn's Golden Ale *(1.040 og; 4.0 w)*
Raspberry Wheat *(1.038 og; 3.8 w)*

1535 Pearl Street
Boulder, Colorado 80302
(303) 546·0886

One block east of Pearl Street Mall.
Mon-Sat 11:30-1. Sun 11-midnight.
Acoustic music on Sunday evenings.

NEW BELGIUM

B *KB*

This Colorado micro is the exemplification of everything that is marvelous about the American craft brewing renaissance! Who could have imagined, a decade ago, that it would be possible to find, on the fringe of the Rocky Mountains, a tiny brewery producing first-rate American versions of Belgian Trappist ales? Who would have guessed that Trappist ales would be produced in a former railroad building, beside the tracks where freight trains still pass in the summer dusk on the old Colorado and Southern tracks. The brewery equipment looks as if it's been cobbled together from camping supplies purchased in the local hardware store, and the young brewtenders in charge of the current batch, when we visited, looked as if they would know more about Nintendo games than Hallertau hops. But the bottom line is the quality of the product, and New Belgium brews some of the best and most individualistic beers available in America today.

Even more astonishing, Fort Collins is also home to three more excellent craft breweries!

New Belgium Brewing Company

Fort Collins, Colorado USA

BEERS & RATINGS	**SG**	**CF**
Fat Tire Ale *(1.049 og; 4.2 w)*	▮▮▮▮	▮▮▮▮
Abbey Ale *(1.063 og; 5.5 w)*	▮▮▮▮	▮▮▮▮
Tripple *(1.073 og; 6.8 w)*	▮▮▮▮½	▮▮▮▮½
Sunshine Wheat *(1.048 og; 5.0 w)*		
Old Cherry Beer *(1.052 og; 5.0 w)*		
Seasonals:		
Abbey Grand Cru (1.080 og)		
Forbidden Fruit (kegs only)		

Scott: "Wonderfully complex brews."
Chris: "Fruity and aromatic. Exceptional!"

350 Linden Street
Fort Collins, Colorado 80524
(303) 221-0524

Hwy. 14 to Riverside, turn right; right on Linden and we're the second building on the right. Open M-F 8-5; Sat 2-5.

OASIS BREWERY

BP *KB*

The Oasis was opened in January 1992 by George and Lynne Hanna, with Bill Sherwood as brewmaster. As brewpubs go, this one is large and extremely elegant. The Egyptian theme of its decor is carried through with both imagination and taste. The food is good, there is a large, airy game room, and the T-shirts are outstanding. But what about the beer? Happily there is no letdown in this department. In fact it would be hard to find a brewpub that offers a more satisfying range of beers than the Oasis. There is nothing especially novel about the selection, but the quality is uniformly excellent and each brew is a well-articulated example of a given style. Highly recommended.

BEERS & RATINGS	SG	CF
Oasis Pale Ale *(12.5 p)*	4	3½
Tut Brown Ale *(14.0 p)*	4	4
Capstone ESB *(13.0 p)*	4	4
Zoser Stout *(14.0 p)*	4	4
Seasonals:		
Oktoberfest Beer	4	4
Terminator Dopplebock (21.0 p)		
Grateful Red (13.0 p)		

Scott: "The Oasis stout has agreeable chocolate accents and a creamy finish."
Chris: "First rate."

1095 Canyon Boulevard
Boulder, Colorado 80302
(303) 449·0363

Corner of 11th & Canyon in downtown Boulder.
Open 11:30-2 am daily.

ODELL BREWING COMPANY

B *KB*

Like New Belgium, Odell Brewing is located beside the railroad tracks in Fort Collins and is one of the four craft breweries that make this beautiful college town a beer fancier's dream. (You could spend a couple of weeks here and drink a different local brew every day without ever repeating yourself.) Doug Odell's plant is located in a former grain elevator that also enjoyed a previous life as a Mexican tile factory. This is not a brewpub, but Odell's beers—brewed with imported English malts—can be bought on-premises for home consumption, a traditional form of retailing that fits right in with the Victorian and Edwardian architecture that typifies Fort Collins' downtown area.

BEERS & RATINGS	SG	CF
Odell's Pale Ale *(1.048 og; 4.2 w)*	▮▮▮½	▮▮▮½
Heartland Wheat *(1.045 og; 3.8 w)*	▮▮▮	▮▮▮
90 Shilling Ale *(1.055 og; 4.8 w)*	▮▮▮▮	▮▮▮▮
Easy Street Wheat *(1.045 og; 3.8 w)*		
Cutthroat Porter *(1.053 og; 4.7 w)*		
Seasonals:		
Riley's Red Ale (1.056 og; 4.6 w)		
Christmas Shilling (1.060 og; 5.1 w)		

Scott: "With its faintly nutty, rich malt character and good balance, the 90 Shilling Ale is well worth seeking out."
Chris: "One of the best wheat beers you'll find anywhere."

119 Lincoln Avenue
Fort Collins, Colorado 80524
(303) 498·9070

Near the corner of Riverside & Lincoln; four blocks weast of Old Town. Open M-Th 9-5; F 9-6; Sat 2-5. Tours & sampling on F-Sat 2-5.

ROCK BOTTOM BREWERY

B BP *K B*

Rock Bottom is a thriving brewpub located on a busy pedestrian mall in downtown Denver. It offers an eclectic menu of above-average pub fare, live jazz and blues, and a selection of between five and seven beers—mostly ales—all made in the fully visible brewing facility.

BEERS & RATINGS	SG	CF
Falcon Pale Ale	▮▮▮½	▮▮▮½
Red Rocks	▮▮▮½	▮▮▮
Molly's Titanic Brown Ale	▮▮▮▮	▮▮▮▮
Rockies Premium Draft	▮▮▮▮	▮▮▮▮
Black Diamond Stout	▮▮▮▮	▮▮▮▮
Seasonal:		
Lager Rhythm	▮▮▮½	▮▮▮½

Chris: "Rock Bottom shares a brewmaster—Mark Younquist—with the Boulder Brewery and Walnut Brewing, but to my taste Rock Bottom's beers are decidedly the best of the three."

1001 16th Street
Denver, Colorado 80265
(303) 534·7616

ROCKIES BREWERY COMPANY

B BP *K B*

Founded in 1979, Rockies (formerly Boulder Brewing Company) has the distinction of being the oldest microbrewery in America. The first batches of Boulder beer to be sold to the public were brewed in a tiny facility installed in a shed on a farm near Longmont, Colorado. In the early eighties, Boulder moved to its present brewery, a handsome, glass-and-brick, post-modern building where the company's beers can be tasted, along with an eclectic selection of food, on a pleasant outdoor terrace or in a comfortable dining room. The name was changed in 1993. In the past, Rockies beers have not always lived up to the pioneering reputation of the brewery, but under brewmaster David Zuckerman they have improved considerably and are especially worth trying when found on draft in their home state.

BEERS & RATINGS	SG	CF
Amber Ale *(1.054 og)*		▮▮▮
Extra Pale Ale *(1.050 og)*		▮▮▮½
Wrigley Red *(14.0 p)*	▮▮½	▮▮▮½
Boulder Porter *(13.0 p)*		▮▮▮½
Seasonals:		
Rockies (12.0 p)	▮▮▮	▮▮▮½
Fall Festival (13.5 p)	▮▮▮½	▮▮▮½

Chris: "Boulder beers always had good malt quality. Lately, though, the hopping is more assertive and the balance and finish are much improved."

2880 Wilderness Place
Boulder, Colorado 80302
(303) 444·8448

Between 30th Street & Foothills Parkway, off Valmont Street. Open M-Th 11-7; F 11-5; Sat 11-3; Closed Sundays.

SAN JUAN BREWING COMPANY

BP

Located in the old Rio Grande Southern Depot, this popular brewpub is part of the Colorado brewing renaissance. We have reached the point in American craft brewing where there are many brewpubs that have learned how to maintain their standards from batch to batch. The old hit-and-miss days have not disappeared entirely, however, and it's still possible to find plenty of brewpubs where part of the fun is wondering how much the next keg of brown ale—or whatever—will differ from the last keg. In our experience, this appears to be the case with San Juan's beers. We tasted them several months apart, first at the brewpub (SG) and then at the Great American Beer Festival (CF). Our scorecards speak for themselves.

BEERS & RATINGS	SG	CF
Boomerang Brown *(16.0 p)*		3½
Tomboy Bitter *(14.0 p)*	2	4
Galloping Goose Golden Ale *(14.0 p)*	2	3½

300 South Townsend
Telluride, Colorado 81435
(303) 728·4587

TABERNASH (COLORADO BREWING CO.)

B *Jugs*

Located in the historic Denargo Market section of Denver, this micro specializing in lagers is the brainchild of Eric Warner, Jeff Mendel, Mark Lupa and George Barela. Eric and Jeff are especially well known among American craft brewers, both having been associated with the Institute of Brewing Studies in Boulder, Jeff as director. Eric—who trained at the world-renowned Weinhenstephan Beer Institute in Bavaria—has been one of the driving forces behind the Great American

Beer Festival, and is the author of *German Wheat Beers*, published by the Association of Brewing Studies.

Given the pedigree of this micro, it was to be expected that the beers would be exceptional, and this has proved to be the case. Tabernash is a very welcome addition to the American craft brewing scene.

COLORADO TABERNASH BREWING COMPANY

BEERS & RATINGS	SG	CF
Golden Spike Lager *(11.0 p; 4.5 w)*	4½	4
Denargo Dark Lager *(12.0 p; 5.0 w)*	4	4
Tabernash Weiss *(12.0 p; 5.5 w)*	5	5

Scott: "Eric Warner is a first-rate brewmaster and a dedicated educator in the craft beer movement. If you're curious how to get a 5 on your wheat beer, do like Eric, write the book."

205 Denargo Market
Denver, Colorado 80216
(303) 293·2337

From I-70 & Brighton Blvd, south on Brighton to 29th Street. Right on 29th, 100 yards to stop sign, look left. We are in the Federal Fruit & Produce Building. Tours every Saturday 10-4 or by appointment.

TELLURIDE BEER

B *KB*

Telluride Beer, in its present incarnation, is the brainchild of Steve Peterson, who in 1986 discovered the recipe for a beer that was brewed in Telluride until 1938. Peterson resurrected that brew. It has become a great local favorite, and currently enjoys distribution in 19 states.

BEERS & RATINGS	CF
Telluride Beer	▮▮▮½

Chris: "A smooth, easy-drinking brew with a long, lazy finish."

P.O. Box 819
Telluride, Colorado 81435

WALNUT BREWERY

B BP *K*

The Walnut is a handsome brewpub right in the middle of Boulder, near the University of Colorado campus. (Large paintings of the labels associated with Walnut's brews contribute an unusual but appropriate design element.) The food is very good and the beers—which are in the charge of Mark Youngquist, who is also brewmaster for Rock Bottom in Denver and the Boulder Brewery—are well made and varied.

BEERS & RATINGS	SG	CF
Indian Peaks Pale Ale *(12.5 p; 3.6 w)*	▮▮▮	
Buffalo Gold Premium Ale *(12.5 p; 3.8 w)*	▮▮▮½	▮▮▮½
Big Horn Bitter *(13.2 p; 4.2 w)*	▮▮▮	
Big Horn Bitter *(cask conditioned)*	▮▮▮½	
The James, Red Irish Ale *(14.2 p; 4.2 w)*	▮▮▮▮	

Devil's Thumb Stout *(16.5 p; 4.8 w)* ♦♦♦½
Devil's Thumb Stout
(cask conditioned) ♦♦♦♦
Seasonals:
Blue Note Ale (14. 0 p; 4.2 w) ♦♦♦½
Sub Zero (16.0 p; 4.8 w)
Red Rooster (16.0 p; 4.9 w)
Jazz Berry (14.5 p; 4.8 w)

Scott: "It's an education to visit the Walnut brewpub and taste the difference between the cask-conditioned and non-cask-conditioned versions of Big Horn Bitter or Devil's Thumb Stout. If you think cask conditioning is no big deal, you'll be amazed."

1123 Walnut Street
Boulder, Colorado 80302
(303) 447·1345

One block south of the Pearl Street Mall.
Open M-Sat 11-2 am; Sun 11-11.

WYNKOOP BREWING COMPANY

B BP *K*

The Wynkoop brewpub reflects the expansive personality of John Hinkenlooper, one of the more colorful characters among the many colorful characters on the craft brewing scene. With a BA in English and a masters in Geology, Hinkenlooper worked in the oil industry, but he was out of work when he visited the Triple Rock brewery in California and set his sights on opening an establishment that would have the best characteristics of an upscale English pub and offer both craft beers and quality food. To ensure this, Hinkenlooper (himself a prize-winning home brewer) hired a gifted brewmaster, Russell Schehrer, and entered into a partnership with a highly respected chef, Mark Schiffler.

The brewpub is located in the handsome J.S. Brown Mercantile Building in the historic section of downtown Denver. The premises are spacious and full of character. This is a great place to sit and enjoy Chef Schiffler's eclectic gloss on shepherd's pie or any of the other dishes on the extensive menu, and there is a spectacular pool hall on the second floor. Promotional material boasts of more than forty styles of beer having been brewed at Wynkoop over the years, and half a dozen are usually available at any given time.

With Wynkoop as his thriving flagship, John Hinkenlooper has gone on to involve himself in helping other brewpubs get started. These include CooperSmith in Fort Collins, the Firehouse Brewing Company in Rapid City, South Dakota, and the Crane River Brewing Company in Lincoln, Nebraska. It's Hinkenlooper's belief that brewpubs can help revitalize communities by bringing new life to historic locations.

BEERS & RATINGS	SG	CF
Sagebrush Stout *(1.055 og)*	▮▮▮½	▮▮▮
Seasonals:		
Imperial India Pale Ale (1.044 og)	▮▮▮½	▮▮▮
Elvis Brau	▮▮▮▮	▮▮▮
Wilderness Wheat	▮▮▮½	▮▮▮
Kyle's Dark Brown Ale	▮▮▮	▮▮▮½

Scott: "John is one of the true characters in the business. He's done a fantastic job in helping to bring craft beers to the public."

1634 18th Street
Denver, Colorado 80202
(303) 297·2700

At the corner of 18th & Wynkoop.
Open M-Th 11-1 am; F-Sat 11-2 am;
Sun 11-midnight.

HOLY COW CASINO, CAFE AND BREWERY

BP R *K*

If you want to play the slot machines, eat a three-course meal, and enjoy craft beer, all in one place, this is the spot for you. Located on the Las Vegas strip.

Amber Gambler Pale Ale
Vegas Gold
Rebel Red

2423 Las Vegas Boulevard South
Las Vegas, Nevada 89104
(702) 732·2697

Located on the Vegas strip. Open 24 hours.

PRESTON BREWERY/EMBUDO STATION

B BP R *K B*

Located on Highway 68, forty-odd miles north of Santa Fe and twenty-five south of Taos, Embudo Station—the brewpub in a converted narrow gauge railroad station dating from the 1880's—is a great spot to visit if you're on a rafting trip to the Rio Grande Gorge or sightseeing in the national forests of northern New Mexico. Patio dining on the banks of the Rio Grande features country smoked meats, trout, barbeque, and regional favorites.

Railroaders Stout
Embudo Gold
Narrow Gauge Ale
Rio Grande Green *(green chili ale)*

Rio Grande Ristra *(red chili ale)*
Cervesa Cereca *(cherry ale)*

P.O. Box 154
Embudo, New Mexico 87531
(505) 852·4707

41 miles north of Santa Fe; 25 miles south of Taos on Hwy. 68. Tues-Sun 12-8 (summer hours).

RUSSELL BREWING COMPANY

B *B*

This micro, in operation since 1992, specializes in top-fermented brews.

La Cañada Pale Ale *(1.048 og; 4.5 w)*
Black Cloud Porter *(1.051 og; 5.0 w)*

1242 Siler Road
Santa Fe, New Mexico 87510
(505) 438·3138

Open M-F 9-5.

SANTA FE BREWING COMPANY

B *KB*

The first microbrewery in New Mexico, Santa Fe began operations in June of 1988 in a barn on a former quarter-horse ranch. The brews produced here are all-malt ales, hand-bottled and hand-labeled. The flagship beer (for a long time it was Santa Fe's only beer) is a very hoppy light ale that is widely available in New Mexico and Colorado, and can be found as far away as Washington, D.C.

BEERS & RATINGS	SG	CF
Santa Fe Pale Ale *(1.052 og; 4.3 w)*	▮▮▮	▮▮▮
Fiesta Ale *(1.060 og; 4.8 w)*	▮▮▮½	
Santa Fe Nut Brown Ale *(1.052 og; 4.3 w)*	▮▮▮▮	
Old Pojaque Porter *(1.056 og; 4.3 w)*	▮▮▮½	▮▮▮▮
Chicken Killer Barley Wine *(1.092 og; 7.1 w)*	▮▮▮▮	
Sangre de Frambuesa *(1.058 og; 4.5 w)*	▮▮▮▮½	

Scott: "The basic Santa Fe Pale Ale is the perfect yuppie brew. The name is right, the packaging is good, and the beer itself has the appropriate profile—a respectable entry-level ale. Some of Santa Fe's other brews are outstanding, and the Barley Wine is a real killer."

Flying M Ranch,
HC 75 Box 83,
Santa Fe, New Mexico 87540

I-25 north from Santa Fe, east on Hwy. 285 to Lamy, south on State Road 41 to mile marker #58. First drive on left past mile marker. Open M-F 9-5; Sat 12-2.

ARMADILLO BREWING COMPANY

BP

This new brewpub is located on Austin's main drag in a renovated 1876 building that features stone walls and wood beams, not to mention a bar that the owners claim to be the longest on 6th Street (and this is Texas, remember). Southwestern cuisine is featured, along with pizza, pasta, and sausages made on the premises.

Axe's Pale Ale
Road Kill Red Ale
Dillo's ESB
Barton Springs Blond

6th Street
Austin, Texas 78701
(512) 322·0039

BITTER END BISTRO & BREWERY

BP

This smart, high-ceilinged brewpub is decorated with spectacular neon sculptures. The menu offers upscale regional pub fare (roasted duck quesadillas, spit-roasted kid), which, come to think of it, is almost interchangeable with what the French call bistro food.

BEERS & RATINGS	SG
Sledgehammer Stout	▮▮▮
Downtown Brown	▮▮▮
Bitter Bitter	
Mad Hat Lager	

311 Colorado Street
Austin, Texas 78701
(512) 478·BEER

Open M-Th 11:30-1; F-Sat 11:30-2 am;
Sun till midnight

CELIS BREWERY

B *KB*

This micro is the latest endeavor of Pierre Celis, the Belgian who revived the then-defunct White Beer style in his homeland back in 1966. His initial brewery, in his hometown of Hoegaarden, was a modest, twenty-barrel operation—a true micro—but his beer quickly gained a reputation at home and abroad and in 1978 he built a larger, more modern brewhouse. His reputation in the brewing world began to grow, but in 1985, while he was on a visit to the United States, the brewery burned down and insurance covered only a third of what it would cost to rebuild.

In order to start over again, Celis was compelled to sell out to Stella Artois—the Heineken of the Belgian brewing world. He supervised the rebuilding of the plant and stayed on as head of the brewery even after Stella Artois was swallowed by an even bigger brewing giant, Interbrew. Bored with being a figurehead, however, he negotiated a buyout.

Celis had already been exposed to the American microbrewery movement and was excited by its potential, even though he found a good deal of the beer produced by micros and brewpubs over here to be mediocre, a fact that he attributes to lack of training on the part of young brewmasters. (It should be noted that he has nothing but admiration for the products of companies like Anchor Steam and Sierra Nevada.) In any case, Celis concluded that America was ready for quality beer.

He claims that he settled on Austin as the location for his American brewery because Texans talk slowly enough for him to understand. There were other practical reasons. The central location is ideal for national distribution, and proximity to the seaport of Houston makes international shipping practical. Also, Austin has excellent water for brewing, high in limestone content like the water in Hoegaarden.

In Texas he built a brewhouse furnished with handsome copper kettles, and set out to use first-class American ingredients to produce top-quality Belgian-style beers at affordable prices. He is assisted in this task by his daughter Christine (sales and marketing), his son-in-law Peter (production), and Kim Blackman, one of the growing number of female brewmasters.

These are unusual beers in many ways. By preference, Celis often uses 6-row barley, sometimes looked down on by American craft brewers. His Texas-brewed White Beer is not only hopped with authority but also displays a pungent finish characterized by the use of coriander and other spices. Without any equivocation, it should be acknowledged that this is one of the most exciting breweries in the country.

CELIS
BREWERY
AUSTIN, TEXAS

BEERS &RATINGS	SG	CF
Celis White *(11.5p)*	▮▮▮▮▮	▮▮▮▮▮
Celis Golden *(11.5p)*	▮▮▮▮	▮▮▮▮
Celis Pale Bock *(11.5p)*	▮▮▮▮½	▮▮▮▮
Celis Grand Cru *(17.5p)*		▮▮▮▮½

Scott: "Try Celis White. Delicious!"
Chris: "Celis White is a classic, but try the others too. Grand Cru is a heady treat, with the high alcohol content and pungent dryness found in certain Belgian ales like Chimay White."

2431 Forbes Drive
Austin, Texas 78754
(512) 835-0884

WATERLOO BREWING COMPANY

BP

In May 1993, the Texas legislature passed new laws which made it legal to own and operate brewpubs in the Lone Star State. Waterloo

Brewing was one of the first establishments to take advantage of this legislation. Its casual atmosphere is geared in large part to the local college crowd. The menu is extensive and varied with a down-home accent (chicken-fried steak, chicken thighs with pilaf).

BEERS & RATINGS	SG
India Pale Ale	▮▮▮½
O. Henry's Porter	▮▮▮½
Clara's Clara	▮▮▮
Raspberry Ale	▮▮▮

401 Guadalupe
Austin, Texas 78701
(512) 477·1836

EDDIE McSTIFF'S

B BP *KB*

Eddie McStiff's is a brewpub founded in March 1991, in Moab, at the heart of Utah's Canyonlands.

BEERS & RATINGS	CF
Amber Ale *(1.038 og; 3.2 w)*	▮▮▮½
Blueberry Cream Ale	
Canyon Cream Ale	
McStiff's Stout	

59 South Main
Moab, Utah 84532
(801) 259·2337

At Center and Main in the Western Plaza.
Open 3 pm till closing.

SALT LAKE BREWING COMPANY
SQUATTER'S PUB BREWERY

B BP *K B*

Established by Peter Cole and Jeff Polychtiois, Salt Lake Brewing is the parent company that operates Squatter's Pub Brewery, a brewpub that has been in existence since 1989. A second brewpub is planned in conjunction with a micro that will have the capacity to serve retail outlets in the Salt Lake City metropolitan area.

BEERS & RATINGS	**CF**
Parley's Porter	▮▮▮½
Cole's Special Bitter	
City Creek Pale Ale	
Emigration Amber Ale	
Shandy	
Millcreek Cream Stout	
Black and Tan	

147 West Broadway
Salt Lake City, Utah 84101
(801) 363·BREW

On Broadway between 200 West and West Temple.
Open Sun-Th 11:30-midnight; F-Sat 11:30-1 am.
Sat & Sun brunch till 3:30.

SCHIRF BREWING COMPANY
WASATCH BREW PUB

B BP *K B*

Nestled at the top of historic Main Street in Park City, the Wasatch Brew Pub provides a sports bar atmosphere to relax in after an absolutely stunning day of skiing in Utah's legendary powder. For lunch, pub fare is available and full entrees are served for dinner.

Wasatch Premium *(1.040 og; 3.2 w. For all beers)*
Wasatch Wheat
Wasatch Stout
Wasatch Slickrock Lager
Seasonals:
Wasatch Winter Ale
Wasatch Bock
Wasatch Rassberry Wheat

---

250 Main Street
Park City, Utah 84060
(801) 645·9500

Top of historic Main Street, Park City.
Open 11:00 am till 1:00 am.

NORTHWEST

NOR

5
Spokane
Washington
Coeur D'Alene
Seattle
90
Olympia
Yakima
Moscow
82
Vancouver
84
Portland
Salem
Newport
Corvallis
Eugene
Oregon
Ida
Boise
Roseburg
84
5
Ashland

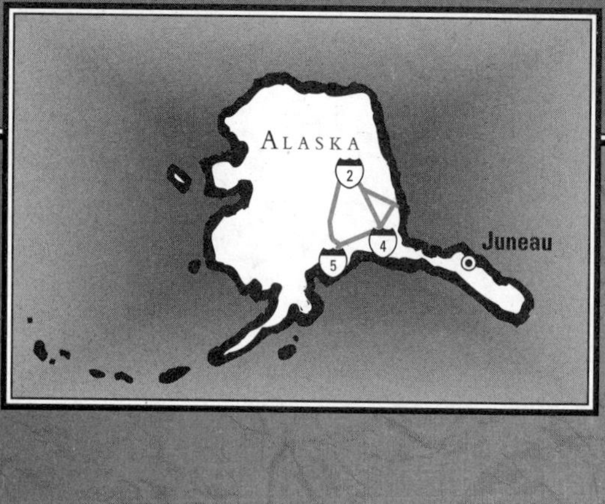

Alaska
2
4
5
Juneau

THWEST

Whitefish
15
Montana
Missoula
Helena
Miles City
94
Bozeman
90
90
90
HO
15
Jackson
Wyoming
25
86
80
Cheyenne

ALASKA

Alaskan Brewing & Bottling Company

Bird Creek Brewery

IDAHO

Coeur D'Alene Brewing Company / T.W. Fisher's A "Brewpub"

Harrison Hollow Brewhouse

M.J. Barleyhoppers Brewery and Public House

The Sun Valley Brewing Company

The Tablerock Brewpub & Grill

Treaty Grounds Brewpub

MONTANA

Kessler Brewing Company

Spanish Peaks Brewing Company & Italian Cafe

OREGON

Bayfront Brewery & Public House

BridgePort Brewing Company & Public House

Deschutes Brewery

Hood River Brewing Company

McMenamins Pubs & Breweries:
- Cornelius Pass Roadhouse
- Edgefield Brewery
- Fulton Pub & Brewery
- High Street Brewery & Café
- Highland Pub & Brewery
- Hillsdale Pub & Brewery
- Lighthouse BrewPub
- McMenamins
- Oak Hills Brewpub
- Thompson Brewery & Pub

Oregon Trail Brewery

Pizza Deli Brewery

Portland Brewing Company

Rogers Zoo & Brew Pub Pizzaratorium

Steelhead Brewery & Cafe

Umpqua Brewing Company

Widmer Brewing Company

WASHINGTON

Big Time Brewing

California & Alaska Street Brewery

Fort Spokane Brewery

Grant's Brewpub / Yakima Brewing

Hale's Ales

Hart Brewing Company

Maritime Pacific Brewing

Noggins Westlake Brewpub

Onalaska Brewing Company

Pacific Northwest Brewing Company

Pike Place Brewery

Redhook Ale Brewery

Thomas Kemper Brewing Company

WYOMING

Otto Brothers' Brewing Company

LEGEND:
***B**—Brewery*
***BP**—Brewpub*
***R**—Restaurant*

B—Available in Bottles
K—Available in Kegs

ALASKAN BREWING & BOTTLING COMPANY

B *KB*

One of the gems of American brewing, the Alaskan Brewing Company—located in Juneau—produces a range of beers that vary from very good to excellent. Managing partners Geoff and Marcy Larson have drawn on historical research to revive styles once popular in Alaska, but the success of this brewery depends, ultimately, on its very international approach to beer. Of necessity, many Alaskans are frequent travelers and so make sophisticated customers for consumer products of all kinds, beer included. Because of this, Alaskan Brewing has been able to take chances on brews such as their splendid Smoked Porter, which is brewed from malts roasted over an alderwood fire—alder being to Alaska what mesquite is to the Southwest. The Alaskan Amber Beer is based on the recipe from a turn-of-the-century brewery in the Juneau area.

BEERS & RATINGS	SG	CF
Alaskan Amber Beer *(4.2 w)*	🍺🍺🍺🍺	🍺🍺🍺½
Alaskan Pale Ale *(3.7 w)*	🍺🍺🍺🍺	🍺🍺🍺
Alaskan Smoked Porter *(1.055 og)*	🍺🍺🍺🍺🍺	🍺🍺🍺🍺½
Seasonals:		
Alaskan Autumn Ale	🍺🍺🍺½	🍺🍺🍺½
Alaskan Winter Stock Ale		🍺🍺🍺🍺
Alaskan Spring Wheat	🍺🍺🍺🍺	🍺🍺🍺🍺
Alaskan Ale	🍺🍺🍺🍺	🍺🍺🍺🍺
Alaskan Breakup Bock	🍺🍺🍺🍺	🍺🍺🍺½

Scott: "Wonderful full-bodied brews. The Smoked Porter is outstanding by any standards. Geoff is a great guy. Every year before the Great American Beer Festival changed locations, Geoff brought a large smoked salmon from his home state of Alaska for the after-event party for all the volunteers to enjoy. Three cheers for Geoff."

Chris: "The nutty Alaskan Ale and delicate Spring Wheat are first-rate."

P.O. Box 241053
Douglas, Alaska 99824
(907) 780·5866

Located in the Lemon Creek area.
Tours every half hour; call for seasonal hours.

BIRD CREEK BREWERY

B *KB*

Opening in December of 1991, Bird Creek is a relative newcomer to the scene. The 7.5 barrel brewhouse was built from converted dairy equipment. If this sounds unorthodox, it should be stated that the conversion was done by someone who knew what he was doing, and the naturally carbonated, cask-conditioned beer produced to date has justified the effort put into the enterprise.

BEERS & RATINGS	SG	CF
Old 55 Pale Ale *(1.048 og; 4.8 w)*	▮▮▮½	▮▮▮½

310 East Seventh Street #B
Anchorage, Alaska 99518
(907) 344·2473

Bird Creek is on the Turnagain Arm about 25 miles south of Anchorage. Open 9-5 M-F.

COEUR D'ALENE BREWING COMPANY
T.W. FISHER'S A "BREWPUB"

B BP *K B*

T.W. Fisher's a "Brewpub" opened in 1987 in response to a change in Idaho law that made brewpubs legal. The public's desire for such an establishment was such that there have been four expansions of the brewing facilities since then, and T.W. Fisher's beer is sold on draft and in bottles in more than 800 locations in Idaho, Washington, Oregon, Wyoming and Montana.

BEERS & RATINGS	SG	CF
T.W. Fisher's Light *(10.3 p)*	▮▮½	▮▮
T.W. Fisher's Full Moon Stout *(12.0 p)*	▮	▮▮½
T.W. Fisher's Centennial Pale Ale		
T.W. Fisher's Festival Dark		

Scott: "It's difficult to brew a really bad stout, but this one comes very close."
Chris: "Hard to explain the popularity of these beers."

204 North Second Street
Coeur D'Alene, Idaho 83814
(208) 664·BREW

Two blocks north of the Coeur D'Alene Resort.

HARRISON HOLLOW BREWHOUSE

B BP *K*

A homey brewpub in burgeoning Boise, handy to the Bogus Basin ski area, the Harrison Hollow Brewhouse was opened in 1992 and offers an eclectic kitchen menu—including "progressive American" items—along with hoppy top-fermented brews.

Fiegwirth *(1.048 og)*
Western Ale *(1.054 og; 3.6 w)*
Ginger Wheat *(1.054 og; 3.4 w)*
Seasonals:
Superior Stout (1.065 og; 4.9 w)
Raspberry Wheat (1.046 og; 3.4 w)
Nighthawk Snowfest (1.063 og; 4.5 w)

2455 Harrison Hollow
Boise, Idaho 83702
(208) 343·6820

North on historic Harrison Blvd., across Hill Road, just off Bogus Basin Road.

M.J. BARLEYHOPPERS BREWERY AND PUBLIC HOUSE

B BP *K*

Established in 1991, M.J. Barleyhoppers is a lively brewpub located in downtown Moscow, a short distance from the University of Idaho campus. Its restaurant serves American entrees "with an English flair"—a phrase seldom used in food circles east of Pocatello. Most of the beers brewed there also aspire to having an English (or Anglo-Irish) flair.

BEERS & RATINGS	SG	CF
Palouse Weizen *(11.5-12.5 p)*		🍺🍺½
Paradise Pale Ale *(11.5-12.5 p)*	🍺🍺½	🍺🍺🍺
Barleyhopper Brown *(11.5-12.5 p)*	🍺🍺½	🍺🍺½
McGinty's Old Irish Stout *(13.5 p)*	🍺🍺🍺½	🍺🍺🍺½
Seasonals:		
Clearwater River Winter Ale		
Paradise Pale Ale (12.5 p)	🍺🍺½	🍺🍺
Snake River Porter		

Scott: "The balance of the ales is generally a little off."

Chris: "As too often happens with brewpubs, Barleyhoppers' brews tend to taste very much like one another. There's nothing wrong with a house style, but these beers would be better if the idioms were better defined."

507 South Main
P.O. Box 8933
Moscow, Idaho 83843
(208) 883·4253

Main & 5th, downtown Moscow, Idaho.

THE SUN VALLEY BREWING COMPANY

B BP *KB*

A contract brewer turned micro that produces several beers distributed in the Rocky Mountain states.

Sun Valley Blonde *(12.0 p; 3.4 w)*
Sun Valley Sawtooth Gold Lager *(12.3 p; 3.6 w)*
Sun Valley White Tooth Ale *(12.8 p)*

Sun Valley White Cloud Ale *(12.8 p; 4.2 w)*

P.O. Box 389
Sun Valley, Idaho 83353
(208) 788·5777

Interstate 84 to Hwy. 75N becomes Main Street.
202 Main Street.

TABLEROCK BREWPUB & GRILL

B BP *K*

Opened in 1991, Tablerock is a comfortably appointed, modern brewpub situated near the old Union Pacific passenger depot and the Boise State campus. The food offered ranges from British pub favorites (Scotch eggs) to Southwestern staples (black bean nachos), with digressions into Cajun and Basque cuisine.

Depot Gold *(1.046 og; 3.7 w)*
Peregrine Porter *(1.055 og; 3.9 w)*
Shillelagh Stout *(1.060 og; 4.2 w)*
Razzleberry Ale *(1.036 og; 3.3 w)*

---

705 Fulton Street
Boise, Idaho 83702
(208) 342·0944

Vista Blvd. exit from I-84, becomes Capital Blvd.; follow to corner of Capital Blvd. & Fulton.

TREATY GROUNDS BREWPUB

BR *K*

Moscow is located near the Idaho/Washington state line, so it finds itself a focus for two major campuses—Washington State, seven miles to the west, and the University of Idaho, just down U.S. 95 to the south. Here Cougars and Vandals meet on neutral ground and, needless to say, the atmosphere of the brewpub is very much student-oriented. The prices are appropriately modest, for both beer and food, which ranges from burgers and sandwiches to fajita salad and teriyaki chicken dinner. Brews are alt style.

Moscow Gold
Border Run Ale
Red Alt
Bulldog Stout

2124 West Pullman Road
Moscow, Idaho 83843
(208) 342·0944

To the front of the Palouse Empire Mall, across from the University of Idaho. Open Sun-M 11-9; T-Th 11-10; F-Sat 11-11. Bar open till midnight.

KESSLER BREWING COMPANY

B *KB*

The original Kessler Brewery was founded in 1865. The more recent micro that now bears the illustrious name was founded in 1984.

BEERS & RATINGS	SG
Larelei Lager *(1.048 og; 4.7 v)*	▮▮▮▮
Centennial Lager *(1.052 og; 4.8 v)*	▮▮▮½
Nicholas Ale *(1.058 og; 6.8 v)*	▮▮▮½
Ale #7 *(1.055 og; 5.2 v)*	▮▮▮½

Scott: "Consistently good beers."

1439 Harris Street
Helena, Montana 59601
(406) 449·6214

At the corner of Harris Street and Railroad Avenue, across from the railway station. Open 9-5:30.

SPANISH PEAKS BREWING COMPANY & ITALIAN CAFE

B BP R *K*

Since it went into business in 1991, the Spanish Peaks ale house, along with the adjacent Italian Cafe, has been one of the busiest spots in Bozeman. Homemade pasta, pizza and other Italian specialties are available, while owner Mark Taverneti and brewer Todd Scott aim to provide customers with quality top-fermented brews.

BEERS & RATINGS	SG
Spanish Peaks Porter *(14.0 p)*	ııı
Yellowstone Pale Ale *(13.5 p)*	ııı
Black Dog Bitter *(12.5 p)*	ııı

120 North 19th Avenue
Bozeman, Montana 59775
(406) 585·2296

OREGON COAST

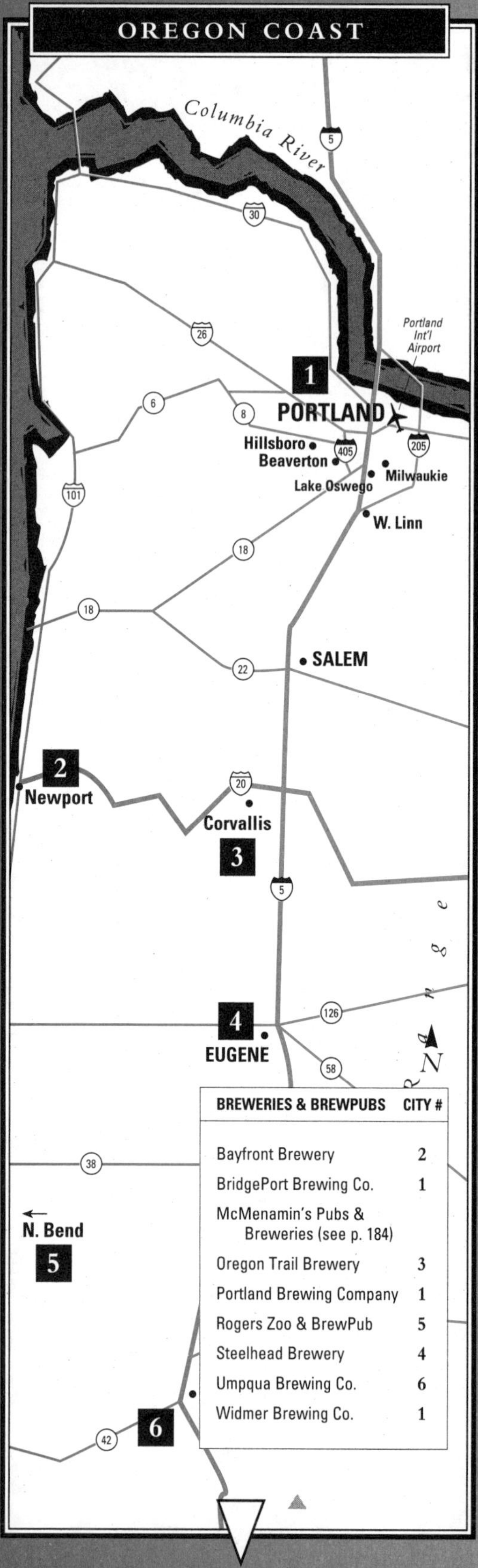

BREWERIES & BREWPUBS	CITY #
Bayfront Brewery	2
BridgePort Brewing Co.	1
McMenamin's Pubs & Breweries (see p. 184)	
Oregon Trail Brewery	3
Portland Brewing Company	1
Rogers Zoo & BrewPub	5
Steelhead Brewery	4
Umpqua Brewing Co.	6
Widmer Brewing Co.	1

BAYFRONT BREWERY & PUBLIC HOUSE

BBPR *KB*

Just north of the California state line, this brewpub occupies a scenically spectacular site, offering fine views of the Rogue River from its outdoor deck. Pizzas, English-style bangers and sandwiches are among the mainstays of the kitchen. The beers brewed by Bayfront are mostly in the Anglo-American tradition, though exceptions such as a seasonal Maierbock are also served.

BEERS & RATINGS	SG	CF
Rogue Ale		▮▮▮½
St. Rogue Red *(1.053 og; 4.6 w)*	▮▮▮▮	▮▮▮▮
Golden Coast Ale *(1.050 og; 4.3 w)*		▮▮▮▮
Mogul Madness *(1.062 og; 5.2 w)*		▮▮▮▮
New Porter *(1.050 og; 4.2 w)*	▮▮▮▮	▮▮▮▮
Shakespeare Stout *(1.055 og; 4.4 w)*	▮▮▮▮	▮▮▮▮
Maierbock *(1.068 og; 6.0 w)*	▮▮▮▮	
Old Crustacean *(1.095 og; 8.05 w)*		
Welkommen *(1.056 og; 4.6 w)*		

Chris: "Robust brews."

748 SW Bay Boulevard
Newport, Oregon 97365
(503) 265·3188

On the bayfront between Circle K and the Rip-tide.
Sun-Th 11-11 pm; F-Sat 11-1 am.

BRIDGEPORT BREWING COMPANY & PUBLIC HOUSE

B BP *K B*

Located in an unpretentiously renovated industrial building, BridgePort is a classic example of the casual but classy Northwest brewpub style. The menu has been deliberately limited to pizza and *foccacia* (Italian bread). The beers are in the predominant Northwest style, British in inspiration but American in inflection.

BEERS & RATINGS	CF
Coho Pacific Light Ale *(1.043 og; 3.6 w)*	▮▮▮▮
Blue Heron Bitter Ale *(1.052 og; 4.2 w)*	▮▮▮▮
Double XX Stout *(1.064 og; 6.0 w)*	▮▮▮▮
Old Knucklehead Barleywine *(1.090 og; 7.8 w)*	

1313 NW Marshall Street
Portland, Oregon 97209
(503) 241·7179

405 to Everett Street exit to 14th N to Marshall. Open M-Th 2-11; F 2-12; Sat 12-12 with live music; Sun 1-9.

DESCHUTES BREWERY

B BP R *K B or In Your Container*

This brewpub produces a wide range of beers that display a distinctive full-bodied, creamy character.

BEERS & RATINGS	SG	CF
Festival Pils *(10.5 p)*	4	3½
Bond Street Brown Ale *(10.51 p)*	4	4
Obsidian Stout *(10.65 p; 5.5 w)*	4	4
Bachelor Bitter *(1.049 og; 4.1 w)*		
Black Butte Porter *(1.054 og; 4.5 w)*		
Cascade Golden Ale *(1.042 og; 3.3 w)*		
Mirror Pond Pale Ale *(1.050 og; 4.4 w)*		
Seasonals:		
Wychick Weizen (10.49 p)		3

1044 Bond Street NW
Bend, Oregon 97701
(503) 382·9242

Downtown Bend, 2 blocks from river.
Open M-Th 11-11:30; F-Sat 11-12:30;
Sun noon-10.

HOOD RIVER BREWING COMPANY

B *KB*

Located in the old cannery district of Hood River, the Hood River Brewery and the associated White Cap Pub have brought fine British-style beers to the eastern end of the Columbia River Gorge. The brewmaster is James Emerson, a graduate of the Siebel Institute.

BEERS & RATINGS	CF
Full Sail Golden Ale *(12.0 p; 4.4 v)*	▮▮▮½
Full Sail Amber Ale *(14.0 p; 5.6 v)*	▮▮▮▮
Full Sail Barley Wine	

506 Columbia Street
Hood River, Oregon 97031
(503) 386·2281

McMENAMINS PUBS & BREWERIES/ HILLSDALE BREWERY & PUBLIC HOUSE

B BP *K*

Having been in business since 1985, the Hillsdale Brewery and Public House is the oldest of the ten brewpubs operated by the McMenamin family. It prides itself upon brewing top-fermented beers that depend upon local ingredients and aspire to a distinctly American character. A dozen different kinds of burger are served, along with hot and cold sandwiches, pizza, and pasta. Food and beer alike are very reasonably priced.

BEERS & RATINGS	SG
Terminator Stout	▮▮▮
Hammerhead	▮▮▮
Transformer	▮▮▮
Ruby	▮▮▮
Black Rabbit Porter	▮▮▮
India Pale Ale	

1505 SW Sunset Boulevard
Portland, Oregon 97201
(503) 246·3938

Open M-Sat 11-1 am; Sun noon-midnight.

Other McMenamins Locations:

Cornelius Pass Roadhouse & Brewery
4045 NW Cornelius Pass Road, Hillsboro
(503) 640·6174

Edgefield Brewery
2126 SW Halsey Street, Troutdale
(503) 669·8610

Fulton Pub & Brewery
0618 SW Nebraska, Portland
(503) 246·9530

High Street Brewery & Café
1243 High Street, Eugene
(503) 345·4905

Highland Pub & Brewery
4225 SE 182nd, Gresham
(503) 665·3015

Lighthouse BrewPub
4157 N Highway 101 Suite 117, Lincoln City
(503) 994·7238

McMenamins
6179 SW Murray Road, Beaverton
(503) 644·4562

McMenamins
2090 SW Eighth Avenue, West Linn
(503) 656·2970

Oak Hills BrewPub
14740 SW Cornell Road, Suite 80 Portland
(503) 645·0286

Thompson Brewery & Pub
3575 Liberty Road, South Salem
(503) 363·7286

OREGON TRAIL BREWERY

B *KB*

This tiny micro, just off Interstate 5, supplies keg beers to local establishments.

Oregon Trail Ale *(1.043 og; 3.5 v)*
Oregon Trail Brown *(1.048 og; 3.8 v)*
Oregon Trail Stout *(1.054 og; 4.5 v)*

341 SW Second Street
Corvallis, Oregon 97339-0070
(503) 758·3527

Open M-F 8-5.

PIZZA DELI BREWERY

B BP

Jerry Miller's pizza restaurant in Cave Junction—not far from the California state line—was already a success with loggers and other locals when, in 1990, he added an 80-barrel brewpub built to the design of Hubert Smith, a filmmaker who is also a beer enthusiast with a taste for British-style ales and other European top-fermented specialties. The house-brewed ales did nothing to hurt business and it was only a matter of time before another brewpub was opened at the Brookings Harbor branch of Pizza Deli, run by Miller's son.

BEERS & RATING	SG	CF
Nut Brown Ale *(1.040 og; 3.5 w)*	4	3½
Original Oregon ESB *(1.060 og; 5.2 w)*	4	4
Harbor Lights Kölsch *(1.048 og; 8.0 w)*	4	4
Hefe-Weizen *(1.038 og; 2.8 w)*	4	3½
Seasonals:		
Snug Harbor Old Ale (1.080 og; 6.5 w)4	4	4
Cave Beer Wheat Wine (1.080 og; 7.0 w)	4	4

Chris: "Brewmaster Hubert Smith is at his best with stronger beers, having the knack of going to higher gravities without losing subtlety and balance. I like the adventurousness he shows with brews like the wheat wine and the kolsch."

249 North Redwood Highway
Cave Junction, Oregon 97538
(503) 592·3556

Deep SW corner of Oregon. On Hwy 199, 20 miles north of California border, 30 miles south of I-5 (Grants Pass) at north town line, Cave Junction, Oregon. Brewery fronts on highway's east side. Restaurant and large, triple-sided parking area at rear of brewery. Open M-Sat 10-10; Sun 12-9:30.

PORTLAND BREWING COMPANY

B BP *K B*

Portland Brewing is a micro, with pub attached, that has been in business since 1986 and is well known and well regarded in the Portland area. The brewery recently moved into a newly built industrial space, where capacity is now in excess of 40,000 barrels per year. Cascade, Mount Hood, and other native hops give Portland's top-fermented brews a distinctly American character—not totally out of touch with the British tradition but very much alert to the northwestern tradition as exemplified by Bert Grant's fragrant ales.

BEERS & RATINGS	SG	CF
Portland Ale *(12.0 p)*	▮▮▮▮	▮▮▮½
Portland Porter *(12.0 p)*	▮▮▮▮	▮▮▮▮
Honeywheat	▮▮▮▮½	
McTarnahan's	▮▮▮▮½	

Scott: "In 1993, before they were in their new brewery, I was at their brewery/pub where they had just run out of McTarnahan's. The customers had a fit. Management had to bring in security to hold back the mobs. Well almost." *Chris:* "An excellent dry porter with a long, slightly floral finish."

1339 NW Flanders
Portland, Oregon 97209
(503) 222·7150

ROGER'S ZOO & BREW PUB PIZZARATORIUM

B BP R *K B*

Despite the fact that it did not exist till 1988, Roger's Zoo has become an Oregon institution and its owner and operator Roger Scott has emerged as a local celebrity. Located at the wrong end of town, in a building that is not likely to be featured in *House & Garden,* the Zoo is the ultimate in funky, down-home brewpubs, attracting an unlikely mixture of yuppies and blue collar workers, all of whom are drawn there by Roger's expansive personality, his crusty pizza, his spicy nachos and whatever beer he brewed this week. We haven't had the opportunity to try all his brews, but if the porter is anything to judge by, you might want to get out your Rand McNally Road Atlas and head for North Bend tomorrow.

The Pizzaratorium is an offshoot of the Zoo. The beer is just as good.

BEERS & RATINGS	CF
North Bend Porter	ıııı½

Chris: "A superb, bitter porter. One of the best I've ever tasted."

Zoo
2037 Sherman Avenue
North Bend, Oregon 97459
(503) 756·1463

Pizzaratorium
2233 Newmark Public Square Shopping Center
North Bend, Oregon 97459

STEELHEAD BREWERY & CAFE

BP *K B*

Steelhead Brewery and Cafe opened to the public in January 1991, brewing a range of beers in a modern 10-barrel brewery that employs a single-step infusion all-grain process. The dining area seats 150 people and the food served is quality American pub fare, nothing over $7.50 besides pizzas.

BEERS & RATINGS	**SG**	**CF**
Oatmeal Stout *(18.7 p; 7.45 v)*	▮▮▮▮½	▮▮▮▮
Riley's Rye *(13.9 p)*	▮▮▮▮	▮▮▮½
Time Warp Weizenbock *(15.0 p)*	▮▮▮½	▮▮▮½
McKenzie Light *(10.2 p; 4.5 v)*		
Amazon Amber *(14.0 p; 5.9 v)*		
Bombay Bomber IPA *(17.5 p; 6.6 v)*		
French Pete Porter *(15.0 p; 5.5 v)*		
Station Square Stout *(20.3 p; 7.7 v)*		
Seasonals:		
Ginger Bells (14.7 p; 6.3 v)	▮▮▮½	
Emerald Irish Ale (14.8 p; 5.2 v)		

Scott: "The use of a touch of rye malt adds character to the oatmeal stout as well as to Riley's Rye, a spicy, well-rounded ale."

199 East 5th Avenue
Eugene, Oregon 97401
(503) 686·BREW

I-5 to Hwy 105 heading west, take exit #11, follow to the left, cross over bridge, then turn left into parking lot immediately. Sun-Th 11-midnight; F-Sat 11-11.

UMPQUA BREWING COMPANY

BP *KB*

Judging by the quality of the brews entered in beer festivals, Roseburg must be well worth visiting. (The logo is part of a petroglyph from the Yoncalla Boulder. What does it mean?)

UMPQUA
EST. 1991
BREWING CO.

BEERS & RATINGS	CF
No Doubt Stout	▮▮▮▮
Downtown Brown	▮▮▮▮
Roseburg Red	

328 SE Jackson
Roseburg, Oregon 97470
(503) 672·0452

Coming into Roseburg from I-5, take City Center exit 124. Turn right on Harvard. Go over the Oak Street Bridge, across the South Umpqua River. Go to the second light past the bridge and turn left onto Stephens Street. Go past the next 2 lights and turn right on Diamond Lake Blvd. (Hwy. 138). Go down one block to Jackson St. and turn right. We're on the right side of the street, across from City Hall parking lot. Open W-Th 5-11; F-Sat 5-1; live music Sat nights.

WIDMER BREWING COMPANY

B *K*

The Northwest is especially well known for its British-style ales, stouts, and porters, but it has also produced some excellent lager breweries, and one of the best of these is the Portland enterprise run by the Widmer Brothers. This micro specializes in beers with a strong German accent. An associated brewpub—B. Moloch—is located in downtown Portland and some Widmer beers are brewed there. After you have enjoyed a liter, you will be able to pronounce their name as Vid-mah, as they do in Deutschland. As of this writing, the beers are available in kegs only.

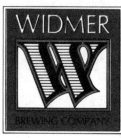

BEERS & RATINGS	SG	CF
Widmer Altbier *(1.048 og; 4.5 w)*	IIII½	IIII
Widmer Hefe-Weizen *(1.047 og; 3.3 w)*	IIII½	IIII
Widmer Weizen *(1.049 og; 3.3 w)*	IIII½	

Seasonals:
Widmer Oktoberfest (fall) (1.052 og; 5.0 w)
Widmer Fest (winter) (1.056 og; 5.4 w)
Widmer Bock (spring) (1.066 og; 5.6 w)
Widmer Maerzen (summer) (1.052 og; 5.0 w)

Scott: "Their Hefe-Weizen is a classic."
Chris: "The Alt starts off with a mouth-filling malty richness, then the authoritative hopping comes through to dominate the finish. American grown hops seem to work especially well with this style."

929 N. Russell Street
Portland, Oregon 97227
(503) 281·BIER

SEATTLE AREA

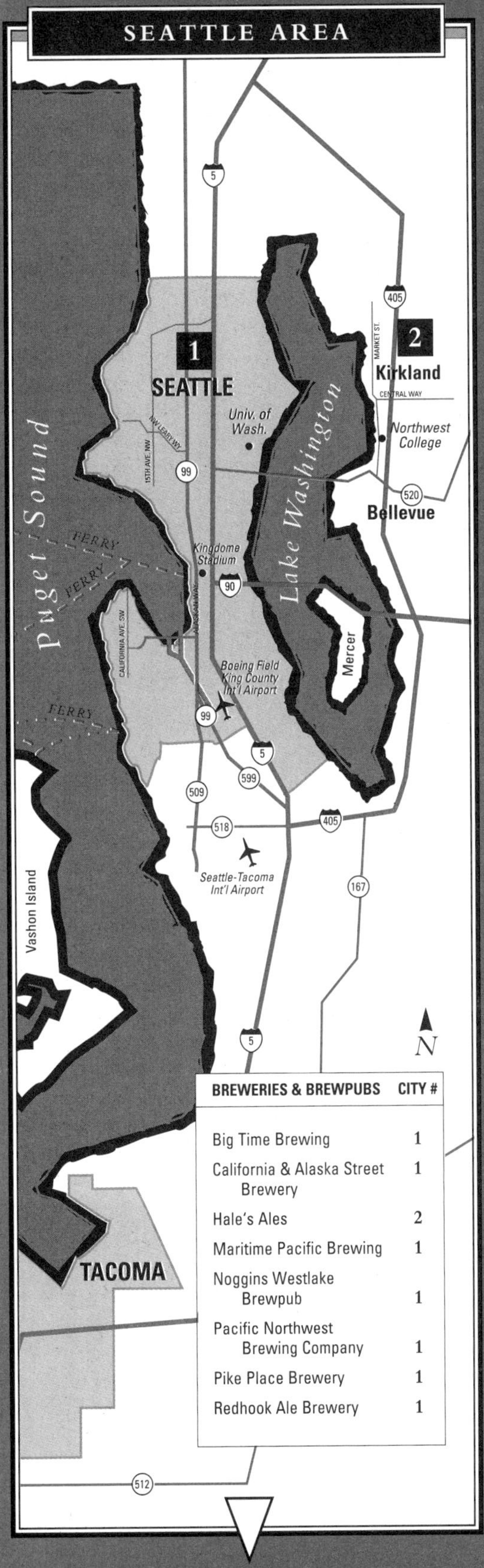

BREWERIES & BREWPUBS	CITY #
Big Time Brewing	1
California & Alaska Street Brewery	1
Hale's Ales	2
Maritime Pacific Brewing	1
Noggins Westlake Brewpub	1
Pacific Northwest Brewing Company	1
Pike Place Brewery	1
Redhook Ale Brewery	1

BIG TIME BREWING

BP *KB*

Established in 1988, and affiliated with the well-known Triple Rock brewpub in Berkeley, California, Triple Rock Big Time is one of the many friendly and free-spirited brew pubs to be found in the Pacific Northwest. Occupying a turn-of-the-century-style building, the pub's decor features a collection of breweriana. Like its California cousin, Big Time specializes in top-fermented beers that are British in inspiration but possess a strong American accent, even by western standards. Like many of his contemporaries, brewmaster Ed Tringali is not afraid to take chances and offers beers not often encountered elsewhere, such as an unfiltered ale accented with rye.

BEERS & RATINGS	SG	CF
Atlas Amber *(13.6 p; 4.2 v)*	▮▮▮½	▮▮▮▮
Old Rip Oatmeal Stout *(17.8 p)*	▮▮▮▮	▮▮▮▮
Bhagwans Best IPA *(15.0 p)*	▮▮▮▮	▮▮▮½
Prime Time Pale *(11.8 p; 3.5 v)*		
Coal Creek *(14.8 p; 4.3 v)*		
HefeRyzen *(13.4 p)*		
Old Wooly *(24.0 p; 8.5 v)*		

Scott: "Flavorful, well-made beers."

4133 University Way NE
Seattle, Washington 98105
(206) 545·4509

Exit I-5 at 45th University District.
Open daily 11:30 am- 12:30 am.

CALIFORNIA & ALASKA STREET BREWERY

BP *K*

This brewpub, across Elliott Bay from downtown Seattle, is an alehouse that serves West Coast pub food and also serves as a retail outlet for home brewing supplies.

BEERS & RATINGS	SG
Admiral ES Bitter *(12.5-13.5 p)*	III
Alki Ale *(11.0-12.0 p)*	II½
Fauntleroy Stout *(13.0-14.0 p)*	II½

4720 California Avenue SW
Seattle, Washington 98116
(206) 938·2476

Located in the Alaska Junction business district of West Seattle. Open T-Sun from 2:00 till 10 or 12:00.

FORT SPOKANE BREWERY

BP *K*

The original Fort Spokane Brewery was established in 1889. The present Fort Spokane brewpub was named in honor of its predecessor and opened for business exactly 100 years later. Snacks, sandwiches, salads, pizza, and full dinners are available, with bratwurst a specialty.

FORT SPOKANE BREWERY INC.

Border Run Ale *(1.054 og)*
Bulldog Stout *(1.058 og)*
Blond Alt *(1.052 og)*
Red Alt *(1.052 og)*

West 401 Spokane Falls Boulevard
Spokane, Washington 99201
(509) 838·3809

Located between Stevens and Washington across from the Riverfront Park. Open 11-1.

GRANT'S BREWPUB/YAKIMA BREWING

B BP *K B*

Active in the brewing business for more than a half century, Bert Grant opened his pioneering brewpub in 1982 in Yakima's former Opera House. In 1990 the operation moved to more spacious quarters across the street, in the old Victorian Railroad Station. It's difficult to imagine a more picturesque setting for the enjoyment of beer and vittles. At Grant's, the food is not as far removed from what you might find in an English or Scottish pub, though Italian, Mexican, and Asian specialties appear on the menu from time to time. The beers that Bert Grant brews are also predominantly in the Anglo-Celtic tradition and are marked by his strong predilection for *very* marked hoppiness. He also produces a very drinkable hard cider.

BEERS & RATINGS	SG	CF
Grant's Scottish Ale *(1.052 og; 4.1 w)*	2	3
Grant's India Pale Ale *(1.047 og; 3.9 w)*		3
Grant's Imperial Stout *(1.068 og; 5.0 w)*	4	4
Grant's Celtic Ale *(1.034 og; 2.0 w)*	3	3
Grant's Weiss Beer *(1.044 og; 3.5 w)*	2	2

Scott: "For hop fanatics only!"
Chris: "Bert Grant says he brews beer the way he likes it, and that's as it should be. Some drinkers may find the very floral hop accents in his beers an acquired taste, but I defy anyone not to enjoy the Imperial Stout."

---

32 North Front Street
Yakima, Washington 98901
(509) 575·2922

HALE'S ALES

B *KB*

Mike Hale developed his taste for British beers while on an extended cycling tour of the south of England, then served an apprenticeship at Gale's of Hampshire, a British brewer noted for its excellent draft beers and its remarkable bottle-conditioned Prize Old Ale. Back in Washington, in 1982, Mike built and opened his first micro in Colville and later supplemented it with another, larger plant. Hale's ales have improved over the years to become classics of the dominant Northwest style, which is to say very British in general idiom, but with that distinctive American accent that gives them a unique stylistic flair.

BEERS & RATINGS	SG	CF
Pale American Ale	4	
Special Bitter	4	4
Stout	5	

Scott: "I was fortunate to sample their Stout on draft hooked up to a nitrogen and CO_2 tank, which gave the beer a lovely creamy texture. An hour later, they had to ask me to leave the booth."

---

109 Central Way
Kirkland, Washington 98033
(206) 827·4359

East 5624 Commerce Street
Spokane, Washington
(509) 534·7553

HART BREWING CO

B *KB*

Hart Brewing is a microbrewery that has been in business since 1984. It produces British-style top-fermented beers as well as a very American interpretation of a German wheat beer, said to be the first draft wheat beer to be produced in the United States since Prohibition. This is a well-established business producing high-quality brews that can be found as far from home as Southern California.

BEERS & RATINGS	SG	CF
Amber Wheat *(1.039 og; 3.19 w)*	4	
Pyramid Wheaten Ale *(1.044 og; 3.7 w)*	4	3½
Best Brown Ale *(1.050 og; 4.0 w)*	5	
Hefeweizen *(1.044 og; 3.7 w)*	4	
Wheaten Bock *(1.068 og; 6.1 w)*	4	
Pyramid Pale Ale *(1.048 og; 3.75 w)*	4½	4½
Pacific Crest Ale *(1.052 og)*	4	4
Sphynx Stout *(1.062 og)*	5	4½
Snow Cap Ale	4½	

Scott: "During the Portland Brewers Festival, I had the opportunity to spend the morning with Jack Schaller, their brewmaster at the brewery. What a thrill sampling these great ales! The brewery puts out about 50,000 barrels per year in a pristine sterile environment. This is very important since none of their beers is pasteurized. Jack personally goes to Yakima and samples 50-60 bales a day for four days picking out choice hops—a rare discipline since most brewers buy directly from brokers. As a stout lover, I appreciated their obsession with producing their stout— they lose money on every bottle, but the chairman of the board, George Hancock, also loves stout and demands exacting and expensive quality standards. They do it out of pride. As a consumer (and marketer), I only wish their package design reflected as much pride as their beers."
Chris: "The pale ale, with its great creamy head, is among the best you'll find. The stout is so good it almost merits five bottles."

110 West Marine Drive
Kalama, Washington 98625
(206) 673·2962

MARITIME PACIFIC BREWING

B *KB*

Maritime Pacific Brewing Company is a small, family-owned brewery established in 1990. A 10-

year dream finally realized, this brewery was built for the purpose of creating a Northwest line of high-quality beers that are distinct from other local microbrews.

BEERS & RATINGS	SG
Flagship Red Ale *(1.052 og)*	▮▮▮½
Clipper Gold Wheat Ale	▮▮▮▮
Islander Pale Ale	▮▮▮½
Nightwatch Ale	▮▮▮▮½

1514 NW Leary Way
Seattle, Washington 98107
(206) 782·6181

Located north of the Ballard Bridge on NW Leary Way, between 17th and 15th Ave NW. Open 7 am-6 pm daily; Sat 11-6. Tours on Saturday only, unless by appointment.

NOGGINS WESTLAKE BREWPUB

BP

Noggins is an offshoot of the highly regarded Spinnakers Brewpub in Victoria, British Columbia, but while Spinnakers enjoys a dockside location with spectacular views of Victoria's Inner Harbor, Noggins is located in the food court of a downtown Seattle shopping center. The atmosphere, then, is very different from that to be found in the typical brewpub, but the lunchtime crowd is lively and both the food and the beer are well above the usual shopping center standards.

BEERS & RATINGS	CF
Best Bitter	III½
India Pale Ale	III½

Seattle, Washington

ONALASKA BREWING COMPANY

B *KB*

BEERS & RATINGS	SG
Onalaska Ale *(1.044 og)*	III
Red Dawg Ale *(1.050 og)*	III

248 Burchett Road
Onalaska, Washington 98570
(206) 978·4253

Visitors welcome, but make an appointment.

PACIFIC NORTHWEST BREWING COMPANY

B BP *KB*

This handsome brewpub is located in the picturesque Pioneer Square neighborhood of downtown Seattle, a block or so from the King Dome. An extensive menu offers an eclectic choice of items with an emphasis on fresh seafood and the flavors of the Pacific rim. The beers have a marked English accent.

BEERS & RATINGS	SG
Pacific Northwest Blond Ale *(1.040 og)*	
Golden Ale *(1.045 og)*	

322 Occidental Avenue South
Seattle, Washington 98104
(206) 621·7002

Near the King Dome, at the corner of Jackson Street and Occidental Avenue. Open M-T 11:30-11; W-Th till midnight; F-Sat till 1 am. Open Sundays for special events. Closed Mondays during winter months.

PIKE PLACE BREWERY

B *KB*

Situated in a former bawdy house, just down the hill from the Pike Place Market—a major attraction on the Seattle waterfront—the Pike Place Brewery is a gem of a micro operated by one of the most important and influential figures in the American beer renaissance.

Charles Finkel had been a pioneer of the boutique winery business when, in the late seventies, he turned his attention to fine beers. His Merchant du Vin company began to import great ales from England and Belgium, splendid pilsners and bocks from Germany. Almost overnight he became the most influential beer importer in the country, representing top brewers like Samuel Smith, Ayinger and Lindemans. Almost single-handedly, he gave Americans an opportunity to taste a wide range of the finest European brews, and his gift for packaging these beers attractively contributed a great deal to his success (as did the business acumen of his wife, Rose Ann).

All this happened in Seattle, already a hotbed of home brewing, and Merchant du Vin's success did much to encourage people like Paul Shipman (Red Hook) and the other young men who sparked the brewpub/microbrewery movement in the Northwest in the early eighties. By any standards, Charles Finkel is a seminal figure.

It was only a matter of time before he took the plunge and opened his own brewery. When he did so, in 1989, he did it on a small scale but he did it right. The Liberty Malt Supply Company was a home-brew supply store that had been at home on Western Avenue, next to a salmon smokehouse, since 1921. Finkel purchased Liberty (keeping it in business) and added a small state-of-the-art brew house designed and installed by Seattle brew guru Vince Cotone.

The brewery is impossible to miss because the gleaming copper kettle is right there in the front window. Under the guidance of brewmaster Fal Allen, production amounts to less than 10,000 barrels a year, but quantity is not the point of this operation, which places its emphasis on crafting beers of the highest possible quality. If you want to taste the real thing, give Pike's Place a visit.

BEERS & RATINGS	**SG**	**CF**
Pale Ale *(1052 og; 4.5 v)*	▮▮▮▮½	▮▮▮▮
XXXXX Stout *(1.072 og; 6.25 v)*	▮▮▮▮▮	▮▮▮▮½
Seasonals:		
East India Pale Ale (1.067 og; 6.5 v)	▮▮▮▮½	▮▮▮▮
Old Bawdy Barley Wine (1.092 og; 9.95 v)	▮▮▮▮▮	▮▮▮▮½
Cervesa Russama (chili) (1.052 og; 4.5 v)		
Old Acquaintance (1.052 og; 4.5 v)		
Birra Preffetto (Italian spiced beer) (1.052 og; 4.5 v)		

Scott: "Outstanding beers. I have the highest regard and admiration for Charles as a creative force and educator in the craft beer category."
Chris: "Pike Place's beers—whatever their gravity—have a rich, creamy, malt character, always balanced by generous hopping."

1432 Western Avenue
Seattle, Washington 98101
(206) 622·3373

On Western Avenue under the Pike Place Market (just south of the Parrot Shop). Open M-Sat 10-4.

REDHOOK ALE BREWERY

***B BP** K B*

One of the earliest and best of American craft breweries, opening for business in 1982, Redhook (formerly the Independent Ale Brewery) is now located in the old Freemont Trolley Barn in what was once the Scandinavian section of Seattle. (The Swedish-inflected "Ya sure, ya betcha" featured on the label of Ballard Bitter is the war cry of the local high school football team.)

Paul Shipman, the founder of Redhook, credits Gordon Bowker, the founder of Starbuck's coffee, with being the first person in Seattle to suggest that the region needed a small brewery brewing high-quality beer. It was Shipman—then in the wine industry—who pursued the idea, however, though at first he had difficulty in convincing potential backers that a boutique brewery had the potential to do just as well as the boutique wineries that had become all the rage. Finally, in 1982, Shipman marketed his first brew, just as Bert Grant was launching his brewery in nearby Yakima. The experts speculated that only one of the two could survive, but in reality the competition between the fledgling breweries stimulated interest and soon other entrepreneurs were helping expand the market.

Shipman is one of those who believes that the craft brewing renaissance is still in its infancy. Having already expanded the Fremont plant twice, he and his partners are about to open a new state-of-the-art brewery in Woodinville—a brewery that will ultimately have a capacity of 200,000 barrels a year.

The Fremont brewery will stay on line as a draft-only facility. The Trolleyman's Pub, which is located in the old car barn, features standard pub fare with an accent on local specialties such as trout and salmon. The beer is very much in the British tradition, always well-crafted and occasionally superb.

BEERS & RATINGS	SG	CF
Ballard Bitter *(1.045 og; 4.0 w)*	4	4
Redhook ESB *(1.054 og; 4.9 w)*	4	3½
Blackhook Porter *(1.050 og; 4.5 w)*	4	4
Wheathook *(1.034 og; 3.3 w)*	3	
Seasonals:		
Redhook Ale (1.050 og)	4	4
Honey Imperial Stout (1.072 og; 6.5 w)	3½	

Scott: "Redhook was the beer that got me excited about microbreweries and in the business. I get a little sentimental talking about it."
Chris: "Redhook ESB is brewed in homage to Fuller's ESB (Extra Special), one of England's greatest ales. Even the original gravity is virtually identical and, despite a slight American accent—Redhook's version is a worthy interpretation of an English special bitter."

3400 Phinney Avenue North
Seattle, Washington 98103
(206)548·8000

At the corner of Phinney Avenue N and N 35th Street. Just west of the Fremont Bridge on the north side of the ship canal. Live jazz and R&B Monday and Saturday night.

THOMAS KEMPER BREWING COMPANY

B *KB*

Thomas Kemper has been around since 1984, which makes it a virtual institution in the microbrewery world, certainly in this picturesque part of Washington, a ferry ride across Puget Sound from Seattle. From the outset, the brewery has devoted itself to German-style lagers, and the fact that its tap room is well-patronized seven days a week, twelve months a year, is some measure of Kemper's success. Unlike ale, quality lager demands long storage periods, and all of Kemper's brews are aged for at least four weeks, some for considerably longer.

FINE BEER
POULSBO
WASHINGTON

BEERS & RATINGS	SG	CF
Thomas Kemper Poulsbo	3½	
Pale Lager *(1.048 og; 3.3 w)*	4	
Thomas Kemper Poulsbo	4	
Pilsner *(1.048 og; 3.8 w)*	4	
Thomas Kemper Hefe Weizen		
Wheat Beer *(1.050 og; 4.0 w)*	4	
Seasonals:		
Thomas Kemper Rolling Bay Bock		
(1.068 og; 5.1 w)		
Thomas Kemper Oktoberfest		
Amber Lager (1.058 og; 4.2 w)		
Thomas Kemper Winterbrau Black		
Roast Lager (1.060 og; 4.3 w)		
Maibock (12.5 p)		4
Vikingfest Vienna-Style Amber		
(13.0 p)		4

22381 Foss Road NE
Poulsbo, Washington 98370
(206) 697·1446

From Seattle-Winslow: Take Seattle to Winslow ferry. At Winslow, travel Hwy. 305 through Poulsbo to Bond Road, turn right onto Bond and travel for 1.5 miles. Turn left onto Foss Road; the brewery is on the left. Open daily 11-8. Tours available.

OTTO BROTHERS' BREWING COMPANY

B

Founded in 1988, Otto Brothers' Brewing Company became the first brewery to operate in the State of Wyoming in a generation. Charlie and Ernie Otto, along with their partner Don Frank, built and equipped the Swiss chalet-style brewhouse themselves and supply draft beer to a number of outlets in northwestern Wyoming. At the time of this writing, they expect to add a bottling line in the near future.

BEERS & RATINGS	CF
Old Faithful Ale *(10.0 p)*	iii
Teton Ale	
Teton Pale Ale	
Moose Juice Stout	

P.O. Box 4177
Jackson Hole, Wyoming 83001
(307) 733·9000

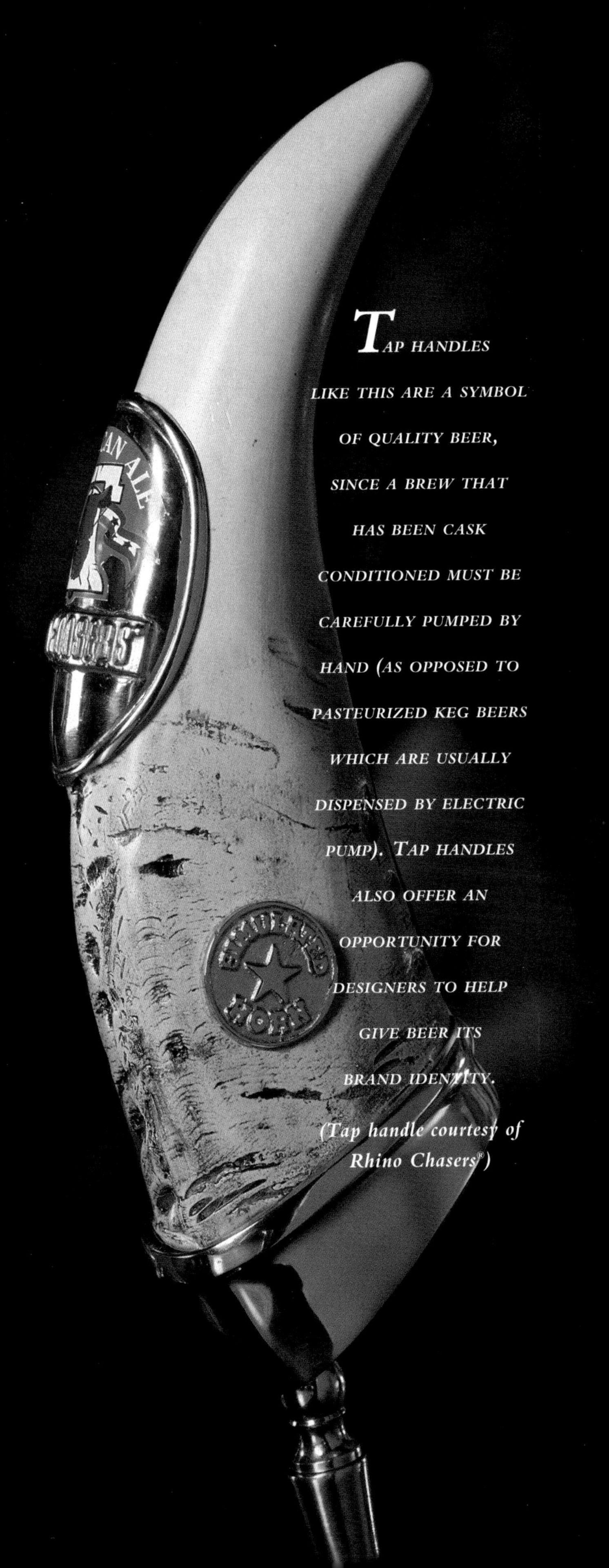

TAP HANDLES LIKE THIS ARE A SYMBOL OF QUALITY BEER, SINCE A BREW THAT HAS BEEN CASK CONDITIONED MUST BE CAREFULLY PUMPED BY HAND (AS OPPOSED TO PASTEURIZED KEG BEERS WHICH ARE USUALLY DISPENSED BY ELECTRIC PUMP). TAP HANDLES ALSO OFFER AN OPPORTUNITY FOR DESIGNERS TO HELP GIVE BEER ITS BRAND IDENTITY.

(Tap handle courtesy of Rhino Chasers®)

DOCK
WILLIAM & SCOTT CO.
CAN ALE™
RHINO CHASERS®
Pure barley malt lager beer.
PENNSYLVANIA
Pilsner
SIGILLVM · GERMANOPOLITANUM · 1691
Brewed and bottled
by the Penna.
MICRO
Reserve
TEXAS
A SPECIAL AMBER
SUMMIT
BREWING COMPANY
ALC. 4.8%
BY WT.
CA REDEMPTION VALUE
5¢ OR DEP.
FULL SAIL
AMBER
Made fro
ful hearty brew to
the winter season.
BREWERY, INC.

THE AMERICAN CRAFT BEER REVOLUTION HAS PROVIDED THE OCCASION FOR AN EXPLOSION OF CREATIVE ACTIVITY IN THE FIELD OF PACKAGING, INSPIRING A RANGE OF APPROACHES THAT VARY FROM PRE-PROHIBITION NEO-BAVARIAN RETRO TO POST-MODERN URBAN COWBOY KITSCH.

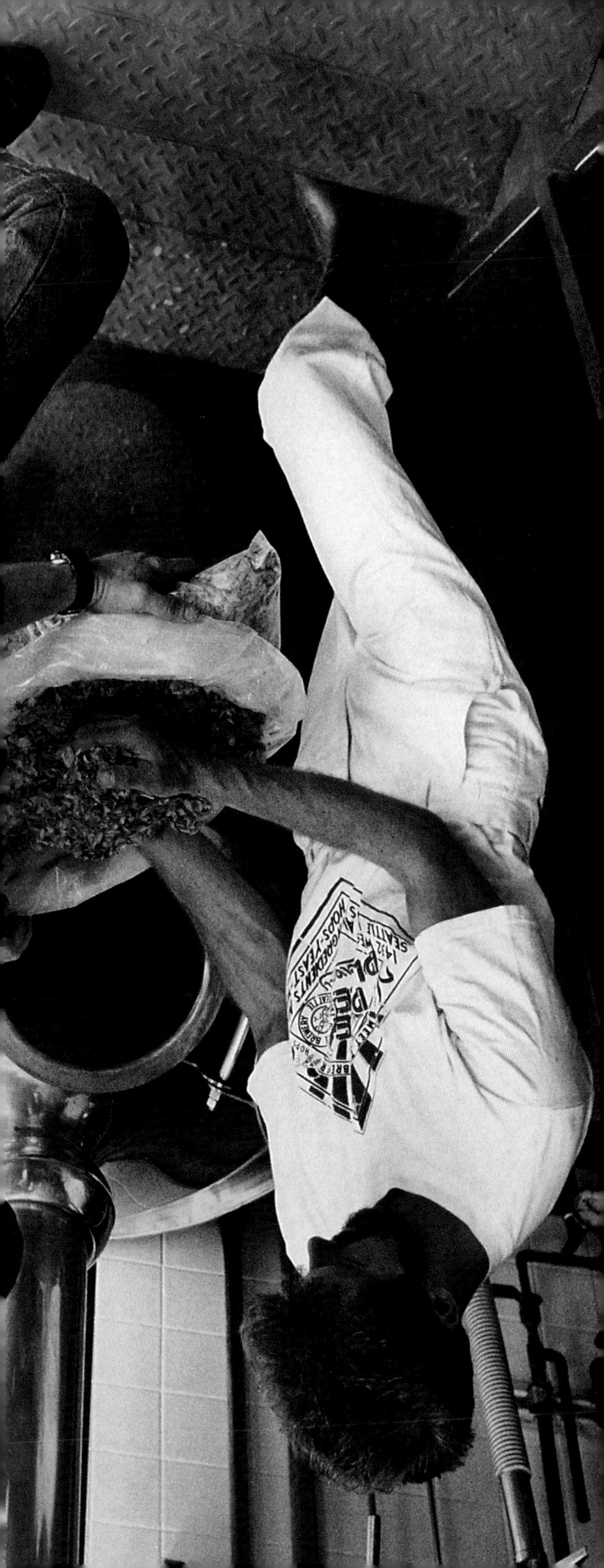

MIDWEST

M

North Dakota
Bismarck
94
29
Minnesota
94
St. Pau
Minneapolis
New Ulm
South Dakota
Pierre
Rapid City
90
29
Iowa
Nebraska
Omaha
Des Moines
80
Lincoln
29
35
Mi
Kansas
Topeka
Kansa
70
Lawrence
135
35
Wichita
Jeffe
Sprin

IDWEST

Lake Superior
MICHIGAN
WISCONSIN
Lake Michigan
Lake Huron
35
94
Eau Claire
Appleton
43
75
90
Oshkosh
Milwaukee
Madison
Frankenmuth
Kenosha
Lansing
Dubuque
196
Amana
Galena
Kalamazoo
Iowa City
Chicago
80
Davenport
80
74
57
65
69
ILLINOIS
Lafayette
Champaign
INDIANA
SSOURI
Springfield
Indianapolis
s City
70
55
St. Louis
64
rson City
64
44
gfield
55

ILLINOIS

Chicago Brewing Company

Goose Island Brewing Company

Joe's Brewing Company

Mill Rose Brewing Company

Pavichevich Brewing Company

Weinkeller Brewery

INDIANA

Broad Ripple Brewing Company

IOWA

Babe's

Fitzpatrick's Brewing Company

Millstream Brewing Company

KANSAS

Free State Brewing Company

Miracle Brewing Company

River City Brewing Company

MICHIGAN

Detroit & Mackinac Brewery

Frankenmuth Brewery, Inc.

Kalamazoo Brewing Company

MINNESOTA

August Schell Brewing Company

Cold Spring Brewing Company

James Page Brewing Company

Sherlock's Home

Summit Brewing Company

MISSOURI

Boulevard Brewing Company

The Signature Beer Company

St. Louis Brewery / The Taproom

NEBRASKA

Lazlo's Brewery & Grill

SOUTH DAKOTA

Firehouse Brewing Company

WISCONSIN

Appleton Brewing Company

Brewmaster's Pub, Ltd.

Capital Brewery Company, Inc.

Cherryland Brewery

Lakefront Brewery

Mid-Coast Brewery

Specialty Brewing Company

Water Street Brewery

LEGEND:
***B**—Brewery*
***BP**—Brewpub*
***R**—Restaurant*

B—Available in Bottles
K—Available in Kegs

CHICAGO BREWING COMPANY

B *KB*

This is one of the craft breweries that is restoring Chicago's honor—after Al Capone did so much to accustom the midwestern palate to inferior beer—and making the Windy City a haven for serious beer fanciers. Housed in a renovated Capone-era pickle factory, Chicago Brewing has an annual capacity of 30,000 barrels. The folks we must thank for these fine beers are Stephen Dinehart, his wife, Jennifer, and his brother, Craig, who began bottling in July 1990.

BEERS & RATINGS	SG	CF
Legacy Lager *(1.052 og; 3.8 w)*	4	4
Legacy Red Ale *(1.050 og; 4.0 w)*	3½	4
Heartland Weiss *(1.048 og; 3.2 w)*	3½	3½
Big Shoulders Porter		

Scott: "Flavorful, full-bodied brews."
Chris: "Legacy Lager is one of the best American lagers I've tasted, mouth filling and smooth with a clean, hoppy finish."

1830 North Beasly Court
Chicago, Illinois 60622
(312) 252·BREW

Just east of the Armitage exit, off I-90/94 (Kennedy Expressway) and ½ block west of the intersection of Elston and Cortland.

GOOSE ISLAND BREWING COMPANY

B BP *K B- 64oz*

Chicago has become home, once more, to some first-rate breweries, and Goose Island rates right up there at the top of the list. Housed in the old Turtle Wax factory, this is one of the rare craft breweries that is genuinely at home with both ales and lagers. The brewery is named for nearby Goose Island, created in 1890 when the Chicago Land Company cut a channel in the north branch of the Chicago River. The island was settled by the Irish, who raised geese and were known for their beer. All the beers we tasted displayed both a sure technical expertise and a very well articulated knowledge of international styles.

The cuisine is a mixture of international ethnic with a pub atmosphere and beer garden. Be sure to try their homemade root beer.

BEERS & RATINGS	SG	CF
Golden Goose Pilsner *(1.043 og; 4.3 w)*	III½	III½
PMD Mild Ale *(1.041 og; 3.0 w)*	III½	IIII½
Oatmeal Stout *(1.068 og; 5.5 w)*	IIII½	IIII
RAF Best Bitter *(1.054 og)*	III½	III½
Seasonals:		
Winter Warmer Barley Wine (1.066 og)	III½	IIII

Scott: "The Oatmeal Stout is exactly what an oatmeal stout should be—rich and chewy."
Chris: "PMD Mild is something of a miracle, a really good midwestern version of the kind of brew that still has a following in the British Midlands and evokes fond memories elsewhere in the British Isles. Malty and soothing."

1800 North Clybourn
Chicago, Illinois 60614
(312) 915·0071

From 90/94: exit North Avenue. Go east toward the lake on North Ave. past river. Go north/left on Sheffield.

JOE'S BREWING COMPANY

B BP

Joe's has made its home in a former textbook warehouse on the campus of the University of Illinois, where undergrads and faculty alike educate their palates. Pub grub describes the menu—sandwiches, wings, nachos, etc.—and there's room for dancing, darts, pool tables and pinball.

India Pale Ale *(1.064 og)*
Seasonals:
Porter (1.060 og; 5.5 v)
Oatmeal Stout (1.068 og; 6.5 v)
Barleywine (1.102 og; 9.5 v)

---

706 South Fifth Street
Champaign, Illinois 61820
(217) 384·1790

On the campus of the University of Illinois.

MILL ROSE BREWING COMPANY

B BP R

This brewpub brings a southwestern atmosphere to the suburbs of Chicago. Lunch and dinner is served, along with bar appetizers.

Dark Star
Country Inn Ale

---

45 South Barrington Road
South Barrington, Illinois 60010
(708) 382·7673

Open M-F 11-1 am; Sat-Sun 11-2 am.

PAVICHEVICH BREWING COMPANY

B *KB*

Ken Pavichevich's main product is Baderbräu Pilsner, a pale, all-malt pilsner that has enjoyed considerable popularity in the Chicago area since its introduction in 1988. (For what it's worth, its fans are said to include George Bush and players of the former Soviet Red Army hockey team.) Ken has recently introduced a bock beer as well. Pavichevich is one of the few microbreweries that is publicly traded on a stock exchange. Ken, by the way, is an ex-Chicago police officer, so it might be wise to be very complimentary when visiting his brewery.

BEERS & RATINGS	SG	CF
Baderbräu Pilsner Beer *(3.59 w)*	▮▮▮	▮▮▮½
Baderbräu Bock Beer *(4.52 w)*		

Scott: "This rating was based on a sample tasted in Southern California. I have liked Baderbräu better on other occasions. Also, I think Ken makes a fine beer, but I am a little curious as to why his name and packaging looks so much like an import."
Chris: "A nice lager, but not quite sharp enough to be a real pilsner."

383 Romans Road
Elmhurst, Illinois 60126
(708) 617·5252

Five miles south of O'Hare Airport.
Romans Road is off County Line Road.

WEINKELLER BREWERY

B BP *K B*

It's safe to assume that when Al Capone ran his empire out of Cicero—which happens to be next door to Berwyn—the beer with which he supplied his protected outlets was not up to the standards established by Weinkeller at both its Berwyn location and its newer micro in Westmont, a few miles farther west. Brewing both top- and bottom-fermented beers, Weinkeller is one of several craft brewing establishments making Chicago-area beer fanciers very happy.

The cuisine is German, featuring sauerbraten, schnitzel, pork roast in beer and many homemade sausages. The brewpub is a combination of a restaurant, bar, brewery, and liquor store. Udo Harttung does it all: runs the pub, brews the beer, and works the bar.

Weinkeller Brewery

BEERS & RATINGS	SG	CF
Dusseldorfer Doppelbock *(18.5 p)*	▮▮▮▮	▮▮▮
Doublin Stout *(18.0 p)*	▮▮▮▮	▮▮▮
Bavarian Weiss *(12.0 p)*	▮▮▮▮	▮▮▮▮
Seasonals:		
Oktoberfest (1.050 og)	▮▮▮▮	▮▮▮½
Lambic Kriek		
Christmas Ale (1.076 og)		

6417 West Roosevelt Road
Berwyn, Illinois 60402
(708) 749·2276

On the corner of Roosevelt and Ridgeland, 10 minutes from the Loop. Take Eisenhower to the Austin exit.

BROAD RIPPLE BREWING COMPANY

BR *K*

John Hill, the owner of this brewpub, opened in 1990, hails from Yorkshire, England, the county that gave us Samuel Smith ales and Old Peculier. Not surprisingly, his primary ambition is to produce beers in the Yorkshire style (though he's not averse to trying his hand at a top-fermented German beer such as Kolsch), and to this end his brewery staff imports two-row barley from England and uses British-style hops such as Kent and Fuggles, even if the latter are grown on this side of the Atlantic. Six beers are on tap at all times, and the brewpub also carries a wide range of bottled microbrews. The restaurant has an English Pub feeling and boasts a 100-year-old metal ceiling. Enjoy the fireplace or the outside dining during the warmer months. Steaks are their specialty.

BEERS & RATINGS	SG	CF
ESB *(12.25 p)*	▮▮▮▮	▮▮▮
IPA *(15.0 p)*	▮▮▮½	▮▮▮
Porter *(14.25 p)*	▮▮▮½	▮▮▮
Kolsch *(11.5 p)*	▮▮▮½	▮▮▮

84 East 65th Street
Indianapolis, Indiana 46220
(317) 253·2739

In the Broad Ripple entertainment district.

BABE'S

B BP *K B*

Named for "Babe" Bisigano, a prizefighter of the thirties, Babe's was a Des Moines institution from 1939 to 1991, when Babe retired. In 1993, Mike Hammer (no, not that one) reopened Babe's as an ambitious brewpub, with a dining room serving a full Italian/American menu, serving hand-carved meats, pastas, and soups, and a lunch counter serving deli sandwiches and pizza by the slice.

Babe's THE BREWERY

Wood Duck Wheat
Thoroughbred Classic Ale
Ring-Necked Red Ale
Owl's Head Brown Ale
Black Angus Oatmeal Stout

---

417 6th Avenue
Des Moines, Iowa 50309
(515) 244-9319

Next to the Convention Center. Open 7 days, 11-2.

FITZPATRICK'S BREWING COMPANY

B BP *K*

In his own words, Gary Fitzpatrick's establishment is "essentially an Irish pub." The exterior is a replica of a Dublin hostelry and the interior would have encouraged Brendan Behan to feel at home. Food is casual, inexpensive to moderate pub grub, including sandwiches and pizza.

Fitzpatrick's
Brewing Co.

Fitzpatrick Celtic Ale *(1.046 og; 5.0 v)*
Fitzpatrick Golden Lager *(1.036 og; 5.0 v)*
Fitzpatrick Mighty Stout *(1.052 og; 5.0 v)*
Fitzpatrick Wheat *(1.036 og;4.0 v)*
Seasonals:
Christmas Ale (cranberry) (1.050 og; 5.0 v)
Spring Bock (1.040 og; 4.0 v)
Fall Oktoberfest (1.050 og; 5.0 v)

525 South Gilbert
Iowa City, Iowa 52240
(319) 356·6900

Take I-80 to Dubuque Street exit to Jefferson to 525 S. Gilbert. Open M-Sat 11:30 am-2 am; Closed Sundays.

MILLSTREAM BREWING COMPANY

BP *KB*

This is the first brewery ever to operate in the city of Amana. It is also the best. They produce German-style beers of the sort that were popular in the Midwest before Prohibition. Visit the brewery in scenic downtown Amana, where you can enjoy the *gemutlichkeit* of the Millstream hospitality room and sample the beer.

BEERS & RATINGS	SG
Millstream Lager *(3.8 w)*	lll
Millstream Wheat *(4.0 w)*	
Schildbrau Amber *(4.5 w)*	
Seasonal:	
Millstream Oktoberfest (4.0 w)	lll½

284 Amana
Amana, Iowa 52203
(319) 622·3672

Located across from the Woolen Mill in Main Amana. Open daily. Call for summer & winter hours.

FREE STATE BREWING COMPANY

B BP *K*

This brewpub is located in a former trolley depot in the historic section of downtown Lawrence. The pub fare offered includes British, German, and American favorites. The house specialty is Cheddar Ale Soup. Have the Honey-Butter Apple Tart for dessert.

Ad Astra Pale Alt *(1.052 og; 4.0 w)*
Free State Hefe Weizen *(1.045 og; 3.7 w)*
Wheat State Golden *(1.040 og; 3.5 w)*

636 Massachusetts Street
Lawrence, Kansas 66044
(913) 843·4555

Just north of the Liberty Hall Opera House in downtown Lawrence. Open M-Sat 11-midnight; Sun noon-11. Tours: Sat 2 pm.

MIRACLE BREWING CO

B *K*

Dennis and Joseph Boone's recently established microbrewery distributes British-style keg beers throughout the region, making theirs the only distributing microbrewery in Kansas.

Miracle Mild *(1.041 og; 4.8 w)*
Red Devil Ale *(1.042 og; 4.8 w)*
Purgatory Porter *(1.043 og; 4.8 w)*

Scott: "Great logo!"

311 South Emporia
Wichita, Kansas 67202
(316) 265·7256

Three blocks north of Kellog, 300 block between Topeka Avenue & Emporia Street.

RIVER CITY BREWING COMPANY

B BP

Open since March 1993, River City is located in the renovated Old Town district of Wichita. This relaxed brewpub offers British-style beers, along with both British-style pub food and local specialties like elk and buffalo, which seldom show up on saloon bar menus in Fulham or Islington. A comprehensive menu offers English pubfare: bangers and mash and shepherd's pie.

Harvester Wheat *(10.0 p)*
Hockaday Pale Ale *(12.0 p)*
Railyard Amber Ale *(13.0 p)*
Four Horsemen Stout *(14.0 p)*
Two Rivers Bitter *(14.0 p)*

---

150 North Mosley Street
Wichita, Kansas 67202
(316) 362·2739

Old Town. Open M-Sat 11-1, till 2 am on F and Sat.

DETROIT AND MACKINAC BREWERY

B

Detroit's first new brewery since the repeal of Prohibition, Detroit and Mackinac produces draft ales that are available, at the time of this writing, only in southeastern Michigan.

BEERS & RATINGS	CF
India Pale Ale *(13.0 p)*	ııı½
Red Ale *(12.3 p)*	ııı

470 West Canfield
Detroit, Michigan 48201

FRANKENMUTH BREWERY, INC.

B

This company was founded in 1987 to renovate and operate a brewery that had been in existence since 1862, a time when Frankenmuth was settled by German immigrants who turned the town into "Little Bavaria." The town still retains its Bavarian atmosphere, making it a major midwestern tourist attraction. Appropriately enough, most of the beers brewed by the Frankenmuth Brewery are very much in the South German tradition, though ale is also produced. Most of the brewing equipment was imported from Germany and the beers are fire brewed, a method that has its supporters though some brewers feel that it does not provide enough control.

BEERS & RATINGS	SG	CF
Frankenmuth Pilsener	2½	2
Frankenmuth Dark	3	3½
Frankenmuth Bock	3	2½
Frankenmuth Extra Light	1½	1½
Old Detroit Amber Ale	3½	3

Scott: "The amber ale is my favorite here. A tasty beer, even though it has very little true ale character."

425 South Main Street
Frankenmuth, Michigan 48734
(517) 652-6183

Frankenmuth is just minutes east off I-75 between Flint and Saginaw, Michigan, northbound exit 136 or southbound exit 144. Brewery tours daily.

KALAMAZOO BREWING COMPANY

B *KB*

Kalamazoo Brewing is a well-regarded micro located in downtown Kalamazoo. Its specialty is top-fermented brews in the British style.

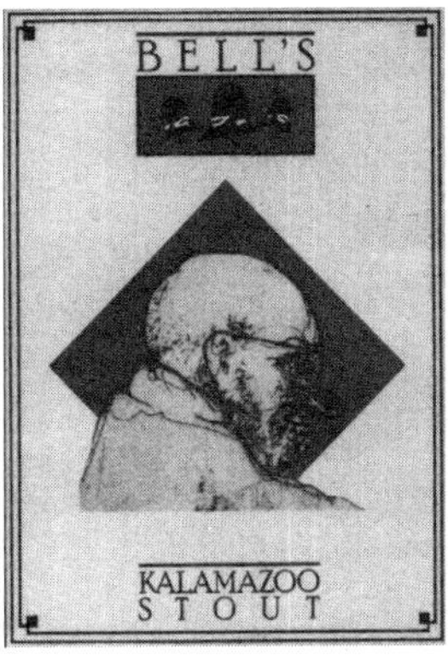

Third Coast Beer
Bell's Amber Ale
Bell's Porter
Bell's Kalamazoo Stout

315 East Kalamazoo Avenue
Kalamazoo, Michigan 49007
(616) 382·2338

Open M-F 9-10; Sat-Sun noon-10.

AUGUST SCHELL BREWING COMPANY

B *KB*

Founded in 1860, and set in a deer park, August Schell is one of the oldest regional breweries in America, and one of the prettiest. That's almost a liability these days when many of our best beers are being brewed by companies that were founded in the past dozen years, often in somebody's garage. Where Schell is concerned, however, tradition does have some real meaning. The brewery was an early participant in the American brewing renaissance, its pilsner and its wheat beer having enjoyed wide distribution for several years.

Lately Schell has been enjoying deserved popularity as a contract brewer, and its house brews, always good, have been reformulated and improved to meet the demands of the burgeoning market of discriminating beer drinkers.

BEERS & RATINGS

	SG	CF
August Schell Weizen *(11.0 p; 3.5 w)*	▮▮▮½	▮▮▮▮
August Schell Pils *(13.5 p; 4.2 w)*	▮▮▮	▮▮▮▮
Schell's Export *(11.2 p; 3.8 w)*	▮▮▮½	
Schell's Deer Brand *(11.2 p; 3.8 w)*	▮▮▮½	
Schell's Light *(8.0 p; 3.2 w)*	▮▮▮	
Seasonals:		
Schell's Bock (13.8 p; 4.5 w)	▮▮▮½	▮▮▮▮
Oktoberfest (13.2 p; 4.1 w)	▮▮▮½	▮▮▮▮½

Scott: "A beautiful old brewery tucked away in the quaint town of New Ulm. Schell's beers I find quite enjoyable on first gulp, but there is a sour note in the finish that I find a little disturbing."
Chris: "If you haven't tried any of these beers lately, you've been missing a treat. The Pils is more full-bodied than it used to be, and displays considerably more character. The same can be said of the Weizen. (Try it with lemon.) The Oktoberfest is outstanding, with lots of hop bite to balance its rich maltiness."

Schell's Park
New Ulm, Minnesota 56073
(507) 354·5528

100 miles southwest of Minneapolis.

COLD SPRING BREWING COMPANY

B *KB*

This small brewery is not a typical micro in that, the Prohibition years aside, it has remained in continuous operation since 1874. Its products are very much in the style that might be considered both Central European and midwestern.

BEERS & RATINGS	CF
Cold Spring	▮▮▮
Cold Spring Export	▮▮▮
Fox Deluxe	
Kegle Brau	

219 North Red River Avenue
Cold Spring, Minnesota 56320
(612) 331·2833

Mon-Fri 8-5.

JAMES PAGE BREWING COMPANY

B *KB*

Anheuser-Busch employs rice as an adjunct when brewing Budweiser. In his microbrewery, James Page has pioneered the use of wild rice as an adjunct. Wild rice has more character than the cultivated form. James Page's wild rice beer has considerably more character than Bud.

BEERS & RATINGS	SG
James Page Amber *(12.0 p; 3.9 w)*	♦♦♦
Boundary Waters Beer *(wild rice) (11.5 p; 3.7 w)*	♦♦♦♦
Burly Brown Ale *(13.0 p; 4.1 w)*	♦♦♦
Mill City Wheat *(11.8 p; 3.9 w)*	♦♦♦
Seasonals:	
Northern Lights Bock (16.0 p; 5.2 w)	♦♦♦

Scott: "The Boundary Waters Beer was my favorite. Wild rice is added for a distinctive taste. According to the brewer, the only wild rice brew in the world."

1300 Quincy Street NE
Minneapolis, Minnesota 55413
(612) 331·2833

On Quincy, north of Broadway off the I-35 W or the I-94. Tours held on the first Saturday of the month from 1-4 pm. Call for special times for groups.

SHERLOCK'S HOME

B BP R

For some reason, restaurateurs in the Twin Cities are very fond of literal impersonations of British institutions. There used to be a half-timbered establishment, on a lake, where a sign announced Sir Brian will park Your Chariot. Sir Brian wore full armor.

More recently, Bill Burdick opened a remarkable reproduction of a British pub near the fabled shores of Lake Minnetonka. Like many British pubs, it features a formal dining room (for the gentry of Wayzata) where game pie and such other delicacies are gracefully presented on bone china. A humbler range of English and Scottish food is available in what, across the pond, would be called the public bar. Four cask-conditioned brews are served at cellar temperature, but chilled beers are also available.

BEERS & RATINGS	**SG**	**CF**
Bishop's Bitter *(1.042 og)*	▮▮▮	▮▮▮▮
Piper's Pride (Scottish Ale) *(1.046 og)*	▮▮▮▮	▮▮▮▮
Palace Porter *(1.042 og)*	▮▮▮	▮▮▮½
Stag's Head Stout *(1.056 og)*	▮▮▮½	▮▮▮▮
Star of India (IPA) *(1.045 og)*	▮▮▮½	▮▮▮½
Gold Crown Lager *(1.040 og)*	▮▮▮	▮▮▮
Queen Anne Light *(1.036 og)*	▮▮▮	▮▮▮

Scott: "A great place to hang out. Start with a Scottish Ale, finish with a Talisker Single Malt."
Chris: "Bad pun. Good beer. Bishop's Bitter is almost as British as the pint glasses it's served in."

11000 Red Circle Drive
Minnetonka, Minnesota 55343
(612) 931·0203

At the northeast corner of the Crosstown Highway and Shady Oak Road. Minnetonka is a suburb of Minneapolis. Open M-Sat 11-1 am; Sun 4 pm-1 am.

SUMMIT BREWING COMPANY

B *KB*

Summit was incorporated in 1984 and began selling beer two years later. This micro is especially proud of its plant, much of which was imported from Germany. (It includes a pre-war, two-vessel brewhouse purchased from a small Bavarian brewery, Hirsch Brau, in Heimertingen.) Seasonal beers are produced, but the pale ale and the porter are the company's basic products. They have tours, but make a reservation.

BEERS & RATING	SG	CF
Summit Extra Pale Ale *(12.0 p; 3.9 w)*	▮▮▮▮	▮▮▮½
Great Northern Porter *(13.4 p; 4.3 w)*	▮▮▮½	▮▮▮▮
Seasonals:		
Summit Sparkling Ale (referred to as their baseball beer) (1.043 og; 3.4 w)	▮▮▮½	
Summit Winter Ale (1.058 og; 4.9 w)	▮▮▮▮	

Scott: "A wonderful micro. Go visit and enjoy the Extra Pale Ale. Also, they asked us to make it clear they, regretfully, are not a brewpub."

2264 University Avenue
St. Paul, Minnesota 55114
(612) 645·5029

Located five blocks east of Highway 280.

BOULEVARD BREWING COMPANY

B *KB*

Boulevard is a recently established micro that shows considerable promise, producing well-crafted, top-fermented beers that deserve to be very popular.

BEERS & RATINGS	CF
Boulevard Wheat	4
Boulevard Pale Ale	3½
Boulevard Bully Porter	4

Chris: "These are high-quality, easy drinking beers that would score higher if they had just a little more personality. The wheat beer is very refreshing in the best American style—perfect for those hot Missouri summers.

2501 Southwest Boulevard
Kansas City, Missouri 64108
(816) 474·7095

Corner of 25th and Southwest Boulevard.
Call for tours.

THE SIGNATURE BEER COMPANY

B *KB*

The original and admirable purpose of this company was to properly handle and deliver, to St. Louis area retail outlets, fresh microbrewery beers. Starting in 1992, Thoney Cardonna, the company's founder, contracted with the Oldenberg Brewing Company to create The Spirit of St. Louis Ale, which Signature now distributes.

BEERS & RATINGS	CF
The Spirit of St Louis Ale *(1.056 og; 4.1 w)*	III

2737 Hereford Street
St. Louis, Missouri 63139
(314) 772·5911

ST. LOUIS BREWERY/THE TAPROOM

B BP *K B*

Opened in 1991, the St. Louis Brewery is located in a 19th-century industrial building that has earned a place in the National Register of Historic Buildings, and like many other brewpubs that have taken root in similar settings, the Taproom serves British-style pub food (though dishes such as goat cheese rarebit add a *nouveau* touch). What makes St. Louis special, however, is that it takes the craft brewing revolution into the heart of Anheuser-Busch territory, and it does so while brewing some of the most outstanding beers it has been our good fortune to taste during the course of preparing this book. President Tom Schlafly, CEO Dan Kopman, and head brewer Dave Miller are to be congratulated.

BEERS & RATINGS	SG	CF
Pilsner *(1.049 og)*		▮▮▮▮
Wheat Ale *(1.038 og)*		▮▮▮▮
Hefeweizen *(1.038 og)*		▮▮▮▮
Pale Ale *(1.045 og)*	▮▮▮▮½	
Cask Conditioned Pale Ale *(1.045 og)*		▮▮▮½
Oatmeal Stout *(1.057 og)*		▮▮▮▮
Seasonals:		
Old Possum Barleywine (1.084 og)		▮▮▮▮½
Robert Burns Scotch Ale (1.055 og)		▮▮▮▮½

Chris: "Pale ales with a nutty hint of Yorkshire bitter, a Scotch ale that would win a following in Aberdeen or Antwerp, a barleywine capable of taming the wildest midwestern winter. Superb."

2100 Locust
St. Louis, Missouri 63103
(314) 241·2337

Located on 21st Street, between Olive & Locust; just 4 blocks northwest of Union Station.
Open M-Th 11 am-12 am; F-Sat 11-1 (live music); Sun noon-10 pm.

LAZLO'S BREWERY & GRILL

B BP R *1-Gallon Containers*

Opened in 1991, Lazlo's became Nebraska's first brewpub. Occupying two adjacent landmark buildings in Lincoln's historic Haymarket neighborhood, this is a casually upscale establishment with a full-service restaurant featuring meats and seafood grilled over a hickory fire.

Lougale's Gold *(10.8 p; 4.0 w)*
Reckless Red's Amber *(11.2 p; 4.2 w)*
Black Jack Stout *(12.0 p; 4.5 w)*

---

710 P Street
Lincoln, Nebraska 68508
(402) 474·2337

Located in Lincoln's historic Haymarket District, easy access off I-80. Open M-Sat 11-1 am; Sun 11-10 pm.

FIREHOUSE BREWING COMPANY

B BP *K*

Anyone who has passed through Rapid City in July or August will acknowledge that the city deserves at least one brewpub. Opened in 1991, Firehouse Brewing occupies the site of a 1915 Fire Station. At the time of writing, brewmaster John B. Kaelberer produces eight different styles of beer, with five on tap at any given moment.

BEERS & RATINGS	CF
Buffalo Bitter *(10.1 p)*	2½
Rushmore Stout *(11.3 p)*	3½
Firehouse Red	
Eagle Pale Ale	
Barely Blond	
Wilderness Wheat	
Roughrider Barley Wine	

Chris: "Although it's true that most British session bitters are lower in gravity and alcoholic content than Americans generally realize, Buffalo Bitter goes a little too far in this direction. The stout is a tad thinnish too, though very pleasant. The T-shirts are among the best in the microbrew world."

610 Main Street
Rapid City, South Dakota 57701
(605) 348·1915

One block north of Alex Johnson Hotel.

APPLETON BREWING COMPANY

B BP *K B*

Adler Brau is located in a 133-year-old brewery building in what was once thought of as the heart of American brewing country. Adler Brau specializes in the lagers that made Wisconsin famous, but serves them up with an enthusiasm and variety that is decidedly refreshing. The company has two brewpubs—Dos Bandidos and Johnny O's Pizzeria—and a range of beers that, while inconsistent, can be excellent.

BEERS & RATINGS	SG	CF
Adler Bräu Amber *(1.047 og; 4.1 w)*	3½	2½
Adler Bräu Double Bock *(1.058 og; 5.5 w)*	3½	3½
Adler Bräu Lager *(1.044 og; 4.0 w)*	3½	2½
Adler Bräu Pilsner *(1.050 og; 4.1 w)*	3½	3½
Adler Bräu Porter *(1.070 og; 4.2 w)*	4	3
Adler Bräu Light *(9.5 p)*	3½	2½
Seasonals:		
Adler Bräu Oktoberfest (15.5 p)	4	3
Adler Bräu Weiss (14.75 p)	3	3½
Adler Bräu Pumpkin Spice (12.5 p)	4	4
Adler Bräu Oatmeal Stout	4½	4

Scott: "The Pumpkin Spice is outstanding—Thanksgiving and Christmas rolled into one. Adler's Oatmeal Stout is one of my favorites."
Chris: "This brewery is at its best—which is very good—when it's being adventurous and having fun."

1004 Old Oneida Street
Appleton, Wisconsin 54915
(414) 735·0507

Between the Locks Mall, southeast end of the Oneida Skyline Bridge. A large, well-lighted parking lot adjoins the Mall.

BREWMASTER'S PUB, LTD.

B BP *K B*

True to the traditions of its region, Brewmaster's specializes in bottom-fermented, German-style beers. Its well-established brewpub serves four styles of lager on a regular basis and offers a different specialty beer every month.

BEERS & RATINGS	SG	CF
Kenosha Gold *(12.0 p; 5.0 w)*	4	3½
Amber Vienna Style *(12.5 p; 6.0 w)*	4	3
Brewmaster's Royal Dark *(15.5 p; 6.0 w)*		

Brewmaster's Southport Light
(12.0 p; 3.7 w)
Seasonals:

Oktoberfest (15.5 p)	🍾🍾🍾🍾	🍾🍾🍾½
Johnson's Honey Lager (14.0 p)	🍾🍾🍾🍾	🍾🍾🍾

Scott: "It might not be in accord with the *Reinheitsgebot,* but Brewmaster's use of honey makes for an interesting taste experience."

4017 80th Street
Kenosha, Wisconsin 53142
(414) 694·9050

CAPITAL BREWERY COMPANY, INC.

B *KB*

Capitol was established in 1986 and has made its reputation as a producer of beers in the German tradition, as is only appropriate given the cultural ties to Germany still very much alive in this part of the country. Five beers are brewed year round, while five more rotate on a seasonal basis.

CAPITAL
BREWERY COMPANY, INC.

BEERS & RATINGS	SG	CF
Wisconsin Amber *(1.051 og; 4.1 w)*	🍾🍾🍾	🍾🍾🍾½
Birch Bay Brown Ale		🍾🍾🍾½
Garten Bräu Special *(1.048 og; 3.8 w)*		
Garten Bräu Dark *(1.054 og; 4.2 w)*		
Garten Bräu Weizen *(1.048 og; 4.0 w)*		
Garten Bräu Oktoberfest *(1.055 og; 4.4 w)*		
Garten Bräu Wiznterfest *(1.057 og; 4.6 w)*		

7734 Terrace Avenue
Middleton, Wisconsin 53560
(608) 836·7100

Open 9-4.

CHERRYLAND BREWERY

BP *KB*

Cherryland is a small lager brewery operating out of a turn-of-the-century Green Bay & Western Railroad station. Located on an inlet of Lake Michigan, Sturgeon Bay is a popular summer resort and is also famous regionally for its cherry crop, hence the name of the brewery and the fact that a cherry-flavored beer is one of its staples. Cherryland's ten-barrel brew system produces three bottom-fermented beers for year-round bottling, as well as rotating seasonal brews.

BEERS & RATINGS	SG	CF
Golden Rail *(1.050 og; 4.5 v)*	🍺🍺🍺	🍺🍺🍺½
Cherry Rail *(1.048 og; 4.0 v)*	🍺🍺🍺½	🍺🍺🍺🍺
Silver Rail *(1.046 og; 3.8 v)*	🍺🍺🍺	🍺🍺🍺½
Apple Bock *(1.052 og; 4.8 v)*		
Seasonals:		
Irish Lager (1.050 og; 4.5 v)		
Weizen (1.042 og; 3.5 v)		

Scott: "The Cherry Rail is a nice surprise."
Chris: "Fresh, crisp lagers. The cherry specialty has an agreeable tartness to its finish."

341 West North Third Avenue
Sturgeon Bay, Wisconsin 54235
(414) 743·1945

From the north, take Egg Harbor Road (42-57 bus.) into Sturgeon Bay. Turn right on Third Avenue. Look for Caboose. Open 7 days a week for tours May-October. Weekends only during winter, 11-4.

LAKEFRONT BREWERY

B *KB*

Located in an old neighborhood bakery building that was built in 1910. Lakefront brews a variety of beers, mostly from a relatively high original gravity.

Klisch Lager Beer *(1.060 og; 5.9 w)*
Riverwest Stein Beer *(1.065 og; 6.3 w)*
Cream City Ale *(1.065 og; 6.3 w)*
East Side Dark *(1.070 og; 6.7 w)*

818A East Chambers Street
Milwaukee, Wisconsin 53212·2601
(414) 372·8800

From I-43 exit on Locust Street and head east 1 mile to Fratney St. Head north on Fratney and the next street is Chambers, which you should turn east on. We are in a brown brick building on the north side of the street, a half block down from Fratney & Chambers. Call for tours.

MID-COAST BREWING

B *KB*

At the time of this writing, Chief Oshkosh Red Lager is Mid-Coast's only brand, though others are planned. Chief Oshkosh is an interpretation, by company founder Jeff Fulbright, of a brew popular in Oshkosh from 1864-1970.

BEERS & RATINGS	CF
Chief Oshkosh Red Lager *(12.0 p)*	III½

Chris: "A satisfyingly malty brew."

35 Wisconsin Street
Oshkosh, Wisconsin 54901
(414) 236·3307

SPECIALTY BREWING COMPANY

B *B*

The Specialty Brewing Company is an interesting experiment in that it is a wholly-owned subsidiary of an industry giant—Pabst—devoted to exploring the possibilities of satisfying the growing demands of beer fanciers who have discovered the pleasures of microbrews and imports. The first results of the experiment show modest promise.

BEERS & RATINGS	SG	CF
Old Tankard Ale	III½	II½
Milwaukee Germanfest Bier *(12.9 p)*		III

P.O. Box 766
Milwaukee, Wisconsin 53233
(313) 831·2739

WATER STREET BREWERY

B R

The Water Street Brewery is located in the Milwaukee neighborhood that was once home to Pabst, Schlitz and Blatz. Water Street makes its home in what was once a florist warehouse (whatever that is) which has been converted into an attractive pub and restaurant where the food is outstanding—both more ambitious than is common with brewpubs and unusually well prepared. It is well complemented by a variety of beers brewed under the supervision of John Dallman.

BEERS & RATINGS	SG	CF
Old World Oktoberfest *(12.75 p)*	4	3½
Weiss *(6.75 p)*	4	3½
Callan's English Red Ale	4	3
Water Street Pale Ale	3½	3

1101 N. Water Street
Milwaukee, Wisconsin 53202
(414) 272·1195

NORTHEAST

NOR

90
79
80
Cleveland
Strongsville
75
Ohio
77
70
Columbus
71
79
Elkins
West Virginia
Louisville
64
Charleston
Kentucky
Frankfurt
64
81
24
65
Roanoke

THEAST

VERMONT
MAINE
95
Montpelier
89
93
Bethel
Augusta
Portland
NEW YORK
Rochester
Albany
Concord
NEW HAMPSHIRE
Boston
90
87
MASSACHUSETTS
81
Adamstown
Allentown
Philadelphia
RHODE ISLAND
CONNECTICUT
Baltimore
NEW JERSEY
DELAWARE
MARYLAND

CONNECTICUT

The Hartford Brewery

New England Brewing Company

New Haven Brewing Company

DELAWARE

Blue Hen Brew Company

DISTRICT OF COLUMBIA

Capitol City Brewing Company

The Olde Heurich Brewing Company

KENTUCKY

Oldenburg Brewery

Silo Brewpub & Restaurant

MAINE

Acadia Brewing Company

Bar Harbor Brewing Company

D.L. Geary Brewing Company

Gritty McDuff's

Kennebunkport Brewing

MARYLAND

Baltimore Brewing Company

Frederick Brewing Condensed

Oxford Brewing Company

Sisson's

The Wharf Rat at Camden Yards

Wild Goose Brewery

MASSACHUSETTS

Boston Beer Company

Boston Beer Works

Cambridge Brewing Company, Inc.

Commonwealth Brewing Co., Ltd.

Ipswich Brewing Company

Massachusetts Bay Brewing

Northampton Brewery at Brewster Court Bar & Grill

Old Marlborough Brewing Company

Olde Time Brewers

NEW HAMPSHIRE

Portsmouth Brewery

NEW JERSEY

Atlantic Brewing Company

Goldfinch Brewing Company

NEW YORK

The Brooklyn Brewery

Buffalo Brewpub

F.X. Matt Brewing Company

Mountain Valley Brewpub

Old World Brewing Company, Inc.

Rochester Brewpub

Shea's Brewery

Syracuse Suds Factory

Woodstock Brewing Company

Zip City Brewing Company

OHIO

The Burkhardt Brewing Company

Columbus Brewing Company

The Great Lakes Brewing Company

Hoster Brewing Company

Melbourne's Brewing Company

PENNSYLVANIA

Arrowhead Brewing Company, Inc.

Dock Street Brewing Company

The Lion Inc.

Neuweiler Brewing Company, Inc.

Pennsylvania Brewing Company / Allegheny Brewery

Philadelphia Brewing Company / Samuel Adams Brew House

Stoudt Brewing Company

VERMONT

Catamount Brewing Company

Latchis Grille & Windham Brewery

McNeill's Brewery

The Mountain Brewers, Inc.

Otter Creek Brewing Company

The Vermont Pub & Brewery

VIRGINIA

Blue Ridge Brewing Company

Old Dominion Brewing Company

Richbrau Brewery

LEGEND:
B*—Brewery*
BP*—Brewpub*
R*—Restaurant*

B—Available in Bottles
K—Available in Kegs

THE HARTFORD BREWERY

BP R

A stone's throw from the State House, this brew-pub offers a relaxed atmosphere, a full menu, and craft beers.

Pitt Bull Golden *(1.042 og)*
Arch Amber *(1.048 og)*
Praying Mantis Porter *(1.052 og)*

---

35 Peary Street
Hartford, Connecticut 06103
(203) 246·2337

Across from the State House.

NEW ENGLAND BREWING COMPANY

B *KB*

Founded in 1989 by Richard and Marcia King, with Paul Markowski and Ron Page as brewers, this is a serious micro producing well-made, very drinkable beers, in the British style, which have gained an enviable local reputation.

NEW ENGLAND BREWING CO.

BEERS & RATINGS	SG	CF
Atlantic Amber *(1.048 og)*	ⅠⅠⅠ½	
Gold Stock Ale *(1.044 og)*	ⅠⅠⅠ½	
Oatmeal Stout		ⅠⅠⅠⅠ

Chris: "New England's oatmeal stout has the full flavor and smoothness one looks for in this style."

25 Commerce Street
Norwalk, Connecticut 06850
(203) 866·1339

Next to the Classic Ice Co. and the Norwalk Garden Center. Open M-F 9-5

NEW HAVEN BREWING COMPANY

B *K B*

A medium-size micro in Yale University's backyard.

BEERS & RATINGS	CF
Elm City Connecticut Ale *(1.047 og)*	ⅠⅠⅠⅠ
Elm City Golden Ale *(1.042 og)*	
Blackwell Stout *(1.051 og)*	

Chris: "Connecticut Ale is full-bodied and fruity, somewhat in the Burton style."

458 Grand Avenue
New Haven, Connecticut 06513
(203) 772·2739

Next to the Classic Ice Co. and the Norwalk Garden Center. Open M-F 9-5.

BLUE HEN BREW COMPANY

B *B*

Brewed for this Delaware company by the Lion Brewery of Wilke-Barre, Pennsylvania, Blue Hen is a good example of the fact that contract brewing has a valuable role to play in the American beer renaissance. This is a style of beer that is often better when brewed by a sizable brewery.

BEERS & RATINGS	CF
Blue Hen Beer *(11.8 p; 3.86 w)*	🍾🍾🍾🍾

Chris: "A chewy, well-balanced brew."

P.O. Box 707
Newark, Delaware 16714-7077
(302) 737·8375

CAPITOL CITY BREWING COMPANY

B BP R *K*

Opened in August 1993, and convenient for the Washington Convention Center, Capitol City Brewing is a welcome addition to the craft beer scene in the nation's capital. A complete menu is featured, along with both British- and German-style brews.

Bitter *(11.8 p)*
Porter *(12.5 p)*
Pilsner *(11.9 p)*
Alt *(11.8 p)*
Kolsch *(12.5 p)*

1100 New York Avenue NW
Washington, D.C. 20005
(202) 628·2222

Located at 11th & 8th streets. Open Sun-Th 11-11; F-Sat 11-12. Large-screen TV for sporting events.

THE OLDE HEURICH BREWING COMPANY

B *KB*

The Olde Heurich Brewing Company is run by Gary F. Heurich, who traces his inspiration to the beers brewed by his grandfather, Christian Heurich, who founded a brewery in Washington, D.C., in 1873 (and was still brewing more than 80 years later at the age of 102!). Contract-brewed in Utica, NY, the company's present product is a Bavarian-style Maerzen beer.

BEERS & RATINGS	SG
Olde Heurich Maerzen	IIII

1111 34th Street NW
Washington DC, 20007
(202) 333·2313

OLDENBERG BREWERY

B BP *K B*

This is said to be the largest brewpub in the world, and is certainly the largest in North America, containing a beer garden, a British-style pub and the so-called Great Hall, which on its own can accommodate 650 for a sit-down meal. The complex also features a gift shop, a bakery, live entertainment, brewery tours and a stupendous collection of breweriana. Hardly cozy, this is a theme park designer's idea of a brewpub. Surprisingly, perhaps, the beers themselves are quite decent—very good in one instance.

OLDENBERG
BREWERY

BEERS & RATINGS	SG	CF
Oldenberg Blond *(3.4 w)*	IIII	IIII
Oldenberg Premium Verum *(OPV) (3.8 w)*	III	III
Oldenberg Weiss Beer	II½	II½

Scott: "The wheat beer displays very little real wheat palate, but is pleasant if undistinguished brew. The OPV is an agreeable everyday beer." ***Chris:*** "Described as dry light pils, Oldenberg Blond is much better than some more highly touted American pilsners. Excellent hop quality and crispness."

I-75 at Buttermilk Pike
Fort Mitchell, Kentucky 41017
(606) 341·2804

Five miles south of Cincinnati exit 186. Open T-Sun 11-10; closed Mondays. Visit this one-of-a-kind attraction: The American Museum of Brewing History & Arts, Tours & Tastings; a spectacular stage show and All-American Buffet.

SILO BREWPUB & RESTAURANT

BP K

Established in 1992, this brewpub offers the citizens of Louisville a menu that ranges from Texas-style chili to Cajun shrimp, along with an eclectic selection of beers.

Silo Premium Light *(1.038 og; 2.9 w)*
Red Rock Ale *(1.050 og; 3.9 w)*
Raspberry Light *(1.038 og; 2.9 w)*
Derby City Dark *(1.054 og; 4.1 w)*

---

630 Barret Avenue
Louisville, Kentucky 40204
(502) 589·2739

Two blocks north of Broadway or two blocks south of Baxter. Open M-Th 11:30-2; F-Sat 11:30-3. Live rock Friday & Saturday nights, digital cable music daily, jazz to rock n' roll.

ACADIA BREWING COMPANY

B BP *K B*

Associated with the Lompoc Cafe and Brew Pub, Acadia is a strong entry in the New England craft brewing scene. The Lompoc Cafe offers "an eclectic international menu," but it's the beer that deserves notice here. With their British malts and their blend of British and American hops, Acadia's brews are very much in the British tradition with just a slight American accent. Seasonal brews, such as a Blueberry Ale, are offered, but it is the classics that provide Acadia with its emerging reputation.

BEERS & RATINGS	SG	CF
Bar Harbor Real Ale *(12.0 p)*	▮▮▮½	▮▮▮▮
Acadia Pale Ale *(12.0 p)*	▮▮▮▮	▮▮▮½
Coal Porter *(12.5 p)*	▮▮▮▮½	▮▮▮½
Acadia Pale Ale		

Scott: "Acadia's beers have a distinctive spicy character. The porter is wonderful."
Chris: "Good brews. The Bar Harbor Real Ale is an authentic British-style session beer."

30 Rodick Street
Bar Harbor, Maine 04609
(207) 288·9392

Conveniently located in the heart of Bar Harbor on Ridick Street (just off Cottage Street) behind Timberland Shoes. Ample parking in the municipal lot adjacent to the café. Open daily 3 pm-1 am.

BAR HARBOR BREWING COMPANY

B *KB*

Established in 1990, by Tod Foster, this micro produces an Imperial-style stout and a couple of ales for local distribution

Cadillac Mountain Stout *(1.075 og; 6.1 v)*
Harbor Light Pale Ale *(1.043 og; 3.6 v)*
Thunder Hole Ale *(1.058 og; 5.2 v)*

---

22 Forest Street,
Bar Harbor, Maine 04609
(207) 288·4592

Tours by appointment. We love talking to beer enthusiasts!

D.L. GEARY BREWING COMPANY

B *KB*

This highly regarded micro distributes one basic product—a Burton-style pale ale—plus a high gravity winter warmer.

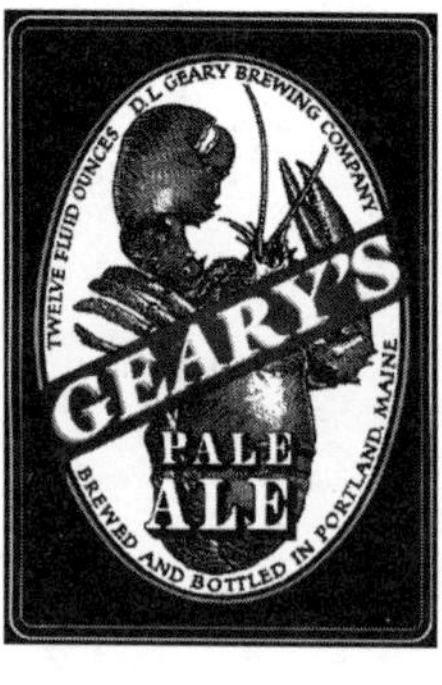

Geary's Pale Ale *(1.047 og; 4.5 v)*

38 Evergreen Drive
Portland, Maine 04103
(207) 878·2337

Two miles north of Exit 8 off Maine turnpike. Open M-F 8-4. Beer available for free sampling in tasting room on tours only. Call for reservations.

GRITTY McDUFF'S

B BP *K B*

Established in 1988, McDuff's was Maine's first brewpub. Located in the Old Port section of Portland, McDuff's boasts a British atmosphere with a copper-topped bar and English pump handles. The food is Anglo-American pub fare (Welsh rarebit, shepherd's pie, New York-style Reuben), and the beer is very much in the British tradition.

Black Fly Stout *(1.045 og)*
Lion's Pride Brown Ale *(1.043 og)*
McDuff's Best Bitter *(1.048 og)*
Portland Head Light Pale Ale *(1.046 og)*

396 Fore Street
Portland, Maine 04101
(207) 772·BEER

In Portland's historic Old Port, one block from the waterfront and harbor. Open M-Sat 11-1; Sun noon-1 am.

KENNEBUNKPORT BREWING

B BP *K B*

This brewpub is located in a picturesque seaside town overlooking Kennebunkport Harbor. Gourmet sandwiches, pizza, and a full line of entrees are served. The brewery produces British-style beers that, at the time of this writing, are distributed to 60 accounts in Maine.

Shipyard Export Ale *(1.052 og; 5.0 w)*
T'aint Town Pale Ale *(1.048 og; 4.6 w)*
Bluefin Stout *(1.052 og; 4.9 w)*
Captain Eli's Kennebunk Porter *(1.046 og; 4.6 w)*
Goat Island Light Ale *(1.034 og; 3.3 w)*

---

8 Western Avenue #6
Kennebunk, Maine 04043
(207) 967·4311

At the shipyard complex overlooking the Kennebunkport Harbor. Open noon to 1 am. Folk music and acoustic music on some nights.

BALTIMORE BREWING COMPANY

B BP *K B*

Although its location is on the edge of Baltimore's Little Italy, this brewpub is decidedly German in atmosphere. The food served includes such German favorites as wiener-schnitzel, sauerbraten, and traditional types of sausage. The beers too are thoroughly German in style.

Weizen *(12.0 p; 4.7 v)*
Pils *(12.8 p; 5.3 v)*
Märzen *(13.0 p 5.3 v)*
De Groen Dark *(13.3 p 5.5 v)*

104 Albemarle Street
Baltimore, Maryland 21202
(410) 837·5000

Next to the Flag House, one block from Little Italy and only a few blocks east of the Inner Harbor. Open T-Th 11-11; F-Sat 11-midnight; closed Sunday and Monday.

FREDERICK BREWING CONDENSED

B *KB*

Formerly a contract brew, Blue Ridge Golden Ale is now the flagship beer of a micro located in the refurbished historic section of Frederick, a long-established community in the Appalachian foothills, and the birthplace of Francis Scott Key, author of "The Star Spangled Banner." The handsome tap room features an extensive beer glass collection.

BEERS & RATINGS

Blue Ridge Golden *(1.047 og)*
Porter *(1.058 og)*
ESB Red Ale *(1.045 og)*
Amber Lager *(1.050 og)*

103 South Carroll Street
Frederick, Maryland

At the corner of Carroll & All Saints in the Historic District. Tours on Saturday 1:00 & 2:30, and Sunday at 1:30.

OXFORD BREWING COMPANY

B *K*

This micro was established in 1992 and brews a variety of keg and cask-conditioned beers for local distribution.

Oxford Class Amber Ale *(1.055 og)*
Cask Conditioned Ale *(1.055 og)*
Eleanor's *(1.060 og)*
Slick Willie Winter Warmer *(1.064 og)*

611-G Hammonds Ferry Road
Linthicum, Maryland 21090
(410) 789·0003

Open 8-5.

SISSON'S

BP R *K & Growlers*

This well-established restaurant and brewery is located in the historic Federal Hill area of Baltimore, opposite the Cross Street Market and a few blocks from the Inner Harbor. The full-service dining room features Cajun and New Orleans Creole specialties.

Cross Street Stout *(1.048 og; 4.9 v)*
Marble Golden *(1.044 og; 5.2 v)*
So Bo HefeWeizen *(1.046 og; 4.7 v)*
Stockade Amber *(1.052 og; 4.9 v)*

---

36 East Cross Street
Baltimore, Maryland 21230
(410) 539·2093

Take Light Street six blocks south past Harborplace. Bear right on Light at the Key Hwy. intersection, and follow for 4 blocks. At the second light, turn right on Cross St. Sisson's is halfway down the block on the right. Parking is available on the street in front of the restaurant or in a lot on nearby West Street: Follow Cross one block and turn left onto S. Charles at the traffic light. Turn left on West Street and pull into the West Street lot. Open M-Sat 11:30-2 am; Sun 5 pm-2 am.

THE WHARF RAT AT CAMDEN YARDS

BP R *K*

A block from the Orioles' new ballpark, the Wharf Rat is a large brewpub in a Victorian cast iron building. There are three full-service dining rooms, plus a patio and a sidewalk café. English pub fare and Maryland seafood is served.

Oliver's Irish Strong *(1.058 og)*
Best Bitter *(1.048 og)*
Blackfriar Stout *(1.050 og)*
Wheat Beer *(1.033 og)*

---

206 West Pratt Street
Baltimore, Maryland 21230
(410) 659·1676

We are on W. Pratt Street opposite the Convention Center. One block from the Oriole Ballpark and 2 blocks from the Inner Harbor. Open daily 11:30-2.

Also: The Wharf Rat at Fells Point
801 South Ann Street
Fells Point, Maryland

WILD GOOSE BREWERY

B

Wild Goose is a micro established in 1989 on the site of an old canning factory. The brewhouse is a British style plant utilizing a constant-infusion mash tun and top-fermenting yeast.

WILD GOOSE
Brewery
Est. 1989

BEERS & RATINGS	SG	CF
Wild Goose Amber Beer *(12.75 p; 5.0 v)*	▮▮▮½	▮▮▮½
Samuel Middleton's Pale Ale *(12.0 p)*	▮▮▮½	▮▮▮

20 Washington Street
Cambridge, Maryland 21613
(301) 221·1121

Take Route 50 east into Cambridge, turn right at Crusader Road and right onto Washington Street. Tours every Saturday noon to 3:00. Please call ahead to reserve a spot!

BOSTON BEER COMPANY

B BP *KB*

The Boston Beer Company is pleased to claim that it brews America's best beer. Then again, Anheuser-Busch is pleased to claim that Budweiser is the King of Beers. The claim made on behalf of Boston's Samuel Adams is justified by the results of polls taken among a few thousand members of the general public attending the Great American Beer Festival. The claim made on behalf of Budweiser is justified by the fact that Budweiser outsells all other beers in the American market, as McDonald's hamburgers outsell all other hamburgers.

Smart advertising and assiduous public relations may well have something to do with all of the above.

That said, most readers of this book would, in all probability, rather wash down the King of Burgers with a Sam Adams brew than with a Bud. Jim Koch's family of beers may not strike all of us as the best in America, but in many restaurants and retail outlets they are the best American brews available. The ultimate contract brewer (and the term is not used pejoratively), Koch has contributed much to the success of the American brewing renaissance by demonstrating to a significant segment of the public that dark beers, malty beers, beers with respectable hop character, have something to offer that goes beyond the thirst-quenching ability of bland quasi-pilsners.

Koch has a genius for marketing, but by attempting, almost from the outset, to go head-to-head with the likes of Heineken and Beck's, he skipped over the folk-art period of the American craft beer revival, and this has left his brews lacking in the earthiness that is often characteristic of America's best beers. Sam Adams' brews wear pinstripes—and not the sort the Yankees were wearing when Babe Ruth was lured to Gotham, leaving the citizens of Boston to weep into their suds.

BEERS & RATINGS	SG	CF
Samuel Adams Boston Lager *(1.052 og; 3.8 w)*	▮▮▮½	▮▮▮½
Samuel Adams Cranberry Lambic *(3.9 w)*	▮▮▮▮	▮▮▮
Samuel Adams Boston Stock Ale *(1.056 og; 3.9 w)*	▮▮▮▮	▮▮▮

	SG	CF
Samuel Adams Cream Stout *(5.0 w)*	▮▮▮▮	▮▮▮
Samuel Adams Doppelbock	▮▮▮½	▮▮▮½
Samuel Adams Winter Brew	▮▮▮½	▮▮▮½

Chris: "Good beers, but with a tendency towards being two-dimensional."

---

30 Germania Street
Boston, Massachusetts 02130
(617) 522·9080

BOSTON BEER WORKS

BP R *K*

Marc Kadish, along with Joe and Steve Slesar, are the owners and founders of Boston Beer Works, an impressive brewpub near the stadium. Marc Kadish is also the owner and founder of one of the best watering holes in town—the Sunset Bar and Grill—which boasts one of the largest beer selections in the country, with over 60 beers on tap. Boston Beer Works, a large, open space with industrial decor, was founded in 1992 and offers a wonderful array of food with their long list of microbrews. Try their savory sour cream-and-chive french fries, marinated raspberry shark sticks, or yankee ribs.

BEERS & RATINGS	SG	CF
Boston Red *(1.050 og; 4.5 w)*	▮▮▮▮	
Buckeye Oatmeal Stout *(1.048 og; 4.0 w)*	▮▮▮½	
Hercules Strong Ale *(1.095 og; 9.0 w)*		
Kenmöre Kolsch *(1.044 og; 4.0 w)*		

Seasonals:	
Back Bay IPA (1.060 og)	IIII
Beantown Nut Brown Ale (1.055 og)	IIII
Curley's Irish Stout	III½
Blueberry Ale (1.038 og)	IIII
Raspberry Ale (1.038 og)	
Baystate ESB	IIII
Father Time Eisbock (1.090 og)	
Centennial Alt (1.090 og)	
Watermelon Ale (1.040 og)	
Fenway Pale Ale (1.045 og)	
Acme Light (1.036 og)	
Climax Wheat (1.044 og)	

Scott: "If you get a chance to visit with Marc, his love of beer and enthusiasm is infectious. For more variety, visit Sunset Grill."

---

61 Brookline Avenue
Boston, Massachusetts 02215
(617) 536·2337

Across the street from Fenway Park, home of the Boston Red Sox. Open daily 11:30-1 am. 3 large TVs to watch sports, etc., CD player.

CAMBRIDGE BREWING COMPANY, INC.

***B BP** K*

It doesn't take a Harvard professor or an M.I.T. graduate to recognize that Cambridge is a good site for a brewpub, and this smallish establishment—150 seats—is in an ideal position to satisfy the thirst of well-educated college palates. Opened in 1989, Cambridge Brewing occupies part of a handsome old industrial building, and its ten-barrel brewery is devoted to a fairly ambitious range of top-fermenting beers, including a Belgian-style, high-gravity Triple that possesses the authentic mellowness that comes from the use of candy sugar in the wort.

BEERS & RATINGS	SG	CF
Cambridge Amber *(1.046 og; 5.5 v)*	2½	3
Charles River Porter *(1.062 og; 6.0 v)*	3½	4
Triple Threat *(21.25 p)*	2½	3½
Regatta Golden *(1.042 og; 5.5 v)*	2½	
Tall Tale Pale Ale *(1.056 og; 5.5 v)*	2½	

One Kendall Square #100
Cambridge, Massachusetts 02139
(617) 494·1994

On the corner of Broadway & Hampshire. Open M-Sat 11:30-1 am; Sun noon-1 am. Features local musicians and area artists whose works hang in the gallery.

COMMONWEALTH BREWING COMPANY, LTD.

BP *KB*

Opened to the public in 1986, Commonwealth Brewing Company—located near Faneuil Hall—can claim to have been New England's first brew-pub. The beer brewed here is in the British ale tradition, and seven to ten brews are available on tap at any given time.

BEERS & RATINGS	SG	CF
Commonwealth Golden Ale *(1.040 og; 4.0 w)*	2½	3
Famous Porter *(1.055 og; 5.3 w)*	3½	3

Special Old Ale *(1.100 og; 9.3 w)* 🍺🍺🍺
India Pale Ale *(10.6 p)* 🍺🍺½ 🍺🍺🍺
Commonwealth Golden Export
(1.042 og)
Commonwealth Classic Stout
(1.050 og; 5.0 w)

Chris: "Easy drinking beers—perhaps a little too easy to have real character."

---

138 Portland Street
Boston, Massachusetts 02114
(617)523·8383

Located at the fork of Merrimac and Portland streets, one block south of Boston Garden and 3 blocks north of Fanueil Hall. Live reggae.

IPSWICH BREWING COMPANY

B *KB*

Founded in 1986, this is a micro specializing in top-fermented brews.

Ipswich Ale *(1.048 og)*
Ipswich Dark Ale *(1.060 og)*
Pilgrim Ale *(1.046 og)*

---

25 Hayward Street
Ipswich, Massachusetts 01938
(508) 356·3329

From the center of town (Rte. 1A & Market Street), head out of town on Market, cross the railroad tracks, turn left at Hayward and follow for a half mile. The brewery is on the right side in the Ipswich Business Park. Tours on Saturdays 1 & 3. Samples during tours.

MASSACHUSETTS BAY BREWING

B *KB*

Mass Bay is both a microbrewery, producing draft beers, and a distributor of contract brews made by F.X. Matt of Utica, New York.

HARPOON
Ale & Golden Lager

BEERS & RATINGS	SG	CF
Harpoon Ale *(1.044 og; 3.7 v)*	4	3½
Harpoon Golden Lager *(1.052 og; 4.5 v)*	4	4
Harpoon Dark *(1.052 og; 4.5 v)*		
Harpoon Light *(1.040 og; 1.9 v)*		
Seasonals:		
Harpoon Stout(1.058 og; 5.5 v)	3½	
Harpoon Oktoberfest (1.058 og; 6.0 v)		
Harpoon Winter Warmer (1.058 og; 6.0 v)	3½	

Chris: "Golden Harpoon Lager is full-bodied and aromatic—one of the best pale lagers produced in America."

306 Northern Avenue
Boston, Massachusetts
(617)574·9551

Down the street from the World Trade Center in the Marine Industrial Park. To reach Northern Ave., follow Atlantic Ave. (parallel to Rt. 93), past the Congress Street intersection, and take the first right onto Northern Ave. We are a mile down the road on the left. From 93, take exit 22 when coming from the south, and exit 23 from the north. We are located on the southeast side of the building, next to the road. Tours every Friday & Saturday at 1 pm (or by special arrangement for large groups).

NORTHAMPTON BREWERY AT BREWSTER COURT BAR & GRILL

BP *K*

Boasting the longest name of any brewpub we have yet encountered, Brewster Court (as we'll call it) is located in a 19th-century carriage house in an attractive town, north of Springfield in the Connecticut River valley. The pub food served includes American and Mexican specialties, and in the summer the fun spills over into an outdoor beer garden.

Northampton Amber *(1.048 og)*
Northampton Golden *(1.048 og)*
Seasonals:
Hoover's Porter (1.050 og)
Black Cat Stout (1.060 og)

---

11 Brewster Court
Northampton, Massachusetts 01061
(413) 584·9903

Off Hampton Ave., between the municipal parking lots and new parking garage in downtown Northampton. Open M-Sat 11:30-1 am; Sun 1-1. Live entertainment in outdoor beer garden (seasonal) and Sunday night acoustic session.

OLD MARLBOROUGH BREWING COMPANY

B *KB*

Old Marlborough is known for one excellent brew—Post Road Real Ale—which is contract-brewed by the Catamount Brewing Company of

Vermont. Since Catamount itself is a small craft brewery, Post Road can legitimately call itself a microbrew beer. The mystery is that Post Road is so much better than any of the Catamount brews we have tasted. Post Road—which won a silver medal at the Great American Beer Festival in 1989—is an outstanding pale ale by any standards.

BEERS & RATINGS	CF
Post Road Real Ale *(1.047 og; 3.7 w)*	▮▮▮▮
Seasonal:	
Le Garde (French country beer)	
(1.062 og; 5.6 w)	

Chris: "Although it is hopped with Willamette and Cascade, this is a very British-tasting ale, meaty and surprisingly complex with a clean, satisfying finish."

P.O. Box 1157
59 Fountain Street
Framingham, Massachusetts 01701
(508) 875·0990

No tours.

OLDE TIME BREWERS

B *KB*

Richard Dugas is one of a number of home brewers who have taken the craft brewing renaissance as a challenge to produce beer on a commercial scale. Ironside Ale is his re-creation of the private reserve ales that New England sea captains once saved for their personal enjoyment.

IRONSIDE ALE

BEERS & RATINGS	CF
Ironside Ale *(12.0 p; 4.02 w)*	▮▮▮

402 Rutherford Avenue
Boston, Massachusetts 02129
(617) 242·4201

PORTSMOUTH BREWERY

BP

Old Brown Dog *(1.055 og)*
Blonde Ale *(1.045 og)*

---

56 Market Street
Portsmouth, New Hampshire 03802
(603) 431·1115

Half block off Market Square in the heart of historic Seaport district. Adjacent to municipal parking garage. Open daily 11:30-1 am. Live music downstairs five nights a week—blues, rock, jazz.

ATLANTIC BREWING COMPANY

B *B*

This New Jersey brewery produces a single lager, named for a former Atlantic City sideshow that—surprisingly perhaps—has not been revived in the age of the Donald.

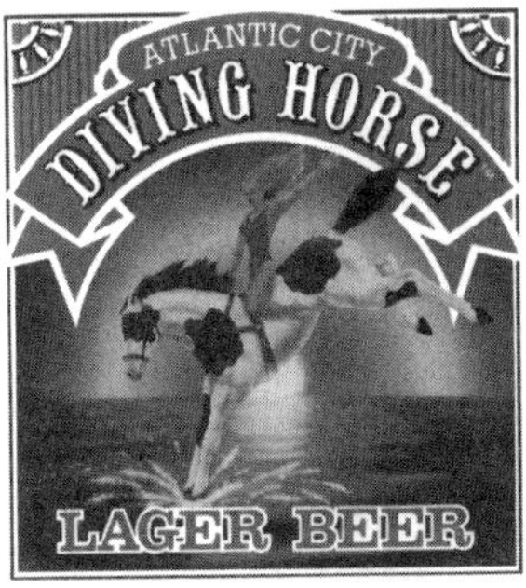

Diving Horse Lager Beer *(12.0 p; 3.9 w)*

P.O. Box 1021
Brigantine, New Jersey 08203
(609) 641·5575

GOLDFINCH BREWING COMPANY

B

Goldfinch is another example of a good contract brew—not great but very acceptable—though the owners are planning to build their own New Jersey microbrewery. In the meantime, Goldfinch Amber is brewed by The Lion in Wilkes-Barre, Pennsylvania, which is close enough to New Jersey to make no big difference.

BEERS & RATINGS	CF
Goldfish Amber Beer *(12.5 p)*	III½

308 Ralston Drive
Mount Laurel, New Jersey 08054

THE BROOKLYN BREWERY

B *KB*

With a label designed by Milton Glazer, Brooklyn Lager is a beer designed for Brooklyn Heights and Cobble Hill rather than Bensonhurst. Contract brewed by F.X. Matt, these brews are described by the owners as being "a revival of Brooklyn's pre-Prohibition-style lagers." The company's distribution arm handles a number of microbrews and imports.

BEERS & RATINGS	SG	CF
Brooklyn Lager *(1.048 og; 4.0 w)*	▮▮▮½	▮▮
Brooklyn Brown *(1.058 og; 5.0 w)*	▮▮▮½	▮▮

Scott: "Easy drinking beers, but not distinctive." ***Chris:*** "As a former Brooklynite, I want these beers to be better."

119 North 11th Street
Brooklyn, New York 11211
(718) 486·7422

BUFFALO BREWPUB

B BP *K*

Located east of downtown Buffalo, not far from the airport, this was a pioneer amongst upstate New York brewpubs. Pub food is served, with English and German favorites featured.

Amber Ale *(1.055 og; 4.5 w)*
Buffalo Bitter *(1.050 og; 4.5 w)*
Oatmeal Stout *(1.060 og; 4.5 w)*
Red Ale *(1.050 og; 4.5 w)*

6861 Main Street
Williamsville, New York 14221
(716) 632·0552

At the intersection of Main & Transit. M-Th 11:30-2 am; F-Sat 11:30-3 am; Sun noon-midnight. Live music (acoustic & German). Call for dates.

F.X. MATT BREWING COMPANY

B *KB*

Once known as the West End Brewing Company, F.X. Matt has been part of the Utica scene for more than 100 years, having been founded there in 1888 by F.X. Matt, a native of Germany's Black Forest. The company is presently run by direct descendants.

As the 12th-largest brewery in the nation, F.X. Matt is hardly a micro. Rather it is a large regional brewer producing its own line of beers, which are in general superior to those produced by most other brewers of its size. The reason it is included in this book, though, is that it has made a distinct contribution to the brewing renaissance as one of the premium producers of contract brews. These have included Rhino Chasers Amber Ale, Samuel Adams Boston Ale, New Amsterdam, Dock Street, Harpoon Ale, Brooklyn Lager, Olde Heurich, and even the venerable Prior Double Dark, one of the few classics that have survived from the pre-Prohibition era.

BEERS & RATINGS	SG
Saranac Adirondack Lager *(12.0 p; 3.9 w)*	
Saranac Black & Tan	

Scott: "The Matts have contributed much to the craft beer movement. They make true quality ales as well as produce beers for many of the top contract brands."

811 Edward Street
Utica, New York 13502·4092
(315) 732·3181

Take exit 31 from I-90. Proceed through toll booth and over the bridge; you will intersect Genesee St. South. You will pass the Children's Museum sign on the left and the Commercial Travelers Ins. Co. on the right. Starting at Oriskany St. pass 7 street lights. Turn right on Court St. Just past the 4th street light is Varick St., and you're at F.X. Matt Brewing Company. The approximate distance from exit 31 to the brewery is 1.75 miles. Tour Center hours are M-Sat 11-4. Call (315) 732·0022 for more info.

MOUNTAIN VALLEY BREWPUB

BP R *K B*

New York City is proving to be a hard nut to crack for the craft beer movement, mostly because overheads there are so high. In the New York hinterlands, however, the movement is catching on after a couple of false starts (such as William Newman's late, lamented micro in Albany, which was just too far ahead of the game). Like most other New York craft breweries, the Mountain Valley Brewpub specializes in top-fermented brews. A full restaurant menu is offered.

Pale Ale
Copper Ale
Porter

---

122 Orange Avenue
Suffern, New York 10901
(914) 357·0101

From the George Washington Bridge, take Rte. 17 north to Franklin Turnpike, bear right and continue for 3.3 miles. The brewery will be on the right side. Bands perform on scheduled nights. Call ahead. Open daily 11-1 am.

OLD WORLD BREWING COMPANY, INC.

B

Old World began life as a home brew supply operation and only recently turned to producing beer for commercial distribution.

BEERS & RATINGS	SG	CF
New York Harbor Ale *(1.052 og; 5.3 v)*	ııı	ııı

Scott: "A well-balanced, easy-drinking brew."

2070 Victory Boulevard
Staten Island, New York 10314
(718) 370·0551

ROCHESTER BREWPUB

BP

This brewpub is located in what was once one of America's greatest ale brewing centers. Breakfast is served, along with lunch and dinner.

Amber Ale
Golden Ale
Oatmeal Stout
Dunkel
Flower City Dark

800 Jefferson Road
Henrietta, New York 14623
(716) 272·1550

A half mile west of I-390, near the airport and the Rochester Institute of Technology.
Open daily 6 am-1 am. Live music on some nights.

SHEA'S BREWERY

B

Ireland produces great stouts and once produced famous porters. It has never been notable for its ales, let alone for its "amber beers," so perhaps this company's only known product is simply named for its color and the brewer's ethnic background. Let's hope so.

BEERS & RATINGS	CF
Michael Shea's Irish Amber Beer	🍺🍺½

445 Saint Paul Street
Rochester, New York 14605

SYRACUSE SUDS FACTORY

B BP

Situated in a handsome old bank building, listed on the National Register of Historic Buildings, the Suds Factory is heavy on atmosphere. The food is straightforward and inexpensive. This is traditional ale country and the beer, made from malt extract, is top-fermented in the style that was appreciated in these parts before Prohibition.

Pale Ale
Amber Ale

210-216 West Water Street
Syracuse, New York 13202
(315)471·2253

Located in downtown Syracuse, across the street from Federal Plaza. M-Sat 11-2 am; Sun noon-2 am.

WOODSTOCK BREWING COMPANY

***B** K*

Before Prohibition, the Hudson Valley was famous for its breweries, and Kingston was home to several of them. The last one closed a half century ago but the Woodstock Brewing Company is doing its best to revive the honorable tradition.

BEERS & RATINGS	SG	CF
Hudson Lager	ııı½	ııı½

20 St. James Street
P.O. Box 1000W
Kingston, New York 12401
(914) 331·2810

From the New York State Thruway, take Exit 19 (Kingston). After the toll booth, enter the traffic circle and take the third right (Rte. 587, Colonel Chandler Drive). Proceed one mile and remain in the right lane as you approach the traffic light. Go straight through the intersection onto Broadway (32S) and signal immediately for a right turn onto St. James Street. The brewery is on the left just after the corner of Prospect Street. Park in our lot just past the building. The brewery is open for tours. Call for schedule. We are handicapped accessible.

ZIP CITY BREWING COMPANY

BP *K B*

A welcome addition to the New York scene, Zip City is located in a loft building once occupied by the National Temperance Society. Founder Kirby Shyer worked with O. Salm and Co. of Vienna to put together a brewpub that is in tune with today but that still manages to conjure up the best of New York's past. As noted often in this book, top-quality lagers are harder to brew than top-quality ales, but judging by its early efforts Zip

City may be one of the American craft breweries that has the personnel and patience to succeed with this family of beers.

ZIP CITY BREWING Co

BEERS & RATINGS	SG	CF
Zip City Märzen *(1.057 og; 5.1 w)*	3	4
Zip City Pilsner *(1.048 og; 4.3 w)*	3½	3½
Zip City Dunkel *(1.053 og; 4.6 w)*	3½	4
Zip City Vienna *(1.053 og; 4.6 w)*		
Zip City Helles *(1.057 og; 5.1 w)*		

3 West 18th Street
New York, New York 10011
(212)366·6333

Zip City is located in Manhattan's "Flatiron" district on 18th Street, between 5th & 6th Avenues. Open daily for lunch and dinner. Late nights Thursday through Saturday. Brewery Tours are scheduled weekend afternoons at 2 pm and Tuesday evenings at 7 pm. Other times by appointment.

THE BURKHARDT BREWING COMPANY

B BP *KB*

The Burkhardt family began brewing in the Akron area in 1877. The present pub and its next-door micro were established in 1991 on the site of an old brewery, with a fifth-generation brewer—Thomas Burkhardt, Jr.—as brewmaster. The atmosphere is relaxed and the menu features steaks and burgers along with British, Irish, and German specialties.

Eclipse Ale *(4.4 w)*
White Cliff Ale *(4.2 w)*
North Star *(3.9 w)*

3700 Massillon Road
Union Town, Ohio 44685
(216) 896·9200

Take I-77 to Route 241, Massillon Road inside the "Shops of Green." Open M-Sat; closed Sundays.

COLUMBUS BREWING COMPANY

B BP *KB*

This micro was established in 1989 in the historic brewing district of Columbus, Ohio. Most of the brewing equipment was brought over from England and for the most part brewmaster Scott Francis, trained at the Siebel Institute, brews top-fermented beers in the British manner, though a krausened lager is also available.

BEERS & RATINGS	SG	CF
Columbus Pale Ale *(1.044 og; 3.5 w)*	ııı½	ııı½
Columbus Nut Brown Ale *(1.046 og; 3.5 w)*	ııı½	ııı
Blackforest Porter *(1.052 og; 4.0 w)*		

Scott: "Pleasant, clean-tasting beers."
Chris: "I'd like these ales better if they were a little hoppier, but that's a matter of taste and many people will find them very much to their liking."

476 South Front Street
Columbus, Ohio 43215
(614) 224·3626

THE GREAT LAKES BREWING COMPANY

B BP *KB*

Founded in 1988, by Patrick and Daniel Conway, Great Lakes is not only a lively brewpub—housed in a century-old building that features an outdoor beer garden (for those Arcadian Cleveland summers) and a Victorian tap room (for those Alaskan Cleveland winters)—but also one of the best places in America to sample beer. The Conways really know what they're doing and, although their brews are distributed only in the Greater Cleveland area, their reputation in the craft brewing community is impeccable. They seem incapable of producing beers that are less than excellent.

BEERS & RATINGS	SG	CF
Dortmunder Gold *(1.056 og; 4.3 w)*	IIII	IIII
The Commodore Perry IPA *(1.064 og; 5.5 w)*	IIII½	IIII
The Edmund Fitzgerald Porter *(1.060 og; 4.7 w)*	IIII	
The Eliot Ness *(1.056 og)*	IIII	IIII
Moon Dog Ale *(12.5 p)*	IIII	IIII
Holy Moses Ale *(16.5 p)*	IIII	

Scott: "Great Lakes beers combine balance and bite. Plus Pat and Dan are two of the nicest guys in the business."
Chris: "With good reason, the favorite brews of both Clark Kent and Howard the Duck."

2516 Market Street
Cleveland, Ohio 44113
(216) 771·4404

Across from the West Side Market on West 25th Street & Lorain Avenue. Open M-Th 11:30-midnight; Sun 3-10. Entertainment is the local patrons.

HOSTER BREWING COMPANY

B BP *K*

Located in an old streetcar barn, this is a large brewpub boasting an atmosphere that recalls the era when trolleys still clanged by outside. The food is Middle American. A pale ale is featured among the seasonal specialties, but the regular beers are in the Bavarian styles.

Hoster Eagle Light *(1.032 og)*
Hoster XX Pale *(1.048 og)*
Hoster Gold Top *(1.048 og)*
Hoster Amber Lager *(1.052 og)*

---

550 South High Street
Columbus, Ohio 43215
(614) 228·6066

On the corner of High & Hoster streets, in the old brewery district. Open M-Sat 11-2 am; Sun 4-11.

MELBOURNE'S BREWING COMPANY

BP

Strange, perhaps, to find a brewpub with an Australian accent on the outskirts of Cleveland. Even stranger—given the popularity of things Australian—that we haven't seen more Down Under influence in the craft brewing movement. Melbourne's offers a range of foods from snacks to full dinners, and beers that are more interesting than the undeservedly well-known antipodean brew sold in containers that look like oil cans.

Bondi Beach Blonde Beer *(1.050 og)*
Wombat Wheat Beer *(1.046 og)*
Down Under Brown Ale *(1.048 og)*

12492 Prospect Road
Strongsville, Ohio 44136
(216) 238·4677

Open M-Sat 10-10; Sun 4-10.

ARROWHEAD BREWING COMPANY, INC.

B

Founded in 1991, Arrowhead's brewhouse has a capacity of 6,000 barrels a year.

BEERS & RATINGS	SG	CF
Red Feather Pale Ale *(11.75 P)*	▮▮½	▮▮▮

1667 Orchard Drive
Chambersberg, Pennsylvania 17201
(717) 264·0101

DOCK STREET BREWING COMPANY

B BP *BK*

Founded by Jeffrey Ware, Dock Street offered bottled beer—contract brewed by F.X. Matt–starting in 1986. In 1990, Ware opened a Dock Street brewpub in Philadelphia. A Washington, DC., branch should be open by the time this book appears in print. The Philadelphia outlet is a large, handsome establishment with one of the most imaginative menus in the brewpub world. How many brewpubs offer an appetizer that could compete with Trio Fries (fried shoestring potatoes, leeks and sweet potatoes)? Other offerings range from Buffalo Chili and Pulled Pork Sandwich to

Muffaletta and Cambodian Pork Spare Ribs.

British brewmaster Nick Frennell is proud of the fact that his kettles are used to produce, on a regular basis, no fewer than 55 styles of beer! We list only those which we have had the opportunity to taste, either at the brewpub or in bottled form.

BEERS & RATINGS	SG	CF
Dock Street Amber *(12.3p)*	III½	III½
Dock Street Dortmunder *(14.1p)*	III½	
Dock Street Old Ale *(16.1p)*	III½	
Pale Ale	IIII½	
Red Ale	IIII½	
Dubbel	IIII	
Bohemian Pils	IIII	
Helles	IIII	III½
Weiss Beer	III½	

Scott: "The cask-conditioned and unfiltered Pale Ale is my favorite. It's well balanced and has a nice fruitiness with spicy overtones."

Two Logan Square
18th & Cherry Streets
Philadelphia, Pennsylvania 19103
(215) 496·0413

THE LION INC.

B

This is another example of a pre-Prohibition brewery that has found a new lease on life thanks to the craft-beer renaissance.

BEERS & RATINGS	CF
Stegmaier Porter *(12.6 p)*	IIII
Stegmaier 1857 Lager *(11.8 p)*	III½
Stegmaier 1857 Light *(8.4 p)*	
Stegmaier Gold Medal *(10.5 p)*	

700 North Pennsylvania Avenue
Wilkes-Barre, Pennsylvania 18703
(717) 823·8801

NEUWEILER BREWING COMPANY, INC.

B *KB*

Louis F. Neuweiler founded a brewery in Allentown back in 1891. It was a typical local brewery of the first Golden Age of American brewing, producing a wide range of beers in both the German and British style. Prohibition put a damper on things, but the brewery survived until 1968, and in 1991 the Neuweiler name was re-established by Barry J. Szmodis and a consortium of local investors to market beers contract-brewed by the Lion Brewing Company in nearby Wilkes-Barre.

NEUWEILER
Traditional Lager · Brewed Porter
Nix besser!

BEERS & RATINGS	SG
Neuweiler Brewed Porter *(13.0 P)*	III
Neuweiler Black and Tan *(12.2 P)*	II½

2310 S.W. 26th Street
Allentown, Pennsylvania 18103

PENNSYLVANIA BREWING COMPANY
ALLEGHENY BREWERY

B BP R *K B*

The oldest microbrewery in the state, Pennsylvania Brewing was founded in 1986 and makes its home in a Victorian-era brewery building that is now home to state-of-the-art equipment from Germany. Appropriately enough, Pennsylvania Brewing specializes in the lager beers that have long been favored in this part of the country. Having lived in Germany for twelve years, owners Tom and Mary Beth Pastorius certainly understand their market. A brewery-owned restaurant and beer garden was added to the operation in 1989 and, thanks to the imaginative way in which the attractive old building has been adapted to this purpose, diners find it easy to imagine themselves in Bavaria.

BEERS & RATINGS	SG	CF
Penn Pilsner *(12.5 p)*	4½	3½
Kaiser Pils *(11.8 p)*	4½	
Penn Dark *(12.8 p)*	4	3½
Oktoberfest *(14.0 p)*	4	

Scott: "Very few microbreweries are producing top quality, bottom-fermented products. Tom Pastorius' brewery makes absolutely superb pilsners, maerzens, bocks, and double bocks. If you don't believe me, ask his clientele, which includes many Germans based in Pittsburgh. Some top German corporations are insisting that Tom's beer be available at company functions instead of flying in German beer by corporate jet."

Troy Hill Road and Vinial Street
Pittsburgh, Pennsylvania 15212
(412) 237·9402

From downtown, cross 16th Street Bridge to third light, right on Troy Hill Road. M-Sat 11-midnight. Live music T-Sat (strolling accordion players, German bands, R & B and Dixieland jazz bands).

PHILADELPHIA BREWING COMPANY SAMUEL ADAMS BREW HOUSE

B BP *KB*

Philadelphia was once the brewing capital of America, boasting more than 90 breweries back in the 1870s. Philadelphia Brewing is the first brewery to open in the City of Brotherly Love since Prohibition. To be more specific, Philadelphia Brewing is a cheerful neighborhood brewpub that provides freshly brewed ales to go with reasonably priced food and live music.

As the name suggests, the Sam Adams Brewhouse has affiliations with the Boston Beer Company, purveyor of widely distributed craft brews (see p. 258). It should not be assumed, however, that the Philadelphia brewhouse offers only Boston Beer Company brews, or even clones. It is very much its own entity with its own brewmaster (William Reed) and its own line of top-fermented brews. There is a complete kitchen menu with an emphasis on steaks and burgers.

BEERS & RATINGS	SG	CF
Ben Franklin's Golden Ale *(12.0 p; 3.5 w)*	▮▮▮½	▮▮½

George Washington's Porter
(15.0 p; 4.0 w) ▮▮▮½ ▮▮▮½

1516 Sansom Street
Philadelphia, Pennsylvania 19102
(215) 563·ADAM

On the second floor of 1516 Sansom Street in downtown Philadelphia. Open M-Sat 11-2 am. Regular live music F-Sat nights from 9-1 am, with acoustic musicians and vocalists— folk, blues and jazz, and rock n' roll. Thursdays are popular Open Mike Nights.

STOUDT BREWING COMPANY

B BP *KB*

Ed and Carol Stoudt hatched the idea for this brewery while they were honeymooning in Germany, the country from which Ed's ancestors emigrated in the 18th Century. Ed opened Stoudt's Beer Garden in the summer of 1987, but it is Carol who is the brewer, having studied at Siebel and UC Davis. She declines the label "master brewer," but it is no accident that her beers have won a total of fourteen medals to date at the Great American Beer Festival.

Carol Stoudt is dedicated to the idea of being a true microbrewer, her output limited to fewer than 15,000 barrels a year. The local German community provides her with plenty of tough critics. The brewery is perhaps best known for its bocks, but the authentic-tasting helles is not to be missed, and top-fermented beers have become part of the repertoire.

BEERS & RATINGS	SG	CF
IPA *(13.5 p)*	▮▮▮½	▮▮▮
Stout *(13.0 p)*	▮▮▮	▮▮▮
Fest *(12.5 p)*	▮▮▮½	▮▮▮
Amber Ale	▮▮▮▮	▮▮▮▮

Scott: "Carol Stoudt is a pioneer, being one of the few female brewmasters, as well as a leader of the craft brew movement in the Northeast."

Route 272 P.O. Box 880
Adamstown, Pennsylvania 19501
(215) 484·4387

CATAMOUNT BREWING COMPANY

B *KB*

Founded by Steve Mason, who is also the brewmaster, Catamount has been brewing since 1986 and, after a 1991 expansion, now produces upwards of 12,000 barrels of beer a year, marketing them throughout the Northeast.

BEERS & RATINGS	**SG**	**CF**
Catamount Amber *(1.048 og; 4.0 w)*	▮▮▮	▮▮▮½
Catamount Gold *(1.042 og; 3.6 w)*	▮▮½	▮▮▮
Catamount Porter *(1.052 og; 4.2 w)*	▮▮½	▮▮▮½

Seasonals:
Catamount Christmas Ale (1.056 og; 4.3 w)
Catamount Bock (1.058 og; 4.4 w)
Catamount Oktoberfest (1.052 og; 4.0 w)

Scott: "Thin brews without much character or flavor. Beautiful tap handles, though."
Chris: "Light-bodied but pleasant beers."

58 South Main Street
White River Junction, Vermont 05001
(802) 296·2248

Junction of Rte. 89 and 91,
Downtown White River Junction.

LATCHIS GRILLE & WINDHAM BREWERY

BP K

While most other craft brewers seem to seek out Victorian railroad stations or Edwardian button factories in which to locate their brewhouses, the Windham Brewery finds itself happily at home in a newly restored art deco hotel, the Latchis, in downtown Brattleboro. The Latchis Grille (a good example of art deco spelling) is the ideal spot to sample Windham's beers, which are produced in a seven-barrel brewery designed by Greg Noonan of Burlington's Vermont Pub and Brewery. John Korpita is in charge of brewing operations.

BEERS & RATINGS	SG	CF
Moonbeam Pale Ale *(11.3 p; 4.5 v)*	3½	3
Whetstone Golden Lager *(12.5 p; 5.4 v)*	3½	3
Windham Porter *(11.5 p)*		
Ruby Brown Ale *(11.5 p; 4.5 v)*		
Seasonals:		
Old Guilford Porter		
Maibock		
Leftrapper Lager (Oktoberfest)		

50 Main Street
Brattleboro, Vermont 05301
(802) 254·6300

In the Latchis Hotel, downtown Brattleboro.
Open 11:30-midnight.

McNEILL'S BREWERY

BP *K*

Not too many years ago, the best American craft brews came almost exclusively from the West Coast, and specifically from the San Francisco/Portland/Seattle corridor. The Northwest is still a mecca for serious beer drinkers, but fine ales and fresh-tasting lagers can now be found in many parts of the country, with the Rocky Mountain states, the Midwest and New England meeting the challenge with special enthusiasm. Among the New England states, Vermont seems to have become a leader both in terms of quantity of breweries and quality of brews. The beers issued by McNeill's Brewery can only help the state's growing reputation in the microbrew world.

Housed in the former town jail, McNeill's has been modified to a style that owner and brewmaster Reagin McNeill describes as "early Victorian fire station—floor-to-ceiling oak and mahogany." The emphasis is on relaxed atmosphere, inexpensive pub food, and reasonably priced real ale.

BEERS & RATINGS	**CF**
Nut Brown *(12.0 p)*	🍺🍺🍺🍺
McNeill's Special Bitter *(13.5 p)*	🍺🍺🍺½
Dead Horse IPA *(14.5 p)*	🍺🍺🍺🍺
Duck's Breath Bitter *(11.0 p)*	
Mudpuddle Mild *(11.0 p)*	
Slopbucket Brown *(14.0 p)*	

Chris: "An authentic taste of England in the heart of New England."

90 Elliot Street
Brattleboro, Vermont 05301
(802) 254·2553

Located at exit numbers 1, 2 & 3 on I-91.
Open daily 4 pm to late. Tours on weekends at 5 pm.

MOUNTAIN BREWERS, INC.

B *KB*

This micro produces the satisfying Long Trail beers that are becoming well-known to skiers who flock to this part of New England in the snow season. The low-calorie light ale is a sop to the vanity of those who worry about their après-ski appearance and should be avoided by serious beer drinkers. The other Long Trail products, however, are well worth seeking out.

The Mountain Brewers

BEERS & RATINGS	SG	CF
Long Trail Light Ale *(1.036 og)*		▮▮½
Long Trail IPA *(1.058 og)*		▮▮▮½
Long Trail Ale *(1.050 og)*		▮▮▮½
Long Trail Stout *(1.046 og)*		▮▮▮▮

Chris: "Long Trail beers tend to be light-bodied but flavorsome with a good hoppy finish. The IPA is somewhat reminiscent of the venerable Ballantine IPA. The stout lacks the creamy density you would expect from Guiness or Beamish. Stylistically it's more of a porter, but none the worse for that. Very tasty."

The Marketplace at Bridgewater Mill
Route 4
Bridgewater, Vermont 05034
(802) 672·5011

Route 4 on Bridgewater/Woodstock line, Central Vermont. Open 12-5 daily.

OTTER CREEK BREWING COMPANY

B *K*

Launched in 1991, Otter Creek offers a seasonally changing selection of top-fermented brews that are available on draft at a number of establishments in the Lake Champlain area.

Copper Ale *(12.5 p)*

---

74 Exchange Street Unit 1
Middlebury, Vermont 05753·1105
(802) 388·0727

Tours held each Friday from 4-6, or by appointment.

THE VERMONT PUB AND BREWERY

BP

Another fine Vermont craft brewery, said to be the state's first brewpub and located in downtown Burlington, hard by Lake Champlain. Nancy Noonan is in charge of the robust pub food that complements the generally meaty beers brewed under the supervision of Glenn Walter and Greg Noonan. Patrons will find brews—both ales and lagers—suitable to those long Vermont winters, those sudden springs, those steamy summers, and especially those glorious New England autumns.

BEERS & RATINGS	SG
Glen Walter Wee Heavy *(1.090 og; 6.4 w)*	▮▮▮▮

Avid Barley Bree Wee Heavy
(13.5 p) ⅠⅠⅠⅠ
Black Bear Lager *(11.0 p)* ⅠⅠⅠⅠ
Farmall Wheat Beer *(13.5 p)* ⅠⅠⅠⅠ
Zatec Red *(12. 0 p)* ⅠⅠⅠ½
O'Fest *(14.0 p)* ⅠⅠⅠⅠ
Vermont Smoked Porter
(1.048 og; 3.4 w) ⅠⅠⅠⅠⅠ
Grand Slam Baseball Beer
(1.046 og; 4.0 w) ⅠⅠⅠ½

Scott: "Quality beer can also be fun. The Vermont Pub and Brewery takes risks and produces beers that are unusual and even unique. The smoked porter is outstanding, its malt roasted over a smoky apple, hickory and maple wood fire."

---

144 College Street
Burlington, Vermont 05401
(802) 865·0500

In the heart of downtown Burlington.
Open M-Th 11:30-1 am; F 11:30-2; Sat 11:30-1; Sun 11:30-12:30.

BLUE RIDGE BREWING COMPANY

B BP R

This brewpub features both ales and lagers, and offers a full menu in its spacious restaurant.

Afton Ale *(5.9 v)*
Hawksbill Golden Lager *(5.9 v)*
Humpback Stout *(6.0 v)*
Piney River Amber Lager *(5.7)*

---

709 West Main Street
Charlottesville, Virginia 22901
(804) 977·0017

OLD DOMINION BREWING COMPANY

B *KB*

The Nation's capital is known as a good market for quality beers and has long been home to the Brickskeller, a cheerful specialty bar on the outskirts of Georgetown. Located about twenty miles from the Loop, Old Dominion is a microbrewery well located to take advantage of the educated thirsts that are to be found in Washington, D.C.

BEERS & RATINGS	SG	CF
Dominion Lager *(13.7 p; 5.4 v)*	▮▮½	
Dominion Ale *(12.5 p)*	▮▮▮	▮▮▮▮
Hard Times Select *(13.7 p)*	▮▮½	▮▮▮▮½

Chris: "Dominion Ale and Hard Times are both easy drinking brews with a very distinctive hoppy fragrance."

44633 Gulford Drive Bay 112,
Ashburn, Virginia 22011
(703) 689·1225

To get to the brewery: Take the Beltway (I-495) to route 267 West (the Toll Road next to the Dulles Access Road). Take Route 267 to exit 1 and turn right (N) onto Sully Road. Go to Route 625, turn left to Ashburn. Go 1.2 miles to the flagpoles marking the entrance to Beaumeade Corp. Ctr. Turn right onto Panorama Pkwy. and follow the stone posts. At the first intersection, turn left onto Beaumeade Circle. Follow this road until you see a red brick building on the left. Turn left there, Guilford Drive. There are three red brick buildings in a row. Old Dominion Brewing is at the end of the third building. Parking is available in front of the brewery.

RICHBRAU BREWERY

BP

This brewpub is located in Shockoe Slip, near the Tobacco Company Building. Along with British-style beers it offers inexpensive food featuring pub favorites and cajun specialties.

Light Ale
Pale Ale
India Pale Ale
Porter
Oatmeal Stout

1214 East Cary Street
Richmond, Virginia
(804) 644·3018

This brewpub is located in Shockoe Slip, near the Tobacco Company Building. M-T 11:30-midnight; W-Sat 11:30-2 am; Sun 12-9. Live music on Tuesday, Thursday-Saturday nights.

SOUTHEAST

Sou

Nashville
Tennessee
24
Fort Smith
40
Memphis
Chattanooga
Arkansas
Little Rock
65
30
59
Mississippi
Birmingham
55
20
Alabama
20
Jackson
Louisiana
Montgomery
59
49
Abita
Baton Rouge
10
New Orleans

THEAST

81
77
Greensboro
Durham
Manteo
40
North Carolina
Raleigh
75
Charlotte
85
40
South Carolina
75
Columbia
Atlanta
20
Georgia
26
16
95
Tallahassee
10
Florida
75
4
Tampa
95
Fort Lauderd ale
75

ALABAMA

Birmingham Brewing Company

ARKANSAS

Vino's

Weidman's Old Fort Brew Pub

FLORIDA

Beach Brewing Company

Florida Brewery, Inc.

Gator Lager Beer, Inc.

Irish Times Pub & Brewery

Market Street Pub

McGuire's Irish Pub & Brewery

Mill Bakery, Eatery & Brewery

Sarasota Brewing Company

GEORGIA

Georgia Brewing Company Ltd.

LOUSIANA

Abita Brewing Company

Crescent City Brewhouse

NORTH CAROLINA

Dilworth Brewing Company

Greenshields Brewery & Pub

Loggerhead Brewing Company

The Mill Bakery, Eatery & Brewery

Spring Garden Brewing Company

TENNESSEE

Bohannon Brewing Company

LEGEND:
***B**—Brewery*
***BP**—Brewpub*
***R**—Restaurant*

B—Available in Bottles
K—Available in Kegs

BIRMINGHAM BREWING CO.

B *KB*

This micro opened in 1992—the first brewery to operate in Birmingham since an earlier Birmingham Brewing Company was forced out of business by local Prohibition 85 years earlier.

BEERS & RATINGS	SG	CF
Red Mountain Red Ale *(12.5 p; 4.5 w)*	▮▮▮½	▮▮▮
Red Mountain Golden Lager *(11.5 p; 4.5 w)*	▮▮½	▮▮½
Red Mountain Golden Ale *(11.75 p; 4.5 w)*	▮▮▮	▮▮½
Red Mountain Wheat *(11.5 p; 4.0 w)*		

Scott: "Easy drinking beers, but not distinctive."
Chris: "Why are so many beers named after mountains?"

3118 3rd Avenue South
Birmingham, Alabama 35233
(205) 326·6677

Near intersection of Third Avenue South and 32nd Street. Tours by appointment.

VINO'S

BP

This downtown brewpub serves appetizers, sandwiches and pizza. Its main beers are in the British tradition.

Seventh Street Pale Ale
Big House Brown Ale
Lazy Boy Stout

923 West Seventh Street
Little Rock, Arkansas 72201
(501) 375·8468

Located downtown. Open M-Wed 11-10; Th-Sat 11-midnight.

WEIDMAN'S OLD FORT BREW PUB

B BP R

Established in 1992, Weidman's is a brewpub installed in an original 1848 brewery building. A complete kitchen menu is offered along with Weidman's own brews.

Irish Red Ale
Pilsner
Pale Ale
Smoked Porter

422 North Third
Fort Smith, Arkansas 72901
(501) 782·9898

Located at the edge of the Fort Smith Historic District, five blocks north of Garrison Avenue and two blocks east of the Clayton Expressway. Open M-Sat. 11-11. Entertainment on Friday & Saturday nights.

BEACH BREWING COMPANY

B

After a long day at Disney World, good beer is very welcome. Beach Brewing is on the right track in that Florida needs refreshing, German-style beers, and it's dark Magic Brew is agreeably thirst-quenching.

BEERS & RATINGS	SG	CF
Knight Light	▮▮▮½	▮▮½
Red Rock	▮▮▮	▮▮½
Magic Brew	▮▮▮½	▮▮▮

5905 South Kirkman Road
Orlando, Florida 32819
(407) 345·8802

FLORIDA BREWERY INC.

B *B Cans*

With annual output in the region of 170,000 barrels a year (1993), the Florida Brewery is on its way to becoming a sizable regional presence. It does not pretend to compete with the smaller craft breweries, but it does produce very respectable beers that can be enjoyed by serious beer drinkers. Its canned all-malt lagers are surprisingly good.

BEERS & RATINGS	CF
Master's Choice *(11.4 p; 4.8 w)*	▮▮▮½
Miami Beer	▮▮▮½

ABC (American Lager) *(11.6 p; 5.0 w)*
Dunk's *(11.6 p; 5.0 w)*
Fischer's Ale *(11.5 p; 4.9 w)*
Fischer's Beer *(11.6 p; 5.0 w)*

---

202 Gandy Road
Auburndale, Florida 33823
(813) 965·1825

GATOR LAGER BEER, INC.

B *KB*

Growlin' Gator Lager is brewed as a pretext for the existence of a mail-order catalogue that features a whole range of Gator Lager T-shirts, baseball caps, varsity jackets, beach umbrellas, key chains, wrist watches, etc. (The Gator mailbox can be yours for a mere $79.00.) If you believe this the worst reason yet for going into the beer business, you probably didn't invest in Microsoft either. And if you think Gator Lager must be a dismal beverage, think again. Contract-brewed by Florida Brewing, Gator is actually an above-average pilsner-style beer, clean and crisp with a long, hoppy finish.

BEERS & RATINGS	SG	CF
Gator Lager *(11.2 p; 3.4 w)*	ııı	ııı
Old West Light *(8.0 p; 3.4 w)*		
Old West Amber *(13.1 p; 4.1 w)*		
Gator Light		
Flying Aces Light		

Scott: "These guys are clever marketers. It's great to see them having so much fun."

---

645 West Michigan Street
Orlando, Florida 32805
(407) 423·2337

Open daily 8-6.

IRISH TIMES PUB AND BREWERY

BP

Founded in 1990, and located in a busy shopping plaza, Irish Times features an extensive menu that not surprisingly includes Irish-style breads (baked on the premises), Irish salmon, Irish potato-leek soup, Irish stew, lean Irish bacon, Irish coffee, Irish spring water, Irish whiskey (properly spelled with an 'e'), and even the legal version of Irish potcheen (which is to Ireland what moonshine is to the American South). Not to mention Boxty potato cakes, a kind of griddle cake that originated in the windswept villages of Cavan and Donegal. Needless to say, the styles of beer found at Irish Times are primarily those that might be encountered in a public house in Dublin or Limerick, though the brewmaster is not averse to an occasional experiment.

Irish Red Ale *(1.060 og)*
Irish Pale Ale *(1.040 og)*
St. Patrick's Special *(1.060 og)*
Red Raspberry *(1.034 og)*

9920 Alternate A1A, Suite 810
Palm Beach Gardens, Florida 33410
(407) 624·1504

Open daily 11:30-2 am.

MARKET STREET PUB

BP

Outside you'll discover the mandatory Florida palm trees. Inside you might fancy yourself in an English pub in some village where thatched roofs are more common than billboards. The kitchen offers fish and chips (naturally), along with salads, sandwiches, burgers, homemade sausages, and off-beat specialties—such as tuna gyros—that you won't find in Much-Binding-Under-the-World.

Downtown Brown Ale
Gainesville Gold
Bullgator
Terminator

SW First Avenue
Gainesville, Florida 32601
(904) 377-2927
Corner of SW First Avenue and SW Second Avenue.
M-Sat 11-2 am; Sun 11-11. Live music W-Sat.

MCGUIRE'S IRISH PUB AND BREWERY

B BP *K B*

Founded by McGuire Martin and his wife Molly, this is a friendly brewpub located in an old fire-house. For the most part, its beers are brewed on premises, in small batches, and sold on draft only. The bottled McGuire's Irish Red, available in many parts of the Southeast, is actually a contract beer brewed for McGuire's by the Oldenberg Brewery in Kentucky.

McGUIRE'S
IRISH PUB
& BREWERY
FEASTING, IMBIBERY & DEBAUCHERY

BEERS & RATINGS	CF
McGuire's Porter *(1.055 og; 5.3 v)*	▮▮▮½
McGuire's Irish Red *(1.048 og; 4.5 v)*	▮▮▮

McGuire's Stout *(1.060 og; 5.2 v)*
McGuire's Light *(1.055 og; 5.3 v)*

Chris: "Another fine stout, very much in the Dublin and Cork tradition, with chocolate depths and Espresso highlights."

---

600 East Gregory Street
Pensacola, Florida 32501
(904) 433·6789

On Hwy. 98 (Gregory Street) between the Bay Bridge and the Civic Center. Open daily 11-2 am.

MILL BAKERY, EATERY & BREWERY

BP

The Mill specializes in freshly prepared fare for health conscious baby boomers. Soups, salads, and sandwiches—all checked for nutritional value—share space on the menu with home-baked breads and pastries. The hand-crafted beers are brewed under the supervision of brewmaster John Stuart, who also supervises the brewing operations at Mill Bakery's other branches, in Orlando, Florida, and Charlotte, North Carolina.

Harvest Light *(3.5 w)*
Magic Brew *(4.0 w)*
Red Rock *(3.8 w)*

---

330 West Fairbanks Street
Winter Park, Florida 32789
(904) 644·1544

In the New York Plaza. Open daily 6:30 am- 2 am.

SARASOTA BREWING COMPANY

BP

Located several hundred miles from the nearest ski slope and no inconsiderable distance from the nearest hill of any description, Sarasota Brewing's brewpub—behind the Gulf Gate Mall—is decorated in the style of an Alpine chalet. This is a sports bar with typical American pub food and an ambitious selection of beers.

Sequoia Amber *(13.0 p; 4.0 w)*
Cobra Lite *(12.0 p; 3.5 w)*
Seasonals:
Blackbeard's Dark (14.5 p; 4.5 w)
Killer Bee's Honey Maibock (18.5 p; 6.0 w)

6607 Gateway Avenue
Sarasota, Florida 34231
(813) 925·2337

Take I-75 south to exit 37 to Gateway Avenue; behind Gulf Gate Mall. Sun-Th 11-midnight; F-Sat till 2 am.

GEORGIA BREWING COMPANY LTD.

B *B*

Rob Nelson and Bob Clark founded Georgia Brewing in 1989 to provide the Atlanta area with its own craft brewed beer. In fact Wild Boar Special Amber is contract-brewed quite some distance from Atlanta by the Dubuque Brewing and Bottle Company. But that should not be held against it, because this is a very respectable brew that can hold its own with the products of many micros and brewpubs.

BEERS & RATINGS	CF
Wild Boar Special Amber *(12.8 p)*	ııı½

Chris: "Well balanced and refreshing."

P.O. Box 8239
Atlanta, Georgia 30306
(404) 633·0924

ABITA BREWING COMPANY

B *KB*

This micro has been supplying draft and bottled beers to the New Orleans area since 1986.

BEERS & RATINGS	SG
Abita Amber Lager *(1.045 og; 4.0 w)*	▮▮▮½
Abita Golden Lager *(1.042 og; 4.0 w)*	▮▮▮½
Turbodog *(1.054 og; 5.0 w)*	

P.O. Box 762
Abita Springs, Louisiana 70420
(504) 893·3143

In the center of town, at the railroad tracks.
Open M-F 8-5. Tours by appointment only.

CRESCENT CITY BREWHOUSE

BP

Situated in an 1840's warehouse in the Vieux Carre, the Crescent City Brewhouse offers such regional specialties as crab cakes Tchoupitoulas, and savory alligator and andouille pie, along with more conventional pub fare. The beer is Bavarian with a Cajun accent.

BEERS & RATINGS	**SG**
Red Stallion *(1.048 og; 4.2 w)*	IIII½
Pilsner *(1.046 og; 4.5 w)*	IIII½
Blackforest Dark Lager *(15.0 p; 5.5 w)*	IIII½

Scott: "This brewpub alone is worth the trip to New Orleans."

527 Decatur Street
New Orleans, Louisiana 70130
(504) 522·0571

Across the street from the Jax Brewery, near Jackson Square. Open daily 11 am to whenever (kitchen closes at 11 pm weekdays and midnight on weekends). Live jazz and Latin music on some nights.

DILWORTH BREWING COMPANY

BP

Charlotte's first brewpub, Dilworth serves reasonably priced full meals and pub snacks.

BEERS & RATINGS	**CF**
Reed's Gold *(10.44 p)*	II½

Dilworth Porter *(13.0 p)* 🍺🍺🍺
Albemarle Ale *(10.48 p)*
Wild Wheat *(10.44 p)*

1301 East Boulevard
Charlotte, North Carolina 28203
(704) 377·2739

GREENSHIELDS BREWERY AND PUB

BP *KB*

This well-established brewpub is located in an attractive brick structure–part of the old Market House Building. Greenshields offers a British atmosphere and mostly British-style beers, though a pilsner and a wheat beer are also available. Not surprisingly, the menu features British pub favorites, like fish and chips and shepherd's pie, but a variety of other dishes, from pastas to steak, are also served.

Golden Ale
Amber
Stout
India Pale Ale
Stout

---

214 East Martin Street
Raleigh, North Carolina 27601
(910) 829·0214

Open daily 11:30-midnight.

LOGGERHEAD BREWING COMPANY

B *KB*

This small micro brews a variety of beers for local distribution.

Loggerhead Pilsner
Loggerhead Light

2006 West Vandalia Road
Greensboro, North Carolina 27407
(919) 292·7676

Open M-Friday 8-5 pm.

THE MILL BAKERY, EATERY AND BREWERY

BP

It is the admirable aim of the owners of the Mill Bakery to offer fine food and beverages made from wholesome, natural ingredients. In Charlotte, the Mill is known for homemade pastas, fresh bread, fresh seafood, tasty salads and an imaginative range of pizzas made in the bakery's own brick oven. It has often been remarked that bread and beer are more than casually related—just take a look at the ingredients—so that it should not be surprising that the Mill also features handcrafted beers made with the classic ingredients permitted by the *Reinheitsgebot*.

BEERS & RATINGS	CF
Copper Creek Ale *(11.25 p)*	🍾🍾🍾
Red Oktober *(11.9 p)*	🍾🍾½
49er Gold *(11.2 p)*	🍾🍾½
Nut Brown Ale	🍾🍾🍾

122 West Woodlawn Avenue
Charlotte, North Carolina 28217
(704) 525·2530

SPRING GARDEN BREWING COMPANY

BP *K*

This brewpub serves American pub fare and brews a variety of lagers.

Hummin' Bird Light *(8.0 p)*
Red Oak Lager *(11.0 p)*
Battlefield Black Lager *(14.0 p)*
Blackbeard Bock *(16.0 p)*

The Brewery:
714 Francis King Street
Greensboro, North Carolina 27410
(910) 299·3649

Across from Friendly Ave. at Guilford College.

Spring Garden Bar & Grills:
1205 Spring Garden Street, Greensboro
(910) 379·0308

2704 Battleground Avenue, Greensboro
(910) 288·0163

111 East Main Street, Carrboro
(910) 929·2708

1500 West First Street, Winston-Salem
(910) 722·6950

295 Talbert Boulevard, Lexington

BOHANNON BREWING COMPANY

B *KB*

The Bohannon Brewing Company provides worthwhile alternatives to the mass-market brands that still dominate almost to the point of exclusion in the land of the Grand Ol' Opry. In business since 1989, Bohannon now produces a range of bottom-fermented Market Street beers that are distributed in eight states—"mostly," says Lindsay Bohannon, "to the Northeast." The present micro is on the site of Nashville's first brewery, established in 1859, and occupies a building built in 1888 for the Greenbriar Brewery. The oak-paneled tasting room overlooks the Cumberland River.

BEERS & RATINGS	SG	CF
Market Street Pilsner	3½	4
Market Street Oktoberfest	4	3½
Market Street Wheat Beer	2½	3
Market Street Golden Ale	3½	3

Scott: "The Oktoberfest beer is full-bodied and satisfying."
Chris: "One of the better American pilsners, dry with a crisp, clean finish."

134 Second Avenue North
Nashville, Tennessee 37201
(615) 242·8223

Historic district in downtown Nashville.
Free tours at 2 pm M-F.

THE SPECTR

THIS CHART DEMONSTRATES THE WIDE DIVERSITY OF BEER STYLES, WITH COMMERCIAL EXAMPLES, FROM A COLOR AND TASTE PERSPECTIVE. COLORS RANGE FROM GOLDEN TO BLACK. TASTES RANGE FROM VERY SWEET AT THE TOP TO VERY BITTER AT THE BOTTOM.

BEER: A fermented cereal beverage which traditionally is made from malted barley, hops, water and yeast. Most beer styles are derivatives of ales and lagers. Other ingredients such as wheat, fruit and spices are used for unique styles of beer. Corn and rice are used as sources of fermentable sugar.
ALES: Ales are fermented at higher temperatures. Fruity aromas are a common characteristic.
LAGERS: Lagers are fermented at lower temperatures and are aged for a longer period of time. Smooth, crisp and fizzy tastes and aromas are characteristics.
COLOR: Color comes from the amount and type of

UM *of* BEERS

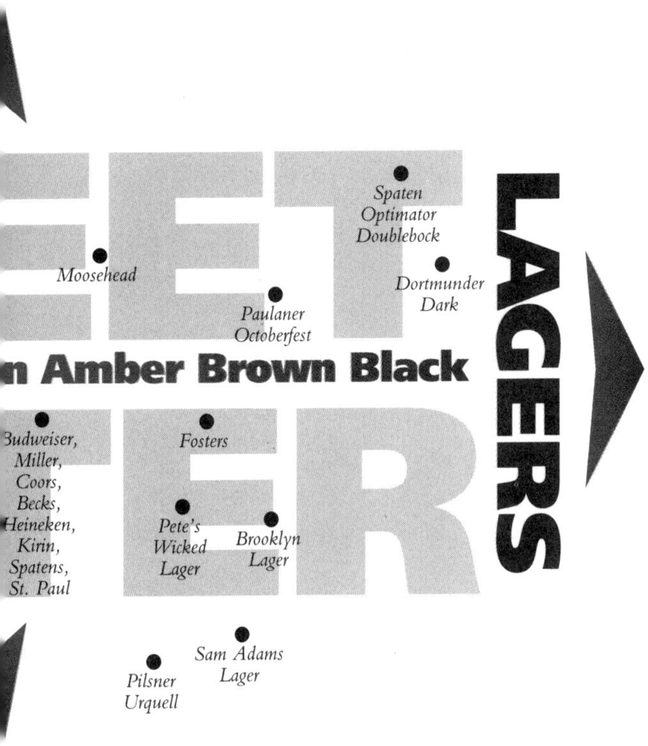

roasted barley used. Caramel, Chocolate and Black Patent are "color" descriptors of roasted barley; the colors range from gold to amber to brown to black.

TASTE: The tastebuds that concentrate on sweet are located at the front of the mouth and pick up the malt tastes in the beer. Bitter tastebuds are located in the back and emphasize the hop characteristics. The aftertaste is also an important factor in beer tasting. The lingering taste should be pleasing, not sour or harsh.

AROMA: Beer should be a savory experience for your senses. Begin enjoying the beer by inhaling deeply. A variety of scents should be detectable based on the beer's ingredients. The aroma of malted barley is sweet and intensifies with dark beers. Hops impart a pleasant, flowery, bitter aroma that balances the sweet smell of malt. Fruity aromas add to the complexity of ales' bouquets.

BODY: As beer rolls across the tongue, the beer can feel watery (light in body) all the way through thick and chewy (full body).

Variety	Average Alpha Acid Content (%)	Stability*	Origin	Comments
Aquila	*6-7.5*	*Fair*	*U.S.*	*Developed as an aroma hop; early 1990s*
Banner	*9.5-10.5*	*Fair*	*U.S.*	*Developed as a bittering hop; early 1990s*
Bramling Cross	*5-6*	*Poor*	*U.K.*	*Crossbred Goldings, traditional ale hop, good for ale flavoring*
Brewers Gold	*8-9*	*Poor*	*U.S./U.K.*	*Traditional ale hop*
Bullion	*8-9*	*Poor*	*U.S./U.K.*	*All-purpose bittering hop, poor aroma*
Cascade	*5-6.5*	*Poor*	*U.S.*	*All-purpose bittering and aroma hop, citrusy character*
Centennial/CFI-90	*7-8*	*Poor*	*U.S.*	*"Supercharged" Cascade; fine aroma hop, citrusy, developed late 1980s*
Challenger	*7-9*	*Poor*	*U.K.*	*Rare*
Chinook	*11-13*	*Very Good*	*U.S.*	*Very bitter, aroma preferred by some*

Cluster	*6-8*	*Excellent*	*U.S.*	*Popular bittering hop, mineral oil, poor aroma and flavor*
Columbia	*9-10*	*Fair*	*U.S.*	*Rare*
Comet	*8-11*	*Fair*	*U.S.*	*Rare*
Eroica	*10-12*	*Fair*	*U.S.*	*Very bitter*
Fuggles	*4-5.5*	*Fair*	*U.S./U.K.*	*High seed content, traditional British ale bittering and aroma hop*
Galena	*12-13*	*Very Good*	*U.S.*	*Very popular bittering hop, very bitter*
Goldings	*4.5-5.5*	*Fair*	*U.S./Canada*	*Traditional British ale bittering and aroma hop*
Green Bullet	*10-11*	*Good*	*New Zealand*	*Very bitter*
Hallertauer	*4.5-5.5*	*Poor*	*U.S./Germany*	*Excellent aroma; traditional lager spicy flavor and aroma; U.S. and German varieties differ distinctly*
Hallertauer Hersbrucker	*4.5-5.5*	*Poor*	*Germany*	*Excellent aroma; traditional lager hop, spicy flavor and aroma*

Variety	Average Alpha Acid Content (%)	Stability*	Origin	Comments
Hallertauer Mittelfüh	*4-6*	*Poor*	*Germany*	*Excellent aroma; traditional lager hop, spicy flavor and aroma; considered finer than that grown in the Hersbrucker region; softer impact on the palate*
Huller	*4-6*	*Fair*	*U.S.*	*Good aroma and bittering hop*
Kent Goldings	*4.5-5.5*	*Fair*	*U.K.*	*Excellent traditional British ale bittering and aroma hop*
Mt. Hood	*5-6*	*Fair*	*U.S.*	*Very good aroma; bred to resemble Hallertauer character*
Northdown	*7.5-9.5*	*Good*	*U.K.*	*Good bitter, flavor and aroma*
Northern Brewer	*7.5-9*	*Fair*	*U.S./Germany*	*Traditional European lager bittering hop*
Nugget	*11-13*	*Good*	*U.S.*	*Very bitter, good aroma*
Olympic	*10-13*	*Fair*	*U.S.*	*Rare*

Orion	*7-9*	*Fair*	•	•
Perle	*7-9*	*Good*	*U.S.*	*Good bittering and aroma for lagers; bred to resemble German Northern Brewer*
Pride of Ringwood	*7-9*	*Good*	*Australia/Canada*	*Bittering hop*
Progress	*7-8*	*Good*	*U.K.*	*Rare*
Record	*5-7*	*Fair*	*Germany*	*Poor aroma*
Saaz	*4-6*	*Fair*	*Czechoslovakia (old borders)*	*Traditional European (pilsner) lager hop; spicy flavor and aroma excellent*
Saxon	*6.5-8.5*	*Very good*	*U.K.*	*Rare*
Spalt	*6-7.5*	*Poor*	*Germany*	*Traditional German bittering and aroma hop*
Stickelbract	*9-11*	*Good*	*New Zealand/ Australia*	*Very bitter*

Variety	Average Alpha Acid Content (%)	Stability*	Origin	Comments
Styrian Goldings	*5.5-7*	*Fair (old borders)*	*U.S./Yugoslavia*	*Very good British ale hop; good aroma*
Super Styrian	*7-9*	*Good*	*Austria/ Czechoslovakia (old borders)*	*Similar to Styrian Goldings and Saaz*
Talisman	*7-9*	*Good*	*U.S.*	*Similar to Cluster; rare*
Target	*9-11*	*Poor*	*U.K.*	*Widely available in U.K.*
Tettnanger	*4-6*	*Poor*	*U.S./Germany*	*Very good lager hop; American variety floral and very distinct from German variety (more spicy)*
Viking	*6-8.5*	*Good*	*U.K.*	*Rare*

Willamette	*5-6*	*Fair*	*U.S.*	*Developed as a seedless Fuggles; excellent aroma; ale or lager*
Wye Target	*9-11*	*Fair*	*U.K.*	*Very bitter*
Yeoman	*10-11.5*	*Very good*	*U.K.*	*General availability in U.K.*
Zenith	*8.5-10.5*	*Good*	*U.K.*	*General availability in U.K.*

* *Very good: 90% of bitterness remains after 4 months of storage at 70°F (21°C); Good: 80-90%; Fair: 60-80%; Poor: less than 60% and some will suffer dramatic loss within a month.*
Note: Stability is extended when the brew is stored at cold temperatures and in an oxygen-free environment.

	Original Gravity (balling)	% Alcohol by Volume	International Bittering Units	Color (SRM)
Ales				
Barley Wine	*1.090-1.120 (22.5-30 p)*	*8.4-12*	*50-100*	*14-22*
Belgium-style Specialty				
a) Flanders Brown	*1.045-1.055 (11-14 p)*	*5-6.5*	*35-50*	*16-20*
b) Trappist Ales	*1.060-1.100 (15-25 p)*	*6-10*	*25-50*	*15-30*
House Brew	*1.060-1.065 (15-16 p)*	*6-6.5*	*25-40*	*15-25*
Double Malt	*1.075-1.085 (19-21 p)*	*7.5-8*	*30-45*	*17-30*
Triple Malt	*1.090-1.100 (22.5-25 p)*	*8-10*	*35-50*	*20-30*
c) Saison	*1.052-1.080 (13-20 p)*	*5.5-7.5*	*25-40*	*4-10*
d) Lambic	*1.040-1.050 (10-12.5 p)*	*4-6*	*3-7*	*4-8*
Faro	•	*4.5-5.5*	•	•
Gueuze	•	*5.5*	•	•
Fruit (Framboise, Kriek, Peche…)	•	*6*	•	•
e) White	*1.044-1.050 (11-12.5 p)*	*4.5-5*	*20-35*	*2-4*

Brown Ales				
a) English Brown	*1.040-1.050 (10-12.5 p)*	*4.5-6.5*	*15-30*	*15-22*
b) English Mild	*1.031-1.037 (8-9 p)*	*2.5-3.6*	*14-37*	*22-34*
c) American Brown	*1.040-1.055 (10-14 p)*	*4.5-6.5*	*25-60*	*15-22*
Pale Ales				
a) Classic Pale Ale	*1.043-1.050 (11-12.5 p)*	*4.5-5.5*	*20-30*	*8-10*
b) India Pale Ale	*1.055-1.070 (14-17.5 p)*	*5.5-7*	*30-60*	*6-14*
c) Old Ale/Strong Ale	*1.060-1.075 (15-19 p)*	*6.5-8.5*	*30-50*	*10-16*
British Bitters				
a) Ordinary	*1.035-1.038 (8.5-9.5 p)*	*3-3.5*	*20-25*	*8-12*
b) Special	*1.038-1.042 (9.5-10.5 p)*	*3.5-4.5*	*25-30*	*12-14*
c) Extra Special	*1.042-1.050 (10.5-12.5 p)*	*4.5-5.5*	*30-35*	*12-14*
Porter	*1.040-1.050 (10-12.5 p)*	*4.5-6*	*25-35*	*25-35*
Scottish Ales				
a) Light	*1.030-1.035 (7.5-9 p)*	*3-4*	*9-10*	*10-12*
b) Heavy	*1.035-1.040 (9-10 p)*	*3.5-4*	*10-11*	*11-13*

	Original Gravity (balling)	% Alcohol by Volume	International Bittering Units	Color (SRM)
c) Export	*1.040-1.050 (10-12.5 p)*	*4-4.5*	*11-13*	*12-15*
d) Strong "Scotch" Ale	*1.075-1.085 (19-21 p)*	*6-8*	*14-16*	*14-17*
Stouts				
a) Dry Stout	*1.036-1.055 (9-14 p)*	*3-6*	*25-40*	*35+*
b) Sweet Stout	*1.045-1.056 (11-14 p)*	*4.5-6*	*15-20*	*35+*
c) Imperial Stout	*1.075-1.090 (19-22.5 p)*	*7-9*	*50-80*	*35+*
Lagers				
Bock				
a) Dark	*1.066-1.074 (16.5-18.5 p)*	*6-7.5*	*20-30*	*18-35*
b) Helles	*1.066-1.074 (16.5-18.5 p)*	*6-7.5*	*20-30*	*8-18*
c) Doppelbock	*1.074-1.100 (18.5-25 p)*	*7.5-14*	*20-40*	*12-35*
Bavarian Dark				
a) Munich Dunkel	*1.050-1.055 (12.5-14 p)*	*4.5-6*	*18-27*	*10-20*
b) Schwarzbier	*1.040-1.046 (10-11.5 p)*	*3.5-4.5*	*25-35*	*25-40*

American Dark	*1.040-1.050 (10-12.5 p)*	*4-5.5*	*14-20*	*10-20*
Dortmunder/Export	*1.050-1.060 (12.5-15 p)*	*5-6*	*25-35*	*4-6*
Munich Helles	*1.046-1.055 (11.5-14 p)*	*4.5-5.5*	*18-25*	*2-5*
Classic Pilsner				
a) German	*1.044-1.050 (11-12.5 p)*	*4-5*	*35-45*	*2.5-4.5*
b) Bohemian	*1.044-1.056 (11-14 p)*	*4-5.5*	*35-45*	*2-5*
American Light Lager				
a) Diet/Lite	*1.024-1.040 (6-10 p)*	*2.5-4.5*	*5-15*	*1-4*
b) American Standard	*1.035-1.045 (9-11 p)*	*3.5-5*	*5-17*	*2-4*
c) American Premium	*1.045-1.050 (11-12.5 p)*	*4.5-5*	*13-22*	*2-8*
d) Dry	*1.040-1.045 (10-11 p)*	*4-5*	*15-23*	*2-4*
Vienna				
a) Vienna	*1.046-1.052 (11.5-13 p)*	*4.5-5.5*	*18-30*	*10-20*
b) Märzen/Oktoberfest	*1.050-1.060 (12.5-15 p)*	*4.5-6.5*	*20-30*	*8-14*

	Original Gravity (balling)	% Alcohol by Volume	International Bittering Units	Color (SRM)
Hybrid Beers/Lagers, Ales				
Alt				
a) *German Altbier*	*1.040-1.040 (10-12.5 p)*	*4.5-5.5*	*28-40*	*16-19*
b) *Kölsch*	*1.040-1.045 (10-11 p)*	*4-5*	*16-30*	*4-10*
Cream Ale	*1.044-1.055 (11-14 p)*	*4.5-7*	*10-22*	*2-4*
Fruit Beer				
a) *Fruit Ale*	*1.030-1.110 (7.5-27.5 p)*	*2.5-12*	*5-70*	*5-50*
b) *Fruit Lager*	*1.030-1.110 (7.5-27.5 p)*	*2.5-12*	*5-70*	*5-50*
Herb Beer				
a) *Herb Ale*	*1.030-1.110 (7.5-27.5 p)*	*2.5-12*	*5-70*	*5-50*
b) *Herb Lager*	*1.030-1.110 (7.5-27.5 p)*	*2.5-12*	*5-70*	*5-50*

Specialty Beer				
a) Specialty Ale	*1.030-1.110 (7.5-27.5 p)*	*2.5-12*	*0-100*	*0-100*
b) Specialty Lager	*1.030-1.030 (7.5-27.5 p)*	*2.5-12*	*0-100*	*0-100*
Smoked				
a) Bamberg Rauchbier	*1.050-1.055 (12.5-14 p)*	*5-5.5*	*20-30*	*12-17*
b) Other styles with smoke flavor				
California Common Beer				
a) California Common Beer	*1.045-1.055 (11-14 p)*	*4-5*	*35-45*	*12-17*
b) Anchor Steam brand lookalike	*1.050 (12.5 p)*	*4.6*	*40-50*	*15*
Wheat Beer				
a) Berliner Weisse	*1.028-1.032 (7-8 p)*	*2.5-3.5*	*5-12*	*2-4*
b) Weizen	*1.045-1.050 (11-12.5 p)*	*4.5-5*	*8-14*	*3-8*
c) Dunkel	*1.045-1.055 (11-12.5 p)*	*4.5-6*	*10-15*	*17-22*
d) Weizenbock	*1.066-1.080 (16.5-20 p)*	*6.5-7.5*	*10-15*	*7-30*
e) American Wheat	*1.030-1.050 (7.5-12.5 p)*	*3.5-5*	*5-17*	*2-4*

Southwest

ARIZONA

Casey Moore's Oyster House—850 S. Ash, Tempe	(602) 968.9935
Charley's Restaurant & Pub—23 N. Leroux Street, Flagstaff	
The Crows Nest—	(602) 941.0602
Crystal Creek—1051 S. Milton, Flagstaff	
Gurley Street Grill—230 W.Gurley, Prescott	(602) 445.3388
Mad Italian Public House—101 S. San Francisco St., Flagstaff	(602) 779.1820
Main Street Bar & Grill—4 S. San Francisco St., Flagstaff	
Mill Avenue Beer Co.—605 S. Mill Ave.,Tempe	(602) 829.6775
Monsoons—22 E. Santa Fe, Flagstaff	(602) 774.7929
Murphy's—102 N. Cortez, Prescott	(602) 445.4044
Old Chicago Pub & Pizza—530 W. Broadway, Tempe	(602) 921.9431
The Palace Bar—Montezuma St., Prescott	(602) 778.7980
Pasto—19 E. Aspen, Flagstaff	(602) 779.1937
Penelope ParkenFarkers—220 W.Goodwyn, Prescott	(602) 445.6848
Pinnacle Peak—6713 E. Cypress, Scottsdale	(602) 945.3367
The Satisfied Frog—4321 N. Scottsdale Rd., Cave Creek	(602) 253.6293
The Shanty—401 E. 9th Street, Tucson	(602) 622.9210
Uptown Billiards—1300 S. Milton, Flagstaff	(602) 773.0551
Z's Pizza—6 Street, Tucson	

CALIFORNIA

Northern California

Bolinas Bay Bakery & Cafe—20 Wharf Road, Bolinas	
The Brewery	(916) 623.3000
Country Grill—Fairfield	(707) 434.8090
Dixon's—675 Emerald Bay Road, Lake Tahoe	
Fox & Goose—1001 R Street, Sacramento	
The Grounds—402 Main Street, Murphys	
Harry O'Shortals—304 Lincoln, Napa	
Josephines—Commercial Row, Truckee	
Lord Derby Arms—1923 Lake Street, Calistoga	
Ma Stokelds—464 First Street E, Sonoma	
Mad Dog & Englishmen—211 Spring St., Nevada City	
McNear's—23 Petaluma Blvd., Petaluma	
Old Vic—731 4th Street, Santa Rosa	
The Passage—Commercial Row, Truckee	
Stinson Beach Grill—3465 Shoreline, Stinson Beach	
Wild Hare—3082 Marlow, Santa Rosa	

Northern California-Bay Area

Barclay's—5940 College Avenue, Oakland
Bit of England—1448 Burlingame, Burlingame
Brittania Arms #1—1087 S. Saratoga/Sunnyvale, San Jose
Brittania Arms #2—5027 Almaden Expressway
Cheshire Pub—1494 El Camino, San Carlos

COLORADO

Boulder

The Corner Bar—13th & Spruce	(303) 442.4344
The James Pub & Grill—1922 13th Street	(303) 449.1922
Old Chicago—	(303) 443.5031
West End Tavern—926 Pearl	(303) 444.3535

Denver

Cherry Cricket—2641 E. 2nd Avenue	(303) 322.7666
Duffy's Shamrock—1635 Court Place	(303) 534.4939
Johnny's Pub & Grill—1624 Market	(303) 595.0609
My Brother's Bar—2376 15th	(303) 455.9991
Pearl Street Grill—1477 Pearl Street	(303) 778.6475
Skyline Café—777 W. 29th Avenue	(303) 296.3232
Zang Brewing Co.—2301 7th	(303) 499.2500

WATERING HOLES

Fort Collins

B&B Pickle Barrel—122 W. Laurel	(303) 484.0235
Cables End—165 E. Boardwalk	(303) 223.3553
C.B. & Potts—1415 W. Elizabeth	(303) 221.1139
County Cork—313 W. Drake Road	(303) 226.1212
Cuisine! Cuisine!—130 S. Mason	(303) 221.0399
Jefferson Grill—200 Jefferson	(303) 493.4348
Mountain Tap Tavern—167 N. College Ave.	(303) 484.4974
Mulligan's—2439 S. College Avenue	(303) 482.3553
Old Chicago—147 S. College Avenue	(303) 482.8599
Old Town Ale House—No. 25 Old Town Sq.	(303) 493.2213
Smiling Moose—518 W. Laurel	(303) 484.6336
Town Pump—124 N. College Avenue	(303) 493.4404
Washington's—132 LaPorte Avenue	(303) 493.1603

The Rest of Colorado

Old Chicago—8711 Wadsworth, Arvada	(303) 431.7707
188 N. Tejon, Colorado Springs	(719) 634.8812
7115 Commerce Ctr. Dr., Colorado Springs	(719) 593.7678
3990 Wadsworth, Lakewood	(303) 431.7707
Westminster	(303) 988.3414
The Royal Well—101 N. Tejon, Colorado Springs	(719) 471.1084
Smiling Moose—2501 11th Avenue	(303) 356.7010
Woody Creek Tavern—2 Woody Creek Plaza	(303) 923.4585

NEW MEXICO

Albuquerque

Billy's Long Bar—4800 San Mateo	(505) 889.0573
Brewster's Pub—312 Central Ave. SW	(505) 247.2533
The Dingo Bar—313 Gold Ave. SW	(505) 243.0663
Maria Teresa Restaurant & 1840 Bar—618 Rio Grande Blvd. NW	(505) 242.1122
Oasis Restaurant & Lounge—5400 S. Mateo NE	(505) 884.2324
Quarters—4516 NE Wyoming	(505) 299.9864
Quarters—801 SE Yale	(505) 843.7505
Time Out Restaurant & Sports Club—618 Central Ave. SW	(505) 764.8887

Taos

The Chili Connection—MM #1 Ski Valley Rd.	(505) 776.8787
Murphy's Delicatessen—115 E. McCarthy Plaza	(505) 758.4205
Taos Inn—125 Paseo del Pueblo Norte	(505) 758.2223
Thunderbird Lodge—Taos Ski Valley	(505) 776.2280
Tim's Stray Dog Cantina—Taos Ski Valley	(505) 776.2894

The Rest of New Mexico

Eddie's Bar & Grill—901 Ave de Mesilla, Las Cruces	(505) 524.8603
Evangelo's—200 W. San Francisco St., Santa Fe	(505) 982.9014
Saints & Sinners—2305 Riverside, Española	(505) 753.2757
The Royal Buck—Galisto St., Santa Fe	

TEXAS

Austin

Crown & Anchor—2911 San Jacinto	(512) 322.9168
The Dog and Duck Pub—406 W. 17 St.	(512) 479.0598
Double Dave's—3000 Duval	(512)476.DAVE
The Elephant Room—315 Congress Ave.	(512) 473.2279
Maggie Mae's—512 Trinity St.	(512) 478.8541
The Posse East—2900 Duval St	(512) 477.2111
Scholtz Garten—1607 San Jacinto	(512) 477.4171
Shakespeare's Pub—314 E. 6th St.	(512) 472.1666
The Tavern—922 W. 12th St.	(512) 474.7496
Texas Showdown Saloon—2610 Guadalupe	(512) 472.2010
The Texas Tavern—301 E. 22nd St.	(512) 471.5651

Dallas

The Angry Dog—2726 Commerce St.,	(214) 741.4406
Flip's—1520 Greenville Ave.	(214) 824.9944
The Gingerman—2718 Boll St.	(214) 754.8771
The Green Elephant—2710 Boll St.	(214) 750.6625
London Tavern—2001 Greenville Ave.	(214) 823.7735
The Medieval Inn—7102 Greenville Ave.	(214) 363.1118
Mimi's Pub & Cafe—5111 Greenville Ave.	(214) 368.1994
The Mucky Duck—3102 Welborn St.	(214) 522.7200
Stan's Blue Note—2908 Greenville Ave.	(214) 824.9653

The Tipperary Inn—2818 Greenville Ave.	(214) 823.7167

Houston

The Ale House—2425 W. Alabama	(713) 521.2333
The Ashford Arms—781 Dairy Ashford	(713) 497.5316
The Brewery Tap—717 Franklin	(713) 236.1537
The Crooked Ferret—11835 Jones Rd.	(713) 894.0055
The Gingerman—5607 Morningside	(713) 526.2770
The Hops House—2321A Hwy. 6	(713) 496.0623
Live Bait—3743 Greenbriar Dr.	(713) 520.7771
Local Charm—1501 Telephone	(713) 926.0329
Mathias'—1960 FM 3755 W	(713) 537.5837
Munchie's Cafe—1617 Richmond	(713) 528.3545
The Richmond Arms—5920 Richmond Ave.	(713) 784.7722
Shakespeare's Pub—14129 Memorial Dr.	(713) 497.4625
Sherlock's Baker Street Pub—10001 Westheimer	(713) 977.1857

San Antonio

Dick's Last Resort—406 Navarro	(210) 224.0026
Durty Nellie's—200 S. Alamo Place, Palacio del Rio	(210) 222.1400
Hills & Dales Ice House—15403 White Fawn	(210) 695.8309
Joey's—217 N. St. Mary's	(210) 733.9573
Kangaroo Court—102 W. Crockett St. #800	(210) 224.9051
Mama's Hofbrau—9903 San Pedro	(210) 342.3219

The Rest of Texas

Carney's Pub—3410 S. College, Bryan	
Molly Malone's Pub—7824 Louetta Rd., Clearwater	(713) 370.4949
Pig & Whistle Pub—5731 Locke Ave.	(817) 731.4938

Northwest

ALASKA

Alaskan Hotel & Bar—167 S. Franklin, Juneau	(907) 586.1000
Anchor River Inn—P.O. Box 154, Anchor Pt.	(907) 235.8531
Anchor Tavern—Font Street, Nome	
Fort Seward Saloon—P.O. Box 307, Haines	(907) 766.2009
Overlook Bar & Grill—P.O. Box 70, Denali Nat'l Pk.	(907) 683.2723
Red Dog Saloon—278 S. Franklin, Juneau	
Rumrunners Olde Town Bar—Anchorage Hotel, 330 E Street, Anchorage 99501	(907) 272.4553

Tourist Information

Alaska division of Tourism—P.O. Box 110801, Juneau, AK 99811-0801	(907) 465.2010

IDAHO

Bugatti's Pub—109 S. 1st Ave., Sand Point	(208) 263.4976
Catcher in the Rye—414 Mullan, Coeur D'Alene	(208) 667.7966
Chelsea's—2601 N. 4th, Coeur D'Alene	(208) 667.9836
Coeur D'Alene Resort—	(208) 765.4000
Godfather's—2615 N. 4th, Coeur D'Alene	(208) 765.3767
Iron Horse—407 Sherman, Coeur D'Alene	(208) 667.7314
Lock, Stock & Barrel—4705 Emerald, Boise	(208) 336.4266
Litre House—Overland & 5 Mile Rd., Boise	(208) 466.8089
Koolehal River Inn—Hwy. 99, Bonner's Ferry	(208) 267.8511

MONTANA

Miles Town Brewing—1008 N. 2nd, Miles City	(408) 232.5732
Montana Bar & Cafe—Broadus	(406) 436.2454

OREGON

Eugene

Rennie's Landing—1214 Kincaid	(503) 687.0600
East 19th Street Cafe—1485 E. 19th St.	(503) 342.4025
Bavarian Restaurant	(503) 345.9815

Portland

Barley Mill Pub—1629 SE Hawthorne	(503) 231.1492
Blue Moon Tavern—432 NW 21st St.	(503) 223.3184
Moloch Bakery & Pub—901 SW Salmon	(503) 227.5700
Bogart's Galleria—921 SW Morrison	(503) 224.3369

Bogart's Joint—406 NW 14th	(503) 222.4988
Captain Ankeny's Well—50 SW 2nd	(503) 223.1375
Captain Coyote—2809 NE Sandy Blvd.	(503)234.8573
Dublin Pub—6821 SW Beaverton-Hillsdale Hwy.	(503) 297.2889
Goose Hollow Inn—1927 SW Jefferson	(503) 228.7010
Greenway Pub—12272 SW Scholls Ferry Rd.	(503) 620.4699
Horse Brass Pub—4534 SE Belmont	(503) 223.2202
Kell's Irish Pub—112 SW 2nd	(503) 227.4057
Laurelthirst—2958 NE Glisan	(503) 232.1504
McCormick & Schmicks—(various locations)	
Paddy's—65 SW Yarnhill	(503) 224.5626
Parchman Farm—1204 SE Clay	(503) 235.7831
Pazzo—422 SW Broadway	(503) 228.1515
Produce Row Cafe—204 SE Oak	(503) 232.8355
Raleigh Hills—4495 SW Scholls Ferry Rd.	(503) 292.1723
St. John's Dublin Pub—8203 N. Ivanhoe	(503) 283.6880
Vat & Tonsure—822 SW Park	(503) 227.1845

The Rest of Oregon

The Elusive Trout—39333 Proctor Blvd.	(503) 668.7884
McMenamin's—6179 SW Murray Rd.	(503) 644.4562
McMenamin's Pub—2020 NE Cornell Rd.	(503) 640.8561
Riverwood Pub—8136 SW Hall Blvd.	(503) 643.7189
Old World Deli—341 SW 2nd St.	(503) 752.8549
Suds 'n Suds—935 NW King	(503) 758.3354

WASHINGTON

Seattle

Anthenian Inn—1715 Pike Place	(206) 624.7166
Attic Tavern & Cafe—4226 E. Madison	(206) 323.3131
Blue Moon Tavern—712 NE 45th St.	(206) 545.9775
Bogey's On Eastlake—1540 Eastlake Ave. E	(206) 325.1702
Canterbury Ale & Eats—534 15th Ave. E	(206) 322.3130
Central Tavern—207 First Avenue S	(206) 622.0209
Comet Tavern—922 E. Pike Street	(206) 323.9853
College Inn Pub—4006 University Way NE	(206) 434.2307
Cooper's Alehouse—8065 Lake City Way NE	(206) 522.2923
Cutter's Bayhouse—2001 Western Ave.	(206) 448.4804
Deluxe I Bar & Restaurant—625 Broadway E	(206) 324.9697
Ditto Tavern—2303 Fifth Ave.	(206) 441.3303
Doc Maynard's—600 1st Ave. (Pioneer Sq.)	(206) 682.4649
Duchess—2827 NE 55th Street	(206) 527.0956
Duke's Yacht Club—1111 Fairview Ave. N	(206) 622.0200
F.X. McRory's—419 Occidental Ave. S	(206) 623.4800
Jake O'Shaughnessey's—100 Mercer Street	(206) 285.1897
J & M Cafe—201 1st Ave. (Pioneer Sq.)	(206) 624.1670
Jazz Alley—2033 6th Ave. at Lenora	(206) 441.9729
La Boheme—6119 Phinney Ave. N	(206) 783.3002
Lake Union Cafe	(206) 328.8855
Latitude 47°—1232 Westlake Ave. N	(206) 284.1047
Latona by Greenlake—6423 Latona Ave. NE	(206) 525.2238
Leschi Lake Cafe—102 Lakeside Ave.	(206) 328.2233
McCormick's Fish House & Bar—722 4th Ave. at Columbia	(206)682.3900
McCormick & Schmick's—1103 First Ave.	(206) 623.5500
Metropolitan Grill—802 Second Ave.	(206) 624.3287
Merchant's Cafe—109 Yesler Way	(206) 624.1515
Place Pigalle—81 Pike St. (Pike Place Mkt.)	(206) 624.1756
Ray's Boathouse—6049 Seaview Place NW	(206) 789.3770
Red Door Alehouse—3401 Fremont Ave. N	(206) 547.7521
Roanoke Park Place—2409 10th Avenue E	(206) 324.5882
Romper Room—106 First Street N	(206) 284.5003
74th Street Ale House—7401 Greenwood Avenue N	(206) 784.2955
Santa Fe Cafe Phinney Ridge—5910 Phinney Ave. N	(206) 783.9755
T.S. McHugh's—21 Mercer Street	(206) 282.1910

North Seattle

Anthony's Homeport—6135 Seaview Ave. NW	(206) 783.0708
Backstage—2208 Market Street NW	(206)781.2805
Barnaby's Steak & Ale—11011 Meridian Ave. N	(206) 363.1705
Burk's Cafe—5411 Ballard Ave. NW	(206) 782.0091
Duffy's Tavern—4300 Leary Way NW	(206) 782.3635

Fabulous Buckaroo Tavern—4201 Fremont Ave. N	(206) 634.3161
Pacific Inn Cafe—3501 Stone Way N	(206) 547.2967
Unicorn Restaurant—4550 University Way NE	(206) 634.1115

The Rest of Washington

Ale House Pub & Eatery—2122 Mildred W	(206) 565.9367
Barnaby's—12405 38th SE, Bellevue	(206) 641.9757
Ben Moore's—112 W. 4th, Olympia	(206) 357.7527
Bullie's—1200 Harris, Bellingham	(206) 734.2855
Cromwell's Ale House—5109 Pt. Fosdick Dr.	(206) 851.1050
Domani—604 Bellevue Way NE, Bellevue	(206) 454.4405
Engine House #9—611 North Pine, Tacoma	(206) 272.3435
Fourth Avenue Tavern—210 E.4th Ave., Olympia	(206) 786.1444
Fort Spokane—W. 401 Spokane Falls Blvd., Spokane	(509) 838.3809
Goochi's Restaurant—104 E. Woodin Ave., Chelan	(509) 682.2436
The Harbour—231 Parfitt Way SW, Bainbridge Island	(206) 842.0969
Heron & Beaver—Pacific Hwy. 103 & N.45th St.	(206) 642.4142
Kirkland Roaster—111 Central Way, Kirkland	(206) 827.4400
Lolli's Boiler—32925 First Ave. S, Federal Way	(206) 838.5929
The New Jake O'Shaughnessey's—401 Bellevue Sq., Bellevue	(206) 455.5559
Oyster Creek Inn—190 Chuckanut Drive Bow	(206) 776.6179
Rico's—East 200 Main, Pullman	(509) 334.9958
Public House—1058 Water St., Port Townsend	
The Roost—120 NW Gilman Blvd., Issaquah	(206) 392.5550
Yarrow Bay Bar & Grill—1270 Carillon Pt., Kirkland	(206) 889.9052

WYOMING

Calico Pizza—Teton Village Road, Wilson	(307) 733.2460
Dierrich's Bar & Gistro at the Alpenhof—Teton Village(307) 733.3242	
Flagg Ranch—South entrance to Yellowstone Nat'l Park, Jackson	(307) 733.8761
J.J.'s Silver Dollar Bar & Grill at the Wort Hotel—On Broadway, Jackson	(307) 733.2190
Jackson Lake Lodge—Teton Park, Moran	(307) 733.2811
Many Piglets—On the Square, Jackson	(307) 733.4968
Mogels—Teton Village	(307) 733.6657
The Pub at Sojourner—Teton Village	(307) 733.3657
Shady Lady—Snow King Ski Area, Jackson	(307) 733.5200
Spirits of the West—385 W. Broadway, Jackson	(307) 733.3853
Tag's Restaurant—On Broadway, Jackson	(307) 733.7999
Tortilla Flats—Base of the Snow King, Jackson	(307) 739.9800
Yellowstone—(available at the following inns) Mammoth Hot Springs, Old Faithful Hotel, Canyon Lodge, Grand Village Lake Hotel	(307) 344.7910

Midwest

ILLINOIS

Heartland Hydroponics—115 Townline Rd.,Vernon Hills	(708) 816.4769
J.D. Nick's—1711 W. Hwy. 50, O'Fallon	(618) 624.2100
Joe's Brewery—706-708 S. 5th St., Champaign	(217) 384.1790
Koski Homebrew Fixin's—1415 5th Ave., Moline	(309) 797.2130

INDIANA

Rich O's Barbeque—3312 Plaza Drive, New Albany	(812) 949.2804
Shello's Pub—County Line Mall, Indianapolis	(317) 882.7997
Sonka Irish Pub & Café—1366 Wabash, Terre Haute	(812) 232.9969

IOWA

A Taste of Thailand—215 Walnut Street, Des Moines	(515) 243.9521
Dallas County Brewing—301 S.10th Street,Adel	(515) 993.5064
Fat Tuesday's—1121 University Ave., Dubuque	

MICHIGAN

Brew & Grow Michigan—33523 W. 8 Mile #F-5, Livonia	(800) 442.7939

MINNESOTA

Brit's Pub & Eating Establishment—1110 Nicollet Mall, Minneapolis	(612) 332.3908
Compadres—The Boardwalk, Dorset	(218) 732.7624

Gasthaus Bavarian Hunter—County Rd. 15 at 64, Stillwater	(612) 439.7128
Trumps Deluxe Grill & Bar— 317 S. Main Street, Stillwater	(612) 439.0024

MISSOURI

Bier Haus—602 Washington St., Hermann	(314) 486.5343
Calico's Bar & Grill—420 Olive St.,St.Louis	(314) 421.0708
Hooter's—301 St. Louis, Union Station, St. Louis	(314) 241.8888
John D. McGurk's—1200 Russell Blvd., St. Louis	(314) 776.6309
Kent's Deli—207 Chesterfield Mall, Chesterfield	(314) 532.4405
Maggie O'Brien's—2000 Market St., St. Louis	(314) 421.1388
O'Connell's Pub—4652 Shaw Ave., St. Louis	(314) 773.6600
Riddle's Cafe & Wine Bar— 6307 Delmar, University City	(314) 725.6985

NEBRASKA

Omaha

Fermenters Supply—4472 S. 84th St.	(402) 593.9171
Homy Inn—1510 N. Saddle Creek Rd.	(402) 554.5815
Jaipur—10922 Elm Street	(402) 392.7331
Jones Street—1316 Jones Street	(402) 344.3858
Lazlo's—710 P Street, Lincoln	(402) 474.2337

NORTH DAKOTA

Beer Barrel—32 NE 3, Minot	(701) 839.9029
Downtowner's Pub—301 3rd Ave., Fargo	(701) 232.8851
Happy Harry's Bottle Shop—2215 Gateway Dr., Grand Forks	(701) 772.2671
Liberty Tavern—600 4 Ave. NE, Minot	(701) 852.5013
Ratch's Bar—100 NE 3, Minot	(701) 838.9312
Sergio's Mexican Bar & Grill—I-94 & Hwy. 22, Dickinson	(701) 264.1022

WISCONSIN

Milwaukee

Barrel Riders Pub—1132 East Wright	(414) 372.2929
Begga's Pub—2479 N. Framey Street	(414) 264.7735
Benjamin Briggs—2501 W. Greenfield	(414) 383.2337
Benno's—7413 W. Greenfield	(414) 453.9094
Blastics—3079 N. Holton	(414) 372.4700
Bosoc's—1000 E. Burleigh	(414) 264.3500
Brennan's—19000 W. Blue Mound	(414) 785.6606
Brett's—1501 N. Jackson	(414) 277.0122
Brown Bottle Pub—221 West Galena	(414) 271.4444
Chancery—7615 West State	(414) 458.2300
Chumley's—3612 S. Moorland	(414) 782.2635
Chump's Rusty Bucket—700 S. 2nd St.	(414) 277.0700
Criss Cross—800 E. Chambers St.	(414) 562.8311
Dino's Lounge—808 E. Chambers St.	(414) 263.6033
Elsa's On the Park—833 N. Jefferson	(414) 765.0615
Erv's Mug—130 W. Ryan Road	(414) 762.5010
Gasthaus Nurnberg—3450 E. Layton	(414) 481.9917
Grady's Saloon—3101 W. Lincoln	(414) 643.9819
Grand Hotel—4747 S. Howell Ave.	(414) 481.8000
Hooligan's Super Bar—2017 E. N. Ave.	(414) 273.5230
Jakester's—2311 N. Murray Ave.	(414) 273.5253
John Hawk's Pub—100 E. Wisconsin Ave.	(414) 272.3199
Just Arts Saloon—181 S. 2nd St.	(414) 347.1171
Kait's—2856 N. Oakland	(414) 332.6323
Klinger's East—920 E. Locust St.	(414) 263.9844
Kuchta's—8423 W. Cleveland	(414) 541.1033
Landmark 1850 Inn—5905 S. Howell	(414) 769.1850
Landmark Lanes—2220 N. Farwell Ave.	(414) 278.8770
Larry's Brown Deer Market—8737 N. Deerwood Dr.	(414) 355.9650
Lennenman's Riverwest Inn—2874 N. Weil St.	(414) 263.9844
Likely Story—932 E. Chambers Street	(414) 264.8840
Maiden Voyage—1694 N. Van Buren Street	(414) 278.0700
McBob's—4919 W. North Avenue	(414) 871.5050
McGillycuddy's—1247 N. Water Street	(414) 278.8888
Mel's Corner Tap—158 E. Juneau	(414) 274.7201
Midway Motor Lodge—1005 S. Moorland	(414) 786.9540
Mike & Anna's—1978 S. 8th Street	(414) 643.0072

Milrose Inn—5831 W. Vilet	(414) 774.1322
Milwaukee Athletic Club—755 N. Broadway	(414) 273.5080
Otto's Wine Cask—4600 W. Brown Deer	(414) 354.5381
Pizza Man—1800 E. North	(414) 272.1747
Polish Falcon's Nest—801 E. Clark	(414) 264.0680
The Purple Foot—3167 S. 92nd Street	(414) 327.2130
Riverwest Tavern—900 E. Auer	(414) 265.8389
Rosie's Water Works—1111 N. Water Street	(414) 274.7213
Sanford's—1547 N. Jackson	(414) 276.9608
Saz's State House—5539 W. State	(414) 453.2410
Sequel's—1758 N. Water	(414) 272.7476
Suds Tavern—2979 N. Bremen Street	(414) 263.7837
Thurman's 15—1731 N. Arlington	(414) 224.1080
Tony's Tavern—412 S. 2nd Street	(414) 273.6321
Track's Tavern—1020 E. Locust Street	(414) 562.2020
Treats—221 N. Humboldt	(414) 765.3172
U.W.M Gasthaus—2200 E. Kenwood	(414) 229.6319
Up and Under—1216 E. Brady	(414) 276.2677
Uptowner—1032 E. Center Street	(414) 372.3882
V. Richards—17165 W. Blue Mound	(414) 784.8303
Von Trier—2235 N. Farwell Avenue	(414) 272.1775
West 37th Street—3700-A W. Pierre	(414) 647.1155
West Bank Café—732 E. Burleigh Street	(414) 562.5555
Wheelhouse Melanec's—2178 N. Riverboat Rd.	(414) 264.6060
Whitehouse—2900 S. Kinnickinnic	(414) 483.2900
Y-Not II—706 East Lyon	(414) 347.9972
Zur Krone—839 South 2nd Street	(414) 647.1910

The Rest of Wisconsin

Essen Haus—508 E. Wilson, Madison	(414) 255.4674
Brat & Brau—6654 Mineral Point Road	(608) 833.3680
Lizard Lounge—141 High Avenue, Oshkosh	(414) 426.1290
Randy's Fun Hunters Brewery—841 E. Milwaukee St., Whitewater	(414) 473.8000

Northeast

WASHINGTON D.C.

Capital Hill

Cafe Berlin—322 Massachusetts Avenue NE	(202) 543.7656
The Dubliner—520 N Capitol Street NW	(202) 737.3773
Kelly's Irish Times—14 F Street NW	(202) 543.5433
Tiber Creek Pub—15 E Street NW	(202) 638.0900

Downtown

Brickskeller—1523 22nd Street NW	(202) 293.1885
Cafe Mozart—1331 H Street NW	(202) 347.5732
Chaucer's at Canterbury Hotel—1733 N Street NW	(202) 393.3000
The Crow Bar—1006 20th St. NW	(202) 223.2972
930 Nightclub—930 F Street NW	(202) 393.0930

Georgetown

Chadwick's-Georgetown—3205 K Street NW	(202) 333.2565
J Paul's—3218 M Street NW	(202) 333·3450
Old Europe—2434 Wisconsin Avenue NW	(202) 333·7600
The Saloon—3239 M Street NW	(202) 338.4900

Uptown

Chadwick's-Friendship Hts.—5247 Wisconsin Ave. NW	(202) 362.8040
The Crow Bar—1006 20th St. NW	(202) 223.2972
Four Provinces—3412 Connecticut Ave. NW	(202) 244.0860
Murphy's—2609 24th Street NW	(202) 462.7171

DELAWARE

Buckley's Tavern—Route 52, Centreville	(302) 656.9776
Peddlers Pub—Christiana	
The Rose & Crown—108 2nd Street, Lewes	

MAINE

Castine Inn—Main Street, Castine	(207) 326.4365
3-Dollar Deweys—446 Fore Street, Portland	
Nickerson Tavern—Route 1, Searsport	(207) 548.2220

The Great Lost Bear—540 Forest Ave., Portland
Whig & Courier Pub—Haymarket Square, Bangor

MARYLAND

Annapolis

'74 Schooner Woodwind—Annapolis Marriott Waterfront Hotel	(800) 638.5139
Griffin's West Street Grill—2049 West St.	(410) 266.7662
McGarvey's—8 Market Space	(410) 263.5700
Middleton's Tavern—33 Sands Ave.	(410) 261.2838
Ram's Head Tavern—33 West Street	(410) 268.4545

Ann Arundel County

Blob's Park—8024 Blob's Park Road, Jessup	(410) 799.0155
Bun Penny—1364 Columbia Mall, Columbia	(410) 730.4100
Elsie's Gourmet German Delicatessen—8141 Telegraph Rd., Severn	(410) 551.6000
Last Chance Saloon—Oakland Mills Village Ctr, Columbia	(410) 730.5656

Baltimore

Alonzo's—415 W. Cold Spring Lane	(410) 235.3433
Cafe Tatoo—4825 Bel Air Road	(410) 325.7427
Harryman House—340 Main St., Reistertown	(410) 833.8850
PJ's Pub—3333 N. Charles Street	(410) 243.8844
Racers Cafe—7732 Harford Road	(410) 665.6000

Fells Point

Bertha's—734 South Broadway	(410) 327.5795
Cat's Eye Pub—1730 Thames Street	(410)276.9085
Duda's—1600 Thames Street (410) 276.9719	
The Horse You Came In On—1626 Thames St.	(410) 327.8111
John Stevens, Ltd.—1800 Thames St.	(410) 276.9497
Max's on Broadway—737 South Broadway	(410) 675.6297
Wharf Rat Bar—801 S Ann St.	(410) 276.9034

Montgomery County

Gentleman Jim's—2017 Viers Mill Rd., Rockville	(301) 762.8841
Hard Times Cafe—1117 Nelson St., Rockville	(301) 294.9720
Olde Towne Tavern & Brewing Co.—227 E. Diamond Ave., Olde Towne Gaithersburg	(301) 948.4200
Olney Ale House—2000 Olney-Sandy Spring Road, Olney	(301) 774.6708
Quarry House Tavern—Georgia Ave/Bonifant St., Silver Spring	(301) 587.9406
Suzanne's American Kitchen—9116 Rothbury Drive, Gaithersburg	(301) 990.0995

MASSACHUSETTS

Boodle's Restauarant & Bar—Back Bay Hilton 40 Dalton Street, Boston	(617) 236.1100
Christopher's—1920 Mass. Ave., Cambridge	(617) 876.9180
Doyle's—3484 Washington Street, Jamaica Plain	(617) 524.2345
Jake Wirth's—31-37 Stuart & Eliot	
The Sunset Grill & Tap—130 Brighton Ave.	(617) 254.1331
Woodley's—2067 Mass. Avenue, Cambridge	(617) 576.2240
The Wursthaus—Harvard Square, 4 JFK Street, Cambridge	(617) 491.7110

NEW JERSEY

Andy's Corner Bar—265 Queen Anne Road, Bogata	(201) 342.9887
Front Porch—217 Wagaraw Road, Hawthorne	(201) 427.4331
Hudson's—200 Hudson Street, Hoboken	(201) 420.8686
Laughing Lion—40 North Essex, Dover	(201) 328.1800
Old Bay Restaurant—61-63 Church Street, New Brunswick	(908) 246.3111

NEW YORK

Manhattan

Bergin's Beer & Wine Garden—89 South Street, Pier 17	(212) 693.0535
Brewsky's—41 East Seventh Street	(212) 982.3006
Burp Castle—41 East Seventh Street	(212) 982.4576
Chumley's—86 Bedford Street	(212) 675.4449
Fraunces Tavern—54 Pearl Street	(212) 269.0144
Jekyll and Hyde Pub—91 7th Avenue S	(212) 989.7701
Jeremy's Ale House—254 Front Street	(212) 964.3537
Jimmy Armstrong's Saloon—875 10th Avenue	(212) 581.0606
Lion's Head—59 Christopher Street	(212) 929.0670
McSorley's Ale House—15 E 7th Street	(212) 473.9148
North Star Pub—93 South Street	(212) 509.6757

Peculier Pub—145 Bleecker Street	(212) 353.1327
Prince Street Bar—125 Prince Street	(212) 228.8130
Amsterdam's—454 Broadway	(212) 925.6166
Slaughtered Lamb—182 West 4th Street	(212) 627.5262
White Horse Tavern—567 Hudson Street	(212) 243.9260
Broome Street Bar—363 W. Broadway	(212) 925.2086
The Soho Kitchen—103 Greene Street	
Tribecca Grill—375 Greenwich Street	(212) 941.3900
Brasserie—100 East 53rd Street	(212) 751.4840
Nosmo King—54 Varick Street	(212) 966.1239
Teddy's Bar—96 Berry Street	(718) 384.9787

The Rest of New York

Adobe Blues—63 Lafayette Ave., New Brighton, Staten Island	(718) 720.BLUE
Canterbury Ales—314 New York Ave., Huntington, Long Island	(516) 549.4404
Clark's Ale House—122 West Jefferson St., Syracuse	(315) 479.9859
Company B's—206 Route 303, Orangeburg, Rockland/Westchester	(914) 365.6060
Conrad's Bar & Grill—West Jericho Turnpike, Huntington, Long Island	(516) 751.4840
Henry's End Cafe—44 Henry Street, Brooklyn	(718) 834.1776
Holmes & Watson Ltd.—450 Broadway, Troy	(518) 273.8526
Horsefeathers Restaurant—N. Broadway, Tarrytown	(914) 232.7842
Waterfront Ale House—136 Atlantic Ave., Brooklyn	(718) 522.3794
Weepin Willoby's—Route 17 M, Monroe	(914) 783.2266
Retail:	
Beers of the World—3000 S. Winton Rd., Rochester	(716) 427.2852
Brewster Beer & Soda—Rte. 22, Brewster	(914) 279.7094

OHIO

Gambier Deli—110 Gaskin Ave., Gambier	(614) 427.4324
Great Lakes Brewing—2516 Market St., Cleveland	(216) 771.4404
Hoster Brewing—550 S. High St., Columbus	(614) 228.6066

PENNSYLVANIA

Philadelphia

Artful Dodger—2nd & Pine Street	(215) 922.7880
Bridgid's—726 N. 24th Street	(215) 232.3232
Cavanaugh's—119 S. 39th Street	(215) 386.4889
Cutter's—2005 Market Street	(215) 851.6262
Dicken's Inn—2nd Street Headhouse Square	(215) 928.9307
Friday,Saturday,Sunday—261 S. 21st Street	(215) 546.4232
The Happy Rooster—118 S. 16th Street	(215) 563.1481
Jack's Firehouse—2130 Fairmont Avenue	(215) 232.9000
London Grill—23rd & Fairmount	(215) 978.4545
Moriarty's—1116 Walnut St.	(215) 627.7676
Odeon Restaurant—114 S. 12th Street	(215) 922.5875
O'Hara's Fish House—3900 Chestnut Street	(215) 349.9000
Serrano—20 S. 2nd Street	(215) 928.0770
Tangier Cafe—1801 Lombard Street	(215) 732.5006
Tavern On Green—21st & Green	(215) 235.6767
White Dog Cafe—3420 Sansom Street	(215) 386.9224
Zanzibar Blue—305 S. 11th Street	(215) 829.0300
16th Street Bar & Grill—264 S. 16th Street	(215) 735.3316

The Rest of Pennsylvania

Cooper's Seafood House—701 N. Washington Ave., Scranton	(717) 346.6883
304 Kennedy Blvd., Pittston	(717) 654.6883
Retail Supplies:	
Home Sweet Homebrew—2008 Sansom St., Philadelphia	(215) 569.9469

VIRGINIA

Alexandria

Bilbo Baggins—208 Queen Street	(703) 683.0300
Bullfeathers—112 King St.	(703) 836.8088
Chadwick's Old Town—203 S. Strand St.	(703) 836.4442
Halyards, Radisson Mark Plaza—5000 Seminary Road	(703) 845.1010
Hard Times Cafe—1201 King St.	(703) 683.5340
King Street Blues—112 N. St. Asaph St.	(703) 836.8800
Murphy's Grand Irish Pub—713 King St.	(703) 548.1717
The Old Brogue—Route 193 & Walker Road, Great Falls	(703) 759.3309
Sutton Place Cafe—600 Franklin St.	(703) 739.0404
Trolley Club—430 South St.#4, Portsmouth	

Union Street Public House—121 S. Union St.	(703) 548.1785

Fairfax County

Artie's—3260 Old Lee Hwy.	(703) 273.7600
Fairview Park Marriott—311 Fairview Pk. Dr., Falls Church	(703) 849.9400
Hard Times Cafe—394 Elden St., Hemdon	(703) 318.8941
Old Brogue—760C Walker Rd., Great Falls	(703) 759.3309
Vienna Inn—120 Maple Ave. West, Vienna	(703) 938.9548

The Rest of Virginia

Bardo—2000 Wilson, Arlington	(703) 527.9399
Bistrot Belgique Gourmande—302 Poplar Alley, Occoquan	(703) 494.1180
Hero's—9412 Main Street, Manassas	(703) 330.1534
Tuscarora Mill—203 Harrison St., Leesburg	(703) 478.1141

WEST VIRGINIA

Tari's—123 N. Washington St., Berkeley Springs	(304) 258.1196

Southeast

ARKANSAS

Mr. Dunderbaks—McCain Mall, N. Little Rock	(501) 753.8705
Spectators Grill—3124 Pike Ave., N. Little Rock	(501) 791.0990
Vino's—923 West 7th Street, Little Rock	(501) 375.8468

FLORIDA

Billabong Pub—3000 Country Club Lane, Pembroke Park	(305) 985.1050
Big Daddy's—2721 Bird Ave., Coconut Grove	(305) 445.2132
Buena Vista Palace—Walt Disney World Village, Lake Buena Vista	(307) 827.2727
Hubb's—265 W. Hwy. 436, Altamonte Springs	
Mr. Dunderbak's Deli & Restaurant—Regency Square Mall, 9501 Arlington Exp., Jacksonville	

GEORGIA

Applebee's—6649 Roswell Rd., Abernathy Square, Atlanta	(404) 843.1490
Cash Bar—309 Pharr Road, Atlanta	(404) 841.6446
Crystal Beer Parlor—301 W. Jones,Savannah	(912) 232.1153
Reggie's British Pub—CNN Center, Atlanta	(404) 525.1437
Slocum's Tavern—8840 Roswell Rd.,Atlanta	(404) 587.3025
Town Tavern—16 7th Street, Augusta	(404) 724.2461
Winston's Pub—2100 Upper Roswell Road, Marietta	(404) 971.8877
Zur Bratwurst—529 N. Central Ave., Hapeville	(404) 763.4068

LOUISIANA

Carrolton Station—8140 Willow Street, New Orleans	(504) 865.9190
Cooter Brown's—509 S. Carrolton Ave., New Orleans	(504) 866.9104

NORTH CAROLINA

Bert's Seafood Grille—2419 Spring Garden St., Greensboro	(910) 854.2314
Crocodile's Cafe—329 S. Tate St., Greensboro	(910) 274.5211
The Dog House—666 N. Main St., High Point	(910) 886.4953
Harry's Shrimp & Oyster Bar—1740 Battleground Ave., Greensboro	(910) 273.8944
J. Butler's Bar & Grill—2531 Eastchester Dr., High Point	(910) 454.4398
1106B N. Main St., High Point	(910) 861.5758
The Silver Fox—805 Westchester Dr., High Pt.	(910) 882.0060
Southern Lights Bistro & Bar—105 Smyres Pl., Greensboro	(910) 379.9419
The Sunset Cafe—4608 W. Market St., Greensboro	(910) 855.0349

TENNESSEE

Bosco's Pizzeria & Brewery—7615 W. Farmington, #30, Germantown	(901) 756.7310

BEER GLOSSARY

ADDITIVES: The term *additive* is used to describe chemicals, enzymes, preservatives and such kinds of foreign matter often used by large commercial brewers to "rationalize" the brewing process and to improve the shelf life of their beer. Within the craft brewing tradition represented by microbreweries and brewpubs, such additives are considered highly undesirable except for rare instances, such as the use of candy sugar in the preparation of certain kinds of ale. Most additives merely make for an inferior brew. There have been instances—as with the use (now discontinued) of cobalt sulphate as a way of promoting an impressive head—when additives have actually caused fatalities among consumers.

ADJUNCTS: Adjuncts are a special class of additives, consisting of the various kinds of unmalted grain that are sometimes added to barley malt in the brewing process. Wheat beers, for example, are made by using wheat as an adjunct. This is a perfectly acceptable practice since it produces a distinct style of beer without in any way compromising quality. More often, however, cheap grains such as corn or rice are added to commercial beers to lighten the palate and to make the product less expensive (to the brewer, if not always to the consumer).

ALL MALT: An all-malt beer is a beer made from barley malt without adjuncts and usually without additives.

ATTENUATION: There are two ways to make a beer stronger. You can begin with more fermentable material, or you can "squeeze" more alcohol out of the same amount of fermentable material. If you choose this second route, the beer is said to be more attenuated. Since more of the malt has been converted into alcohol, the beer will be lighter in flavor (which also comes from the malt) and dryer.

BARLEY: The basic grain used by brewers since prehistoric times.

BARREL: In the United States, 31 U.S. gallons. In the United Kingdom, 36 Imperial gallons (43.2 U.S. gallons).

BODY: Body is a somewhat subjective way of describing the "heft" of a beer. A doppelbock will be much "heftier" than a pilsner and thus would be described as having more body. More significant, though, are differences of body within a given style. One pale ale, for example, may have more body than another.

BOTTLE CONDITIONED: A bottle conditioned beer is an unpasteurized beer, usually belonging to the ale family, into which a little yeast has been pitched at the time of bottling so that the beer undergoes a secondary fermentation in the bottle, and hence remains alive till the bottle is opened.

BREW KETTLE: The vessel in which the wort is boiled with hops. Sometimes it's called a copper.

CARBON DIOXIDE: Carbon dioxide is produced naturally during the fermentation process, and gives beer its effervescence and sparkle. Commercial brewers often pump additional carbon dioxide into their beers to exaggerate the effervescence, though always at a cost in terms of quality. Craft brewers who desire a high level of effervescence achieve their ends through natural techniques such as krausening.

CASK: The barrel-shaped containers used to store beer are now usually made of metal, but are supplied with wooden bungs (stoppers), which permits pressure to be released from still-fermenting beers.

CASK CONDITIONED: A beer, usually of the ale family, which has undergone a secondary fermentation in the cask.

CONDITIONING TANK: A brewing vessel, sometimes called a bright beer tank, where a beer matures, clarifies, and can undergo a secondary fermentation.

CONTRACT BREW: One phenomenon of the American brewing renaissance has been the rise of the contract brew. Rather than build their own breweries, some entrepreneurs have gone to existing regional breweries and contracted with them to have a beer brewed to a formula that compares with those favored in microbreweries and brewpubs. The results have been mixed, but the best of the contract brews are very good indeed and there may even be certain kinds of beer that are best brewed in this way. In some instances, microbreweries have themselves offered their services as contract brewers.

FERMENTATION: The process in which yeast organisms act upon the wort to convert sugar into alcohol and carbon dioxide.

GRIST: Ground barley malt.

HAND PUMP: An important symbol of the brewpub movement. In most bars and taverns, commercial tap beers are served with the aid of a cushion of carbon dioxide which forces the beer out of its container. In serious brewpubs—as in British locals, or German beer-gardens—the precious liquid is delivered by means of gravity, usually with the help of a simple, mechanical hand pump. The barman or barmaid is seen to pull repeatedly on the handle. Thus, in Britain, serving real ale is described as "pulling a pint."

HOPS: The female flowers of the hop vine *(humulus lupulus)* are used to flavor beer, to lend it bitterness and aroma, and to serve as a natural preservative.

KEG: A metal, barrel-shaped container, usually carrying beer under pressure and containing 15.5 gallons (half a barrel). Beer aficionados often use the term "keg beer" disparagingly to describe the pressurized commercial form of draft beer—whether pasteurized or not—from the cask conditioned kind favored by craft brewers. By these standards, even the best of the imported draft beers found in America are actually "keg beers." It is one of the great advantages of the microbrewery/brewpub movement that it can supply American beer lovers with authentic, fresh, cask-conditioned beer.

KRAUSENING: Krausening describes a way of conditioning beer by adding unfermented wort, or "green" partly fermented wort, to a fully fermented beer before bottling or kegging. This process produces a very lively, highly carbonated beer.

LIQUOR TANK: There are people who believe that malt liquor is a form of beer to which hard liquor has been added for an extra kick. In fact, liquor is the brewer's word for water and a liquor tank is merely a water reservoir.

MALT: Barley which has been drenched with water, permitted to sprout, then dried.

MASH TUN: The brewing vessel in which grist is mixed with water and heated to promote the conversion of starch into sugar. Also called a lauter tun.

MICROBREWERY: There was a time when microbreweries could conveniently be described as breweries producing no more than 15,000 barrels of beer per year. Some breweries that fit this specification a few years ago now produce well in excess of 20,000 barrels a year. Does this mean that they can no longer qualify as microbreweries? We prefer to think that this makes them successful microbreweries. In common-sense terms, a microbrewery is a small craft brewery which seeks the support of informed beer consumers.

ORIGINAL GRAVITY: The measurement of a brew's density in comparison with the density of water, taken at the time when fermentation is about to begin in the wort. In other words, a description of the proportion of fermentable matter to water in the basic mixture. The higher the original gravity (referred to by aficionados as o.g.), the higher in alcohol content the beer is likely to be.

PASTEURIZATION: The application of heat to beer (or other substances) to halt the activity of microorganisms. Since yeast consists of microorganisms, pasteurization brings the fermentation process to an end. Large commercial brewers often favor pasteurization because it helps prolong the shelf life of their product.

REINHEITSGEBOT: The Bavarian purity law, enacted in 1516, which dictates that beer should be made from nothing but malted barley, yeast, hops and water. A later amendment permitted the use of wheat as an adjunct and in 1919 the *Reinheitsgebot* was adopted as law throughout Germany. In recent years it has been the object of attacks by members of the European Economic Community, who perceive it as protectionist, but even though the law has been struck down it is still voluntarily observed by the vast majority of German brewers, and by most American craft brewers too.

SEASONAL BEER: Traditionally, many beers—such as Maibocks or Winter Warmers—were brewed for consumption at certain times of the year. Strong Christmas beers, for example, are brewed in many European countries, and lately these traditions have been revived in America where, prior to Prohibition, they were commonplace.

SESSION BEER: British in origin, the term "session beer" refers to any beer of low to moderate alcoholic content which can safely be consumed in reasonable quantity during the course of a beer-drinking session. The sweet malt liquid produced by mashing and boiling grist and water during the brewing process.

YEAST: Microorganisms of the fungus family, used to ferment beer.

ZYMURGY: The branch of chemistry dealing with fermentation.

BIBLIOGRAPHY

Charlie Papazian, *The New Complete Joy of Home Brewing* (Avon Books, New York, NY, 1991).

Graphics and captions in the earlier chapters *(The American Tradition, The Brewing Process, Styles of Beer)* provided by the Beer Institute, representing America's brewers, *"Continuing the Great Tradition of Beer."*

David Edgar (Managing Editor), *North American Brewers Resource Directory 1992-1993 & 1993-1994* (Brewers Publications, Boulder, CO, 1993).

"Spectrum of Beers" chart provided by Pete's Brewing Company.

Steve Johnson, *On Tap: The Guide to U.S. Brewpubs* (WBR Publications, South Carolina, 1991).

ALE STREET NEWS *newspaper*
P.O. Box 5339, Bergenfield, NJ 07621. (201) 387·1818. Bi-monthly, 6 issues $14.95. Publishers: Tony Forder, Jack Babin. Covers New York State, New England and D.C. area.

BARLEYCORN *newspaper*
P.O. Box 2328, Falls Church, VA 22042. (703) 573·8970. Bi-monthly, 6 issues $15.00. Publisher: George Rivers. Covers Mid-Atlantic states.

BEER-THE MAGAZINE *magazine*
P.O. Box 9877, Berkeley, CA 94709. (510) 548·0697. Bi-monthly, $24.00. Publisher: William E. Owens. Covers Mid-Atlantic states.

CELEBRATOR BEER NEWS *newspaper*
P.O. Box 375, Hayward, CA 94543. (501) 670·0121. Bi-monthly, 6 issues $14.95. Publisher: Tom Dalldorf. Covers Western U.S.

MIDWEST BEER NOTES *newspaper*
339 Sixth Avenue, Clayton, WI 54004. (715) 948·2990. Bi-monthly, 8 issues $12.95. Editor/Publisher: Mike Urseth. Covers Midwestern states.

SOUTHERN DRAFT *newspaper*
P.O. Box 180425, Casselberry, FL 32718. (407) 327·9451. Bi-monthly, 6 issues $15.00. Editor/Publisher: Jerry Gengler. Covers Southeastern U.S.

SOUTHWEST BREWING NEWS *newspaper*
11405 Evening Star Drive, Austin, TX 78739. (512) 467·2225, (512) 282·4935. Bi-monthly, 6 issues $12.00. Publishers: Joe Barfield, Bill Metzger. Covers Southwestern U.S.

YANKEE BREW NEWS *newspaper*
P.O. Box 8053, JFK Station, Boston, MA 02114. (617) 522·2182. Tri-monthly, 4 issues $7.95. Publisher: Brasseur Publications. Covers Northeastern U.S.

INDEX